Published in 2023 to coincide with
the 200th anniversary of the death of
Sir Henry Raeburn
1756 - 1823

A history of Stockbridge

&

50 portrait sketches

Imagined view of early Stockbridge by Cumberland Hill

Barclay Price
© 2023

Deanhaugh Street, c.1910 (Capital Collections)

CONTENTS

Introduction — 1

Part One - The History
Stockbridge village — 6
Henry Raeburn — 12
Developing Stockbridge — 16
Homes for working families — 28
St Bernard's Well — 30
Industrial Stockbridge — 32
Churches — 36
Charitable institutions — 38
Schools — 40
Libraries — 44
Laundries — 46
Community halls — 48
Fire — 54
Law & Order — 58
Transport — 62
Edinburgh Academy Sports Ground — 68
Grange Cricket Club — 72
Stockbridge Park — 74
Other sports venues — 76
Entertainments — 82
First & Second World Wars — 86
Drugs & Drink — 90
Shops — 94

Part Two - 50 Portrait sketches — 106

Appendix - Street Names — 208

Author's other Edinburgh histories — 212

Index — 213

Sir Henry Raeburn self portrait, c.1820

INTRODUCTION

Two hundred years ago, on 10 July 1823, two days after his death, Sir Henry Raeburn left Stockbridge for the last time. His cortege travelled a route he would have walked numerous times, crossing the bridge over the Water of Leith and making its way up through the New Town to the Church of St John the Evangelist, where his body was interred. Raeburn was born in Stockbridge and it was his home for all of his life. As well as being one of Scotland's greatest portrait painters, he was a key figure in the area's development. He envisaged an enlarged Stockbridge that would retain a village atmosphere and I like to imagine that the neighbourhood's most distinguished resident would consider today's Stockbridge to have developed much as he desired.

Stockbridge often is loosely defined, especially by estate agents and tourist guides, but for this history I have kept to Edinburgh Council's delineation of the district as shown on the map below. Although Raeburn Place sports ground, Inverleith Park and St Bernard's Well are just outside the official boundary, I have included them as all are significant in the area's history.

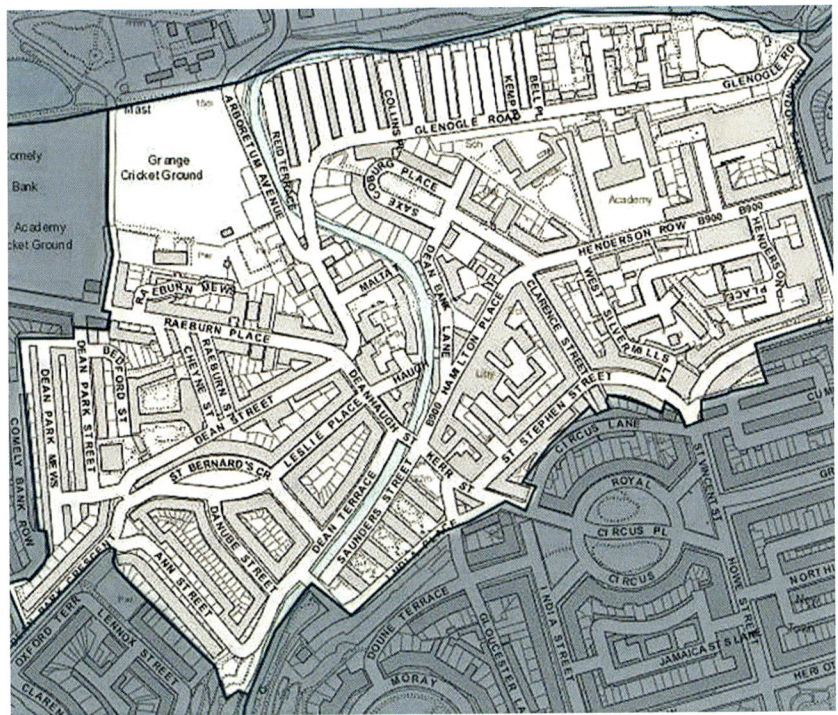

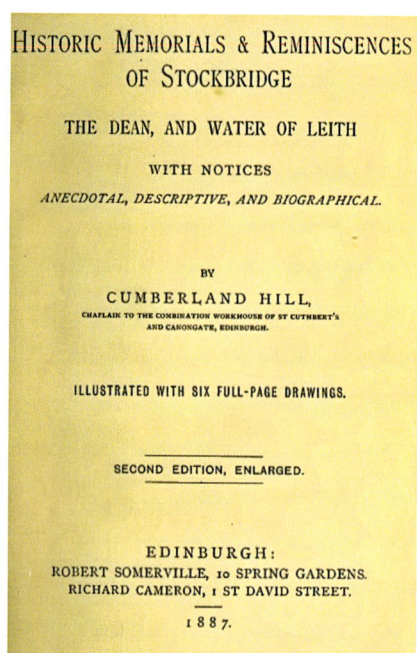

1 *Historic Memorials & Reminiscences of Stockbridge*, second edition, 1887
https://www.electricscotland.com/history/edinburgh/historicmemorialhill.pdf
2 Advert promoting a series of articles in *The Weekly Scotsman* in April and May 1922
3 Envelope of letter sent by George Mackenzie Brown, the Member of Parliament for Stockbridge using House of Commons mail to A. Christison, a cabinetmaker, 1902. In 1901 Brown, who was on the board of Thomas Nelson publishers, was chosen to fight the seat as the Liberal candidate. By chance, standing against him was Arthur Conan Doyle, Liberal Unionist, whose Sherlock Holmes books Thomas Nelson published. Brown won by 569 votes.

The only previous history of Stockbridge is the noteworthy *Historic Memorials & Reminiscences of Stockbridge* by Cumberland Hill, published in 1887. Although long out of print it can be downloaded from the excellent Electric Scotland web site. I had high hopes that a *Weekly Scotsman* series, *True Tales of Stockbridge*, published in 1922 might provide interesting historical snippets but sadly not. The most intriguing character, Pietro the Wizard, 'silent, mysterious and unapproachable as though he lived in the midst of unutterable mysteries', resided (if he existed at all) outwith today's Stockbridge boundary as did almost all of those featured in the 'tales'.

There have been two accounts of Stockbridge streets: *A History of Ann Street* by Andrew Kerr (1982 - out of print) and my own *A History of St Stephen Street* (2022). The latter is complementary to this history. Details of this and my other histories of Edinburgh streets can be found on page 212. *Happy Homes* by Richard Roger (The Word Bank, 2022) provides a comprehensive account of the Stockbridge Colonies and also describes how the idea for improved housing for the working class came in response to the dreadful conditions many in the Old Town were living in at the time.

Hill's book includes 25 'Sketches of Distinguished Natives and Residents' and I decided to replicate that idea. I have doubled the number to 50 - in fact 51, as Henry Raeburn rightly has his own chapter - but do not focus solely on 'distinguished men' as Hill did. A number of eminent names are included, but there also are portrait sketches of infamous residents and of many who are little known – including Cumberland Hill himself - or never documented before. To help ensure that these reflected the diversity of past inhabitants, I set myself the challenge that every individual should link to a different Stockbridge street; those included illuminate the history that makes up the first part of the book. Two are still alive and my thanks to James Simpson and Rachel Hazell for agreeing to be included.

I have trawled widely for images that illustrate Stockbridge's history and my apologies if I have omitted any credits or inadvertently breached anyone's copyright. Please contact me about missing credits or images that require permission, and I will resolve the issue in future print runs.

My thanks to my wife Fiona Dick for her support, Oula Jones for proofing and indexing, and the staff of Golden Hare Books.

Barclay Price
Contact email: albanystreetedinburgh@gmail.com

> 25th December 1819
>
> William Paul Esq. Accountant Edinburgh, and Miss Eliza Deans, Eldest daughter of the late Admiral Robert Deans, residing Ann Street, That they are unmarried persons and not within the forbidden degrees of consanguinity, and that She has resided in this Parish for the space of four weeks previous to the above date is certified by
>
> Robert Paul, Witness, Brother
> Arch. Ferguson, Witness
> 14 Society, Clerk to the Commercial Banking Coy of Scotland

At the house of Mrs Admiral Deans, Anne Street St. Bernard's, on the 28th ult. WILLIAM PAUL., Esq accountant, Edinburgh, to ELIZABETH, eldest daughter of the late Admiral Deans, of Huntingdon.

1&2 Register and newspaper announcement of one of the first weddings in Ann Street. The marriage between William Paul, an accountant who lived in Duke (Dublin) Street, and Elizabeth Deans took place on Christmas Day, 1819. As was common at the time the wedding took place in the bride's home, No. 23. Elizabeth was the daughter of Admiral Robert Deans who died in 1815. Not long before his death Deans, who was a close friend of Horatio Nelson, was painted by Raeburn.

3 *Portrait of Admiral Robert Deans* by Henry Raeburn (National Gallery of Victoria, Melbourne)

PART ONE
A HISTORY OF STOCKBRIDGE

1 Raeburn Place, 1951 (photo - S. G. Jackman, Capital Collections)
2 India Place, view from Church Street looking west, c.1950s. The street sign says, 'Children's playground. No vehicles please. 4pm till sunset.' This was one of a number of Edinburgh streets that restricted motor vehicles at set times to enable children to play in the road safely. (photo - James Neil Saunders)

STOCKBRIDGE VILLAGE

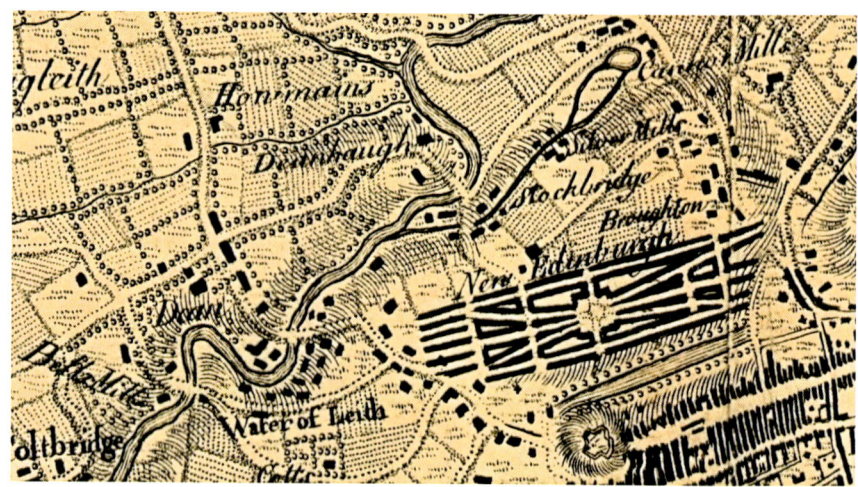

1 Detail from *A plan of Edinburgh and places adjacent.* by John Laurie, 1766 (National Library of Scotland)
2 *Old Stockbridge* by Alexander Campbell, 1811 (National Galleries Scotland)

Cumberland Hill says of Stockbridge that it, 'cannot boast of being a place of great antiquity' as he found no record of it in an account written in the mid-17th century of the various villages that stood on the Water of Leith. It may have been known in earlier times as Deanhaugh, a generic name for the lands that sloped down from The Dean. The map opposite designates the north side of the river as Deanhaugh and the south side as Stockbridge. Hill writes that the area was under the jurisdiction of the Baron-Bailies of Broughton who, 'possessed considerable power within their own bounds. Some of them had the power of life and death, or, as it was termed, of "pit and gallows", so called from the manner in which the criminals were put to death - hanging the men upon a gibbet or gallows, and drowning the women in a pit, or burning them, as in the olden time it was not thought "decent" to hang them.'

The village name of Stockbridge appears by the 1740s and at that time it is recorded as having a population of 524, of which 180 were children. The name 'stock' refers to a timber bridge - usually a footbridge - and the village may have got its name from a rickety bridge across the Water of Leith; possibly sited nearer where St Bernard's Bridge stands today.

When the New Town began to be developed Stockbridge was one of several isolated villages running along the Water of Leith. To the west were the villages of Bells Mills, Dean and Water of Leith and to the east Silvermills and Canonmills. All had grown up as centres of a variety of trades that drew water and power via weirs and a mill lade that ran from Water of Leith village to Canonmills Loch, on the south side of the river through Stockbridge.

The road from Queensferry to Edinburgh that ran through the village was called Deanhaugh. In 1760 a toll gate was erected on the south side by the Road Trustees (where Glanville Place meets Baker's Place today) and all traffic going towards Edinburgh had to pay to pass through. Before the building of the New Town, there were two routes from Stockbridge to the city, both steep and rough. The main one was Stockbridge Brae that ran through the area where Royal Circus is today and the other was the narrow, steep Church Street/Lane (now Gloucester Street/Lane). Both roads met Long Dykes that ran along the north side of the Nor' Loch below the castle. Until the first stone bridge was built in 1785 the Water of Leith at Stockbridge was crossed by a ford that was difficult for carts to navigate, as Hill recounts: 'The road to the ford must have inclined rapidly toward the water, as it is spoken of as being very steep, so much so that Mr Adam Smith, the proprietor of the mills, had to employ a trace horse in order to draw up his carts from the water. The bank seems to have been equally steep on the north side. When the water was high, passage by carts or other vehicles was at once stopped. It is recounted that when coals were brought for those living on the north side of the stream, and the water high,

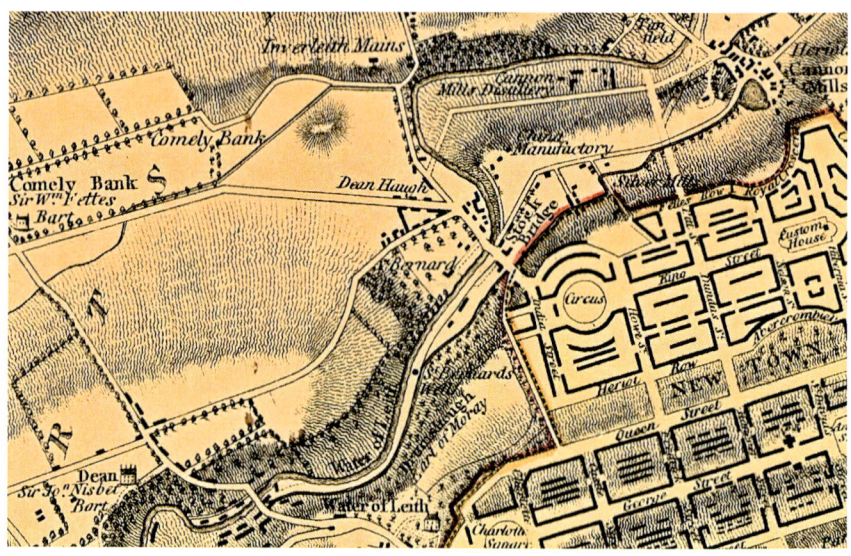

1 *St Bernard's Well*, engraving by W. Byrne, 1803, after G. Walker
2 Detail from 1816 map by James Knox showing Stockbridge and its environs, National Library of Scotland)

the carts had to stop at the water side, and the coals had to be carried over by a wooden foot-bridge which had been erected some years before. The inconvenience to which the inhabitants had been subjected was very great, there having been no proper access to the city, to those going south or to those coming north. Under these circumstances a proper stone bridge was a dire necessity.'

The 1803 map of the village opposite shows a scattering of buildings, mainly on the south side. On the north side was Veitch's Court (later named Veitch's Square), described by Hill as, 'one of the most interesting and picturesque localities in Stockbridge. It was a complete square, each side being composed of the same number of one-storeyed houses. They were generally all thatched, and the fronts covered with honeysuckle and other climbing plants. Roses, daisies, southernwood, and other nice old-fashioned flowers grew on the little plots of ground between the doors and windows. The centre of the square was used as a bleaching green. Everything was kept scrupulously clean and tidy.' Many of the tenants were widows or single women who took in washing.

The Water of Leith was at that time described as, 'a pure, limpid, and beautiful stream' and people fished it for trout. Hill recounts that in earlier times the valley between Stockbridge and the village of Water of Leith had 'on one side the fine plantations of Drumsheugh, the seat of the Earl of Moray, and on the other side, the banks of the river were bounded by tangled brakes of bramble and hawthorn. The mill lade was conveyed in wooden troughs generally very leaky. These were raised upon posts, and being patched, mended up and covered with green moss and tangled creeping water plants, had a most picturesque appearance.' Into this bucolic scene was added St Bernard's Well to the west of the village that is described in a later chapter. Discovered in 1760, the mineral well may have been given its name by Walter Ross who lived in the nearby St Bernard's House. Its water swiftly became reputed for its medicinal qualities, so it was much visited by the nobility and gentry. In 1810 another well, just to the west of St Bernard's Well, was discovered and named St George's Well. The small plain building erected over it still exists today, though in poor condition. For a time a solitary old woman lived there and later the well was used for breeding leeches for medicinal purposes.

A number of country houses and villas were built in the countryside around the village during the 18th century. These included St Bernard's House, Inverleith House, Malta House, Patriot Hall, Deanhaugh House and Deanbank House, and all are shown on the map on page 10. When Deanhaugh House was sold in 1771 it was described as: 'consisting of five bedrooms, four of which have closets, dining room, drawing room, small parlour and kitchen, with a large lumber garret that may be suitable for

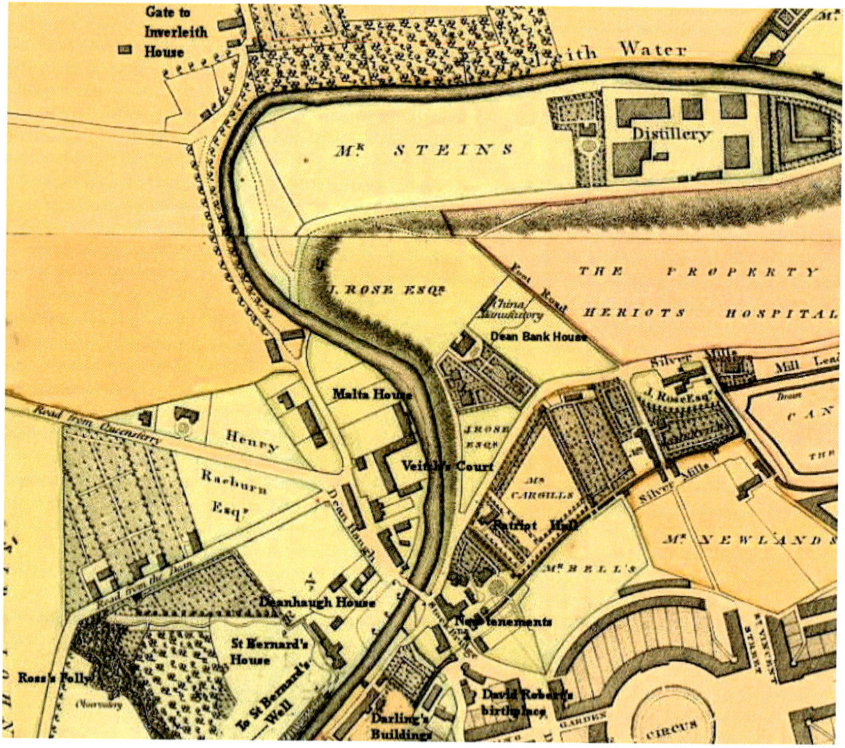

1 Detail from 1804 map by John Ainslie (National Library of Scotland)
2 St Bernard's House, detail from map by James Kirkwood, 1819 (National Library of Scotland)
3 *Ross's Folly* by Cumberland Hill c.1870

servants sleeping in; also an ale cellar, wine cellar, larder, pantry, milk house, coal house, hen house and a coach house. Also a stable for five horses, byre for like number of cows, a parterre in front of the house with a small garden to the west, all lying in a pleasant valley on the banks of the Water of Leith.' The house was purchased by John Leslie, 11th Earl of Rothes when he married Ann Edgar and they moved in the following year. He later was known as the 'Count of Deanhaugh'.

Patriot Hall was advertised to let at £50 per annum in 1775 and described as a 'Mansion House consisting of a large kitchen, and seven rooms, with a stable and hay loft, poultry yard, and other conveniences. A park and convenient kitchen garden, with fine wall-fruit, espalliars and standing trees of different kinds'.

St Bernard's House was built around 1750 for Walter Ross, a Writer to the Signet and Registrar of Distillery Licences in Scotland: 'Two square castellated projections came out upon each side in front, so that the entrance was from three sides of a square. Into the front of one of the castellated projections was built a very fine Gothic window.' Ross was a great collector of antiquities and paintings. He rescued sculptures and other artefacts from Old Town buildings that were being demolished and incorporated some into St Bernard's House, while others were built into a 40 foot high tower he had constructed as part of a garden created on the hill behind his house - where No. 10 Ann Street is today. This was known locally as 'Ross's Folly' and when Ross died in 1789 he was buried there. An obituary said of him: 'Mr Walter Ross was eminently distinguished for his wit and humour. The collecting of antiquities and fine paintings, and ornamental agriculture and gardening were his favourite pursuits, of all which he has left many elegant and some perhaps whimsical specimens. He possessed in a very high degree the talent of ridicule, and his colloquial powers will be long remembered by those who had the pleasure of his company.' Hill recounts that the folklore was that Ross died from choking in a fit of laughter. For a time after his death the upper part of the tower was occupied by a night-watchman for the area and the lower part used as a stable. The tower was demolished in 1825 to make way for further building in Ann Street and Ross's body was moved to St Cuthbert's graveyard. Among the objects were four sculptured heads that formerly adorned the Old Cross of Edinburgh and when the tower was dismantled these were sent to Abbotsford as a present to Sir Walter Scott.

There were a number of industries dotted about the area and one of the larger premises belonged to Robert Raeburn, who was a 'yarn-boiler' (boiling wool to create felted fabric). In 1780 Stockbridge village was still pastoral but that was about to change, and Robert Raeburn's youngest son was one of the main instigators.

HENRY RAEBURN

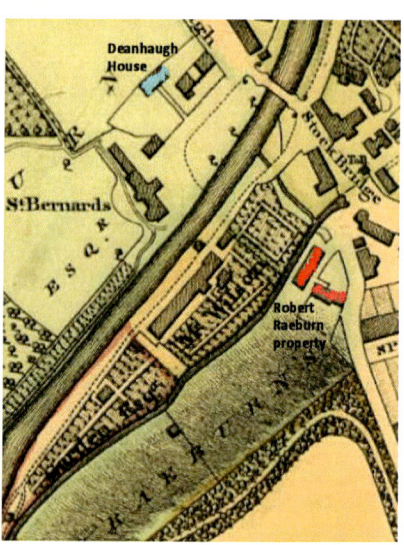

1 *Henry Raeburn as a Youth* by David Deuchar (National Galleries Scotland)
2 Miniature portrait of James Gilliland, goldsmith, by Henry Raeburn, c.1770 (Murray Archive)
3 *Portrait of Ann Raeburn* by Henry Raeburn (private collection)
4 Map showing (in red) Robert Raeburn's Yarn-Boiling workshop and house where Henry Raeburn was born, and land belonging to Robert Raeburn

Robert Raeburn's second son, Henry became one of Scotland's most significant portrait painters, but it is his role as a developer that is particularly relevant to Stockbridge's history. He was born in 1756 the second son of Robert Raeburn, who had married Ann Elder in 1740. Their first child, William, had been born 12 years before. Around 1855 Robert Raeburn purchased land on the east bank of the Water of Leith from George Heriot's Hospital and during the 1750s erected a complex of buildings, including a 114-foot-long yarn-boiling workshop. Next to it was the house where Henry was born. Ann died in 1763 and Robert soon after so William took over the running of the boiling house and looked after his young brother. From 1865 to 1872 Henry attended Heriot's Hospital school, which provided education for the orphaned sons of Edinburgh burgesses.

On leaving school at 16, Henry was apprenticed to a goldsmith, James Gilliland. He began producing portrait miniatures that were much admired and also experimented with larger oil paintings. Although self-taught, his early work was recognised as showing talent and he left Gilliland's employment and by 1776 received his first portrait commission.

In 1780 while sketching in Stockbridge, Raeburn was observed by Ann Leslie of Deanhaugh House; the widow of John Leslie who had died three years earlier. She commissioned the young artist to paint her portrait and clearly it was not only his artistic talent that took her fancy for within a short time they married. Ann had a son and two daughters from her previous marriage - John, Jacobina and Ann –and had two more sons with Raeburn - Peter and Henry. Both John and Peter died in their late teens. Raeburn was keen to visit Italy to extend his art knowledge and expertise; fortunately Ann's wealth enabled them both to travel there.

After two years in Italy they returned to live at Deanhaugh House. When Walter Ross died in 1789 Raeburn purchased St Bernard's House and they moved there. Raeburn also had a studio in the New Town, firstly in George Street and then in a newly built house in York Place that included reception areas, a picture gallery, a workshop for a frame maker, and a studio which took up the whole of the first floor. Raeburn did not lack for clients, as he was quickly recognised as Scotland's primary portrait painter. On his work days he breakfasted with his family about 8am and then walked from Stockbridge to his studio in the New Town to start work at 9am. He had three or four sitters each day, spent an hour or two with each, and normally completed each portrait over four to five sessions. He painted standing and Walter Scott recounted: 'His manly stride backwards, as he went to contemplate his work at a proper distance, and, when resolved on the necessary point to be touched, his step forward, were magnificent.'

DEATH OF SIR HENRY RAEBURN.—It is with sincere regret we announce the death of that eminent artist, Sir Henry Raeburn, who has for a long period occupied the first place among the portrait painters of his country. Sir Henry died at his house at St Bernard's, Stockbridge, early on Tuesday morning.

FOR BEHOOF OF CREDITORS.
To be SOLD by public roup, within Mr Grinly's Sale Rooms, Leith, on Saturday the 21st May inst. at at one o'clock afternoon,
THE GOOD SHIP OR LUGGER, CALLED
THE HARLEQUIN,
As she presently lies in the new dock of Leith, measuring 57 61-94th tons per register, with her Furniture and Apparelling, conform to inventory.
This vessel is well found, a remarkably fast sailer, and particularly adapted for the herring or salmon fishery, or would make a capital pleasure yacht. A great part of the canvas is quite new.—Also
Nine Hhds. of SCALE SUGARS on bond, and six dozen of SHERRY WINE.
After the roup of these articles, and at two o'clock of the same day, there will be sold, in the warehouses of HENRY RAEBURN and Co. North Leith, the following articles—
271 BASKETS or HAMPERS, and 248 Covers to them.
About 20,000 FIRE BRICKS.
3 Brass-barrelled BLUNDERBUSSES.
An excellent six-seated WRITING-DESK, and a parcel of old Boxes, and other articles belonging to a Counting-house.
The articles of roup, and inventory of the vessel, are in the hands of W. Scott Moncrieff, trustee on the sequestrated estate of Henry Raeburn and Co. or John Rofs, W. S. And samples of the Sugar and Wine will be seen at the counting-house of Mr Gilbert Ogilvy, merchant, Leith, who will cause the vessel, stores, and other articles be shown to intending purchasers.

1 *Deanhaugh House* by H Peattie, 1830 - shown in blue on map on page 12
2 *The Skating Minister*, attributed to Henry Raeburn. One of a set of four postage stamps, 'Artistic Anniversaries', issued in 1973 commemorating Joshua Reynolds birth in 1723 and Raeburn's death in 1823
3 Advert for sale of the sequestrated estate, 1808
4 Announcement of Raeburn's death in *The Caledonian Mercury*

Raeburn's marriage brought ownership of land in Stockbridge and on the death of his brother in 1810 Raeburn inherited the land and property that had belonged to his father. As a major local landowner he, along with other property owners, began exploring the potential for housing development, given the building of the New Town was moving down the hill towards Stockbridge. Raeburn visualised an expanded Stockbridge that retained a rural village atmosphere so, unlike houses in the New Town, his houses were designed with front flower gardens. In spite of his own father having established a large yarn-boiling workshop in the area, Raeburn was against industrial development that might spoil this vision. In 1815 he unsuccessfully tried to stop a new steam engine being operated at Stockbridge Mills. In court, Raeburn's lawyer stated: 'So vast a column of smoke comes from this engine, that clothes hung out to dry are made as black as before they were washed. My clients are deprived of the use of their gardens, hot-houses, &c. and the value of their properties are thereby reduced.' To which the mill's lawyer responded: 'In the suburbs of all large and populous cities, disagreeable manufactories of all kinds must exist; and while the nice and elegant part of the community might find it necessary to remove all impolite trades and employments from their vicinity, yet the increase of luxuries required also an increase of manufactures and machinery of all kinds.' The jury sided with the mill: 'The engine is useful, and not offensive'.

    Raeburn underwrote his son's investment in a Leith shipping business and when that failed in 1808 Raeburn was declared bankrupt, owing creditors £36,000. He had to sell his York Place property and the need to pay off his debts spurred his building development. His urgent need for money also affected Raeburn's art, as over-production resulted in many of his later portraits being considered of lower quality than his earlier work. Yet he gained many honours at this time. In 1812 he was elected president of the Society of Artists in Edinburgh and a member of the Royal Scottish Academy, and in 1822 was knighted by George IV and appointed the Royal Limner for Scotland.

    Raeburn died at St Bernard's House on 8 July 1823. Ann Raeburn died in 1832 at Raeburn Cottage in Peeblesshire. Her daughters, Jacobina married Daniel Vere, Sheriff-Substitute of Lanarkshire and Ann wed James Inglis, a merchant in Bengal, India. After Inglis died in 1813 Ann lived with her children at Deanhaugh House. Henry junior married Charlotte White and they and their children lived with Raeburn and Ann at St Bernard's House. After his father's death Henry continued to oversee the developments that Raeburn had initiated. In 1826 he moved out of St Bernard's House so it could be demolished to make way for the new streets, and lived at No. 17 St Bernard's Crescent.

DEVELOPING STOCKBRIDGE

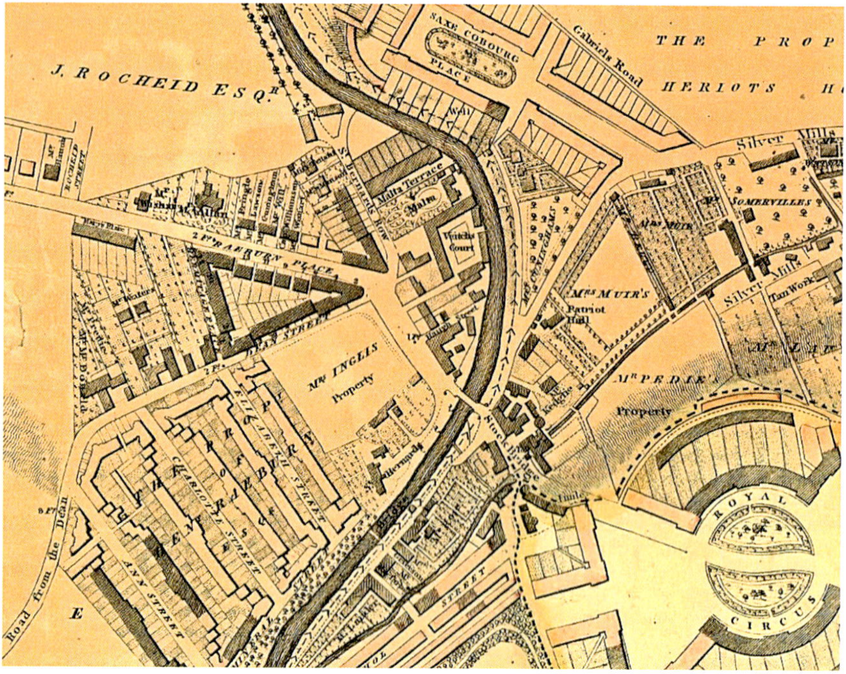

1 Detail from 1821 map by James Kirkwood (National Library of Scotland)

2 Plan showing elevation of tenements submitted to the Dean of Guild Court in March 1823 by Henry Raeburn as part of his proposal to build India Place. The Court's decision came in December: 'We approve of the buildings intended to be erected by Mr. Raeburn on a street leading to Athol Street (renamed Saunders Street), to be called India Place and authorise the same to be erected'. By this time Raeburn was dead and so the plan was taken forward by his son. (Dean of Guild Court records/Dr Joe Rock)

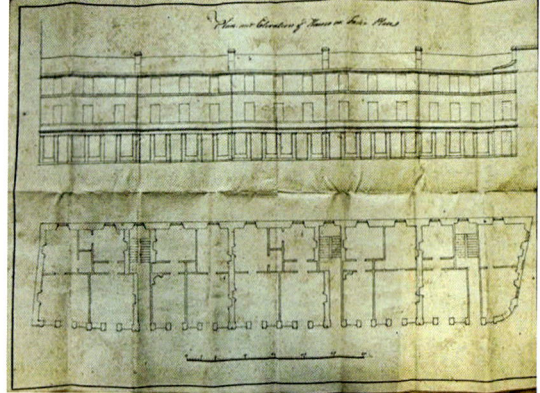

By the 18th century Edinburgh had become one of the most densely populated cities in Europe and many of the wealthier citizens felt the outdated city fabric was no longer suitable for modern living. Concerned at the prospect of many of its influential citizens leaving Edinburgh, the city fathers decided to construct a brand-new suburb. In January 1766 James Craig won the design competition for the New Town to be built on the land beyond the Nor' Loch and building work began in 1767. Demand for properties swiftly led to an enlargement of the original Craig plan and development moved down the hill towards Stockbridge. The vision for the New Town was to create townhouses with a country feel, an aspiration with which the romantic glen created by the Water of Leith to the west of Stockbridge fitted perfectly.

Thus, by the 1780s owners of estates in Stockbridge began to consider feuing land for house building. In addition to the attraction of its pastoral setting, residents of Stockbridge were exempt from Edinburgh's taxes as at the time it was not part of the town. Those looking to develop their land recognised that to enable the necessary building materials to be transported into Stockbridge the ford across the Water of Leith needed to be replaced with a bridge so a group, including Raeburn, petitioned the city in 1784 to pay for a stone bridge. They also proposed that the main road from the north should be re-routed via Stockbridge. However, the council chose Bell's Mills as the site for the new bridge and from then until the opening of Dean Bridge in 1831, all traffic from the north passed through Bell's Mills and travelled up to the city along what are now Belford Road and Queensferry Street. Undeterred, Raeburn and his associates invested in a smaller stone bridge in 1785, although as this was very narrow and steeply arched it was unsuitable for larger carts.

In 1792 early adverts for completed tenements appeared: 'For sale, that large new tenement built by William Wilson at an upset price of £720'. 'Two new tenements lately built by Alexander Melrose', were on offer at £370 for the two or at £190 each. Some, such as one built by Robert Gilchrist, contained retail units: 'a good shop and bake house with an excellent oven.' One of the earliest areas that Raeburn feued was the triangle of land that is shown on the 1804 map on page 10 between the road from Queensferry and the road from the Dean. He named these Raeburn Place and Dean Street. Following his sequestration, to speed up development Raeburn provided some builders with cash advances on the security of the houses they built and sold. The villas Nos. 27 and 29 Raeburn Place (originally Nos. 9 and 10) were completed in 1816 and on sale at £500 each.

Others who owned land quickly saw the chance to make money. In 1818 Matthew Craw, a goldsmith, advertised: 'To be feued by public roup within the Royal Exchange, that field at Stockbridge lying between Dean

> To be fold at the time and place above mentioned, and
> either feparately or together,
> Thefe Two New TENEMENTS at Stockbridge, with
> the pertinents, lately built by Alexander Melrofe, wright,
> confifting in all of fixteen different apartments, or eight each,
> befides garret, clofets, offices, and garden ground. Thefe
> fubjects are at prefent very moderately rented at about 30 l
> yearly. They will be expofed together fo low as 330 l. and
> feparately at 170l. each.
> The fituation of the whole premiffes is commodious and
> delightful upon the banks of the river Leith, adjoining to the
> new Ferry road, and, though beyond the royalty, within a
> few minutes walk of the city of Edinburgh.
> The articles of roup are in the hands of James Drummond,
> writer to the fignet, who will inform as to further particu-
> lars, and is authorifed to conclude a private bargain.

> TO SELL,
> By public roup, within the Royal Exchange Coffeehouse, on
> Wednesday the 18th day of November 1812, at two o'clock
> afternoon, if not previously disposed of by private bargain,
> AN Elegant HOUSE, No. 2, RAEBURN PLACE,
> STOCKBRIDGE. It is finished in a superior style,
> and consists of drawing-room, dining-room, nine bed-rooms,
> water-closet.—On the sunk storey there is a large kitchen, with
> a soft water pipe, larder, scullery, a large front room, and a
> small housekeeper's room, large wine cellar with catacombs,
> strong beer and coal cellar; in the back area, a wash-house
> and other conveniencies; a well laid out garden behind, and a
> beautiful plot before the door.
> If the house is not sold, it will be let, and may be entered
> to at the term of Martinmas.
> For further particulars apply to James M'Robin, solicitor-
> at-law, No. 11, Brown's Square, in whose hands the title-
> deeds are.

1 *View of Stockbridge* by Alexander Robertson, c.1800 (National Galleries Scotland). This shows the first stone bridge with its steep incline that was built around 1784
2 Advert, 1793
3 Advert, 1812

Street and Mary's Place. The field extends to upwards of a Scotch acre and is extremely well situated for building, being almost surrounded with new streets.' The flurry of house building brought an increasing demand for builders. Some invested their own funds or borrowed money to buy feus and built houses for sale or rent; while others worked for architects or responded to adverts such as one in 1827 from William Philip, a watchmaker: 'Estimates wanted for building two houses in Dean Terrace, agreeable to plans and specifications'. As Stockbridge was outside the city boundary the Dean of Guild had no power and thus building was uncontrolled. With some land owners, developers and builders more interested in profit than retaining the rural village atmosphere that Raeburn and others envisioned, the buildings erected were an eclectic mix of detached villas, small terraces with front gardens, townhouses and tenements.

Build quality varied. Some builders like George Trotter who, in 1828 was building a house for himself in Bedford Street, clearly were highly regarded: 'Members of the Decennial Property Company presented George Trotter of Bedford Street, with an elegant snuff box engraved with the following inscription: in approbation of the manner in which he has completed the contract for their two houses at Dean Terrace.' Of course there were other builders whose work was shoddy and received legal writs rather than gifts. In 1879 Alexander Adamson was taken to court by residents of St Bernard's Crescent who complained that the houses he had built were not in conformity with the existing buildings and in breach of the feu conditions. The court agreed and he was forced to take them down and rebuild. Other builders overstretched themselves. In 1818 one builder advertised his new houses: 'Five dwelling houses in Dean Street, Stockbridge, being Nos. 4,8,9,10,11 and 12 of said street. The upset price of No. 4 is reduced to £445, and that of the remaining numbers to £575.' Four did not sell and by 1823 the builder was bankrupt and the remaining houses sold off: 'Four dwelling houses, being Nos. 4, 8, 9 and 12 of Dean Street. The houses were valued by a respected builder at £550 each and are now exposed at £300 to ensure a sale, being part of a bankrupt estate.'

Yet most of those involved in Stockbridge's development made a healthy profit. James Peddie certainly did. He was a Writer to the Signet (solicitor) living in Albany Street and around 1820 bought a plot of land between the edge of Royal Circus and the mill lade that few probably considered as fit for building, as it was low-lying and so prone to flooding from the Water of Leith, while the noxious mill lade ran through it. However, Peddie saw that there was a potential demand for houses that could be rented more cheaply by the less-well-off tradesmen, shop-keepers, artisans etc., and a need for more shops in the area. He commissioned the architect Robert Brown to lay out an overall plan for the development of Brunswick Street

THREE HOUSES at HERMITAGE PLACE, STOCK-BRIDGE, each having a separate entrance and which, from the circumstance of being just without the extended royalty, are not liable to pay the town taxes, which now amount to above 20 per cent. and thus enjoy very considerable advantages.

One of the Houses is entirely finished, and the other two may be finished at a small expence, agreeably to the taste of a purchaser. Each contains six apartments, kitchen, and various conveniences.

1 View of Hermitage Street (renamed Raeburn Street in 1970s), 2022. This terrace with front and rear gardens is in the 'village' style developed by Henry Raeburn.
2 Advert, 1814
3 St Bernard's Bridge, c.1820

(now St Stephen Street) and sold the feus that regulated the builders to follow Brown's overall plan. Rather than being marketed for sale to occupants, the properties were advertised as investments, offering a return from rents of 10% p.a. Raeburn had envisaged Stockbridge attracting what he considered the right type of person and that required home ownership; the building of houses for rent undermined that vision.

The pace of building required large amounts of quarried stone and other materials to be hauled in by horse-drawn carts so around 1820 the stone bridge was widened and levelled: 'Upon the Bridge across the Water of Leith, which is so inconveniently narrow, a number of masons are at present employed; and it is intended to give it an additional width of several feet. Nowhere is the spirit of improvement more conspicuous than in this quarter. The stream above the bridge has been confined within banks of solid masonry, and its margin carpeted with verdant turf. The new Bridge near to St Bernard's Well is considerably advanced; and in all directions buildings are proceeding with great rapidity.'

The 1821 map on page 16 shows the original plan for the development of Raeburn's land to the west of Deanhaugh House, designed with input from the architect James Milne. The three parallel streets between Dean Street and Dean Terrace (then named Mineral Street) were to be Ann Street (named after Raeburn's wife), Charlotte Street (named after Raeburn's daughter-in-law), and Elizabeth Street (named after Raeburn's oldest granddaughter). However, only Ann Street, where building began around 1814, was built to the original plan, In 1822 No. 33 was on the market for £500 and was advertised as being 'plentifully supplied with excellent water from a well on the premises.' St Bernard's Bridge, probably also designed by James Milne, was built in 1824 to provide easy access to the Raeburn Estate. The large Jacobean stairs were added to the bridge in the 1880s.

Raeburn's initial plan was revised to enable the building of St Bernard's Crescent and in 1827 the *Caledonian Mercury* related that the idea for the crescent was suggested to Raeburn by his friend, David Wilkie. 'It is a fact not generally known, that St Bernard's Crescent was built at the suggestion of the celebrated artist, David Wilkie. On a visit to Raeburn Mr Wilkie said he was struck with the picturesque effect of a double row of stately elms, and proposed to his friend to erect on each side of the trees a deep crescent, in the purest style of Grecian architecture.' Although Raeburn died in 1823, his son took forward the idea; to enable its creation, Charlotte St and Elizabeth St were redesigned and renamed Danube St and Carlton St. As more land was now required for construction, Henry junior moved out of St Bernard's House, which was demolished. To link St Bernard's Crescent with Deanhaugh Street Leslie Place was created. However, its completion required the demolition of Deanhaugh House

1 Dean Bridge, engraving c.1840
1 No. 51 St Stephen Street, c. 1900
3 Arboretum Avenue - old entrance to Inverleith House - postcard,1905
4 Shop in Dean Street, rear of St Bernard's Crescent, 2023
5 Ann Street, c.1940
6 Bedford Street, c.1960s

and its gardens, but the widowed Mrs Inglis, Raeburn's step-daughter, who was living there refused to leave, so it was not until her death that Leslie Place was finally completed around 1880.

The majority of early shops were clustered around the bridge. This focus for shopping increased with the building of Brunswick (St Stephen) Street with its rows of shops and the opening of Stockbridge Market in 1826. A few small shops existed in other streets, such as those on Dean Street that were built in 1828 as part of the rear of the properties on the north-west side of St Bernard's Crescent.

Lord Provost Learmonth, who owned the Dean estate to the west of Stockbridge, was also keen to develop his land but the narrow steep roads up from the Water of Leith were a barrier. In 1824 he therefore commissioned the noted civil engineer, Thomas Telford to build the Dean Bridge from the west end of the town across the Water of Leith. This impressive structure, which is 136 metres long and 32 metres above the river, was one of Telford's last major works, being completed in 1831 when he was 73 years old. Although part of the money given towards its construction was on the condition that there would be no toll for traffic passing over it, between completion and the contract hand-over date the bridge builder John Gibb had a toll-gate erected at each end of the bridge and charged pedestrians one penny per head to enjoy the view from the structure.

By good fortune, the northwards development of Stockbridge left the great sweep of open land to the north and west consisting of the sports grounds of Edinburgh Academy and Grange Cricket Club, Inverleith Park and the Botanic Gardens. The creation of the sports facilities are recounted in later chapters. The Botanic Gardens, like Inverleith Park, originally were part of the country estate that had been owned by the Rocheid family since 1665. At the south end of Arboretum Avenue are two pillars, one hidden in trees, and on top of each sits a lion. These, together with the adjacent lodge, were the entrance to the estate and from them a tree-lined avenue led up to Inverleith House, designed by David Henderson in 1773. It was in 1877 that the house and grounds were bought to extend the Botanic Gardens: 'Another great improvement about to be made to the Botanic Garden by the extension of its limits. It already covers fourteen and half imperial acres, and to this area two and a half acres will at Whitsunday next be added on the west side, including within the walls the eastern slope of the finely wooded grounds around Inverleith House, lately purchased by the Crown for the purpose.'

Mary Gordon, the daughter of John Wilson of Elleray, a Scottish advocate and the writer most frequently identified with the pseudonym Christopher North of Blackwood's Edinburgh Magazine, recounted her family moving into No. 29 Ann Street in 1819: 'This little street was at

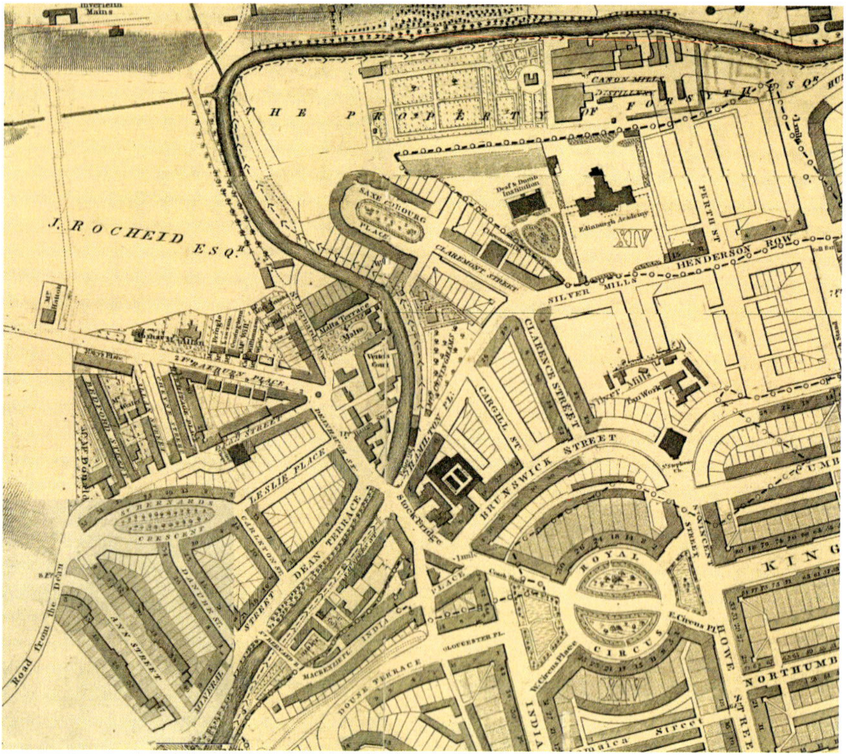

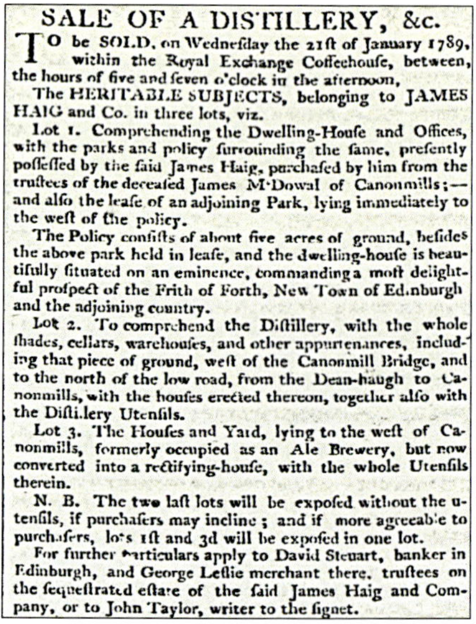

SALE OF A DISTILLERY, &c.

TO be SOLD, on Wednesday the 21st of January 1789, within the Royal Exchange Coffeehouse, between the hours of five and seven o'clock in the afternoon,

The HERITABLE SUBJECTS, belonging to JAMES HAIG and Co. in three lots, viz.

Lot 1. Comprehending the Dwelling-House and Offices, with the parks and policy surrounding the same, presently possessed by the said James Haig, purchased by him from the trustees of the deceased James M'Dowal of Canonmills;— and also the lease of an adjoining Park, lying immediately to the west of the policy.

The Policy consists of about five acres of ground, besides the above park held in lease, and the dwelling-house is beautifully situated on an eminence, commanding a most delightful prospect of the Frith of Forth, New Town of Edinburgh and the adjoining country.

Lot 2. To comprehend the Distillery, with the whole shades, cellars, warehouses, and other appurtenances, including that piece of ground, west of the Canonmill Bridge, and to the north of the low road, from the Dean-haugh to Canonmills, with the houses erected thereon, together also with the Distillery Utensils.

Lot 3. The Houses and Yard, lying to the west of Canonmills, formerly occupied as an Ale Brewery, but now converted into a rectifying-house, with the whole Utensils therein.

N. B. The two last lots will be exposed without the utensils, if purchasers may incline; and if more agreeable to purchasers, lots 1st and 3d will be exposed in one lot.

For further particulars apply to David Stewart, banker in Edinburgh, and George Leslie merchant there, trustees on the sequestrated estate of the said James Haig and Company, or to John Taylor, writer to the signet.

1 Detail from 1861 map by James Kirkwood (National Library of Scotland)
2 Mill lade that ran through Stockbridge, 1858 (photo -Thomas Begbie)
3 Advert, 1789

that time quite out of town. In withdrawing from the more fashionable part of Edinburgh, they did not, however, exclude themselves from the pleasures of social intercourse with the world. They found a pleasant little community that made residence there far from distasteful.' This was exactly how Raeburn had envisaged the new Stockbridge but Bedford Street, just a short walk from Ann Street, and in the 1840s similarly still on the edge of open countryside, was quite different. Here was a street of gardenless tenements occupied by tenants in 'half-flats'- one room and a kitchen. In 1849 a resident wrote: 'Here in the outskirts of the city of Edinburgh, quite rural in its aspect, offensive filth can be seen. There is a strip of ground used by the street inhabitants for bleaching, and which is divided into partitions. Through the medium of a choked up or burst soil-pipe a tenement conveys the contents of its privies and all its filth and waste upon the stripe of ground above mentioned, under the very windows of the residents of Bedford Street, not only destroying the natural amenity of the place, but actually disseminating a stench that is quite intolerable.'

Such insanitary conditions were not unusual. The rapid development of Stockbridge led to contamination of the river and lade: 'The Water of Leith during the whole summer has been a mass of stagnant impurity, sending forth the poison of death to all within its neighbourhood.' The pollution was hardly surprising for in 1853 it was reported that as well as the pollution from mills and other works, many New Town sewers drained into the Water of Leith between St Bernard's Well and Warriston Cemetery. As well as being unhealthy, the river and lade were dangerous; children and, less often, adults frequently drowned in them. In 1828 the Edinburgh and Leith Humane Society announced: 'In consequence of recent accidents at the Water of Leith, we have opened a receiving-house where persons accidentally drowned may be brought and the means of resuscitation employed; and that Messrs Crichton, surgeons, Stockbridge, have kindly undertaken to render professional assistance on such occasions.'

Raeburn's concern about the negative impact of noise and pollution proved real. There were regular complaints about foul odours and residents in those parts of Stockbridge near the mill lade and river had high incidences of illnesses. One complainant in 1858 wrote about 'the nauseous exhalations' from the distillery: 'During one night last week the atmosphere in the vicinity of Stockbridge was so thoroughly impregnated with carbonic acid gas, that it was perceptible in every house and shop.'

Yet these issues did not hold back Stockbridge's development although the disparity in living conditions increased. While the affluent lived in airy accommodation in fashionable streets the under-privileged were crammed into insanitary flats. In 1894, at an Edinburgh Public Health Committee meeting, the deplorable state of properties in Allan Street was raised and

1 Mackenzie Place allotments meeting hut designed by Sutherland Hussey Harris Architects
2 Saunders Street, c.1950
3 *Horse, Rider, Eagle* by Eoghan Bridge
4 Ordnance Survey Map of 1920 showing streets that were redeveloped in 1960s
5 Area today, Google Maps

a local doctor told the committee: 'The houses are small, mostly damp and dark, and are in many cases infested with rats. All fevers are much more frequent in Allan Street. The stairs of some houses are so dark that on one visit. I heard yells below my feet, and found on examination that I had trampled a child lying in the passage.' The conditions in Allan and Bedford streets were judged so bad that all the houses were demolished and new ones built.

Although the mill lade was covered over by the 1890s, the buildings in the streets it had run through had begun to deteriorate, as most were rented flats and few landlords looked after their properties. By the 1960s the overcrowding, lack of basic facilities and poor maintenance in Saunders Street, India Place and St Stephen Street were such that the council decided on major slum clearance. A campaign saved St Stephen Street and its properties were renovated but the two other streets were redeveloped with new flats built. Rather than recreate the long terrace formats, the architects set the blocks side on, creating open public space and views across the Water of Leith from India Place. Many were critical of the decision to demolish the old tenements and opinions on the replacement flats remain mixed. Yet for many who lived there – particularly those who shared an external toilet – the redevelopment was welcomed. In 1962 Janet Wilson who lived in India Place told *The Scotsman:* 'At the age of 70 my ambition is to get a new house with a bathroom and toilet.' A second redevelopment of the area around Bedford Street and Allan Street took place around the same time.

Almost all of Stockbridge's early industrial buildings sites that are explored in a later chapter have been redeveloped as housing or offices. To mark its residential development in Silvermills in 1997 Cala Homes commissioned a striking sculpture, *Horse, Rider, Eagle* by Eoghan Bridge. Another public art work was sited in Stockbridge in 2010 when one of Turner Prize-winning artist Antony Gormley's six figures that watch over the Water of Leith river as it winds its way through and down to the sea – called *6 TIMES* - was placed in the river just to the west of the bridge. Such contemporary public art works often divide opinion, as do architectural projects. A modern shed designed by Sutherland Hussey Harris Architects as part of the allotments on the empty ground where Mackenzie Place buildings once stood stirred up objections from local residents who argued the five-metre high shed could 'destroy' views of Georgian Edinburgh. In spite of the protests it was built and its quirkiness in what was previously a derelict space seems, to this writer at least, to suit Stockbridge. Similarly, while the proposed grandstand for the Edinburgh Academicals ground caused debate, its stylish design by Michael Laird Architects may have appeased most of those who were against its construction.

HOMES FOR WORKING FAMILIES

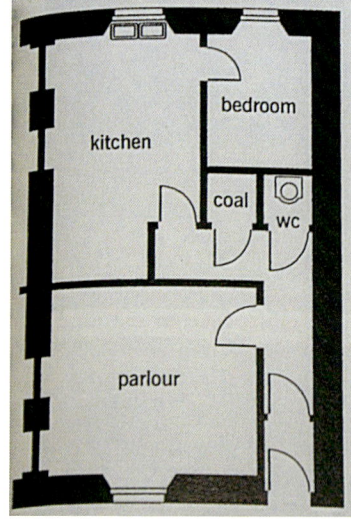

1 Builders' plaque, Stockbridge Colonies
2 Patriot Hall buildings, 2023
3 Layout of an early ground floor house in the Stockbridge Colonies
4 Reid Terrace (frontispiece of *Happy Homes for Working Men* by J. Begg, 1866)
5 The pedestrian bridge and ford at Bridge Place before the Falshaw Bridge was built, 1874 (Capital Collection)

Two significant projects to provide better housing for the less well-off took place in Stockbridge in the 1860s. The Edinburgh & Northern District Co-operative Society built 42 'dwelling places for artisans' on the land where Patriot Hall house and garden had stood. Designed by John Starforth, each contained a large living room where there was a sink and a recess for a bed; two bedrooms, one with a fireplace, and a Water Closet (toilet), exceptional at the time for houses of this type. Communal washing accommodation was provided in a separate building.

At the same time The Edinburgh Cooperative Building Company (ECBC), formed by seven stonemasons following an industrial dispute in which construction workers were barred from work, began building the Stockbridge Colonies, named Glenogle Park, to the north of Saxe-Coburg Place on land that had been part of the Haig distillery. The ECBC issued shares and holders received dividends. The purchase price of each house was between £100 and £130, and buyers only had to put down a £5 deposit and then received a loan for the balance to be repaid over a 15- to 20-year period, thus enabling workers with modest but regular incomes to buy their own house. A condition of purchase was that it was 'unlawful to convert, or permit to be converted, any of the dwelling houses into shebeens or brothels or to have any cow house, pig house, or manufactory.' The innovative design of ground-floor front doors facing in one direction and first floor front doors on the opposite side allowed for external staircases, which made the houses cheaper to build. Each house had a minimum of two rooms, a scullery and a WC. The first row was named Reid Terrace in honour of Hugh Gilzean Reid – a newspaper editor who assisted the striking stonemasons.

Although the aim was to empower working-class families to benefit from private home ownership, many of the earlier houses were sold to investors to finance the building of the other terraces. James Ross, a well-off photographer who in 1849 with his partner John Thomson sent an album of their photographs to Windsor Castle and in return were appointed 'Photographers to the Queen', purchased 20 houses in Hugh Miller Place. The final terraces, Dunrobin, Balmoral and Teviotdale were not completed until the 1890s as that land had been in use as the ECBC's building yard.

A small row of shops to service the colonies' 2,000 residents was built in Bridge Place. For a few years there was no bridge across the river to St Bernard's Row so to get from the Colonies to Stockbridge people either, 'had to cross a frail erection of planks over the Water of Leith, or ascend to the back of Saxe-Coburg Place, by a lane steep, narrow, and tortuous.' In 1863 a wooden footbridge was erected but it was not until 1877 that the current iron Falshaw Bridge, named in honour of the then Lord Provost, was opened.

ST BERNARD'S WELL

ST BERNARD'S WELL..
To be Let,
ST BERNARD'S WELL, in the immediate neighbourhood of the New Town.
Offers to be lodged with Robinson and Ainslie, W. S. who will inform as to particulars.
2, Hill Street, Edinr. Feb. 20, 1810.

ST. BERNARD'S WELL.

The KEEPER of the WELL is in ATTENDANCE from 7 till 9.30 A.M. and from 12 Noon till 6 P.M. (on Sundays from 7 till 9 A.M. and from 3.15 till 6 P.M.) for the supply of the MINERAL WATER to VISITORS, at the Charge of ONE PENNY per Visitor.
The Water is celebrated for its Health-giving and Curative Qualities, and is especially beneficial in cases of Rheumatism and Indigestion, and in Diseases of the Skin, Liver, and Kidneys.
The well laid-out GROUNDS adjoining the Well are OPEN to VISITORS.

1 *St Bernard's Well* engraved by W Poole (Wellcome Collection)
2 Advert, 1810
3 Advert, 1895

St Bernard's Well was discovered in 1760 by three schoolboys and may have been given its name by Walter Ross who lived in the nearby St Bernard's House. Its water swiftly became reputed for its medicinal qualities, and was much visited by the nobility and gentry. 'Few mineral springs in the United Kingdom have proved more efficacious in the prevention and cure of those numerous diseases to which the human frame is liable.' In 1789 the well was purchased by Lord Gardenstone and he commissioned the Scottish painter Alexander Nasmyth to design the ornate structure above it that includes a statue of the Greek goddess of health, Hygeia.

A 'keeper of the well' was employed as those coming to drink its claimed efficacious water had to pay: 'Those who choose to subscribe for the season, from the 1st of May to the 1st of October, shall pay down, before they begin to drink, at least five shillings sterling. Persons who do not choose to subscribe, but choose at their pleasure to drink the water any time of the morning period, occasionally, shall pay before they begin to drink every morning, for grown persons each one penny, and for children each one halfpenny; or at the rate of sixpence and threepence per week respectively. For water drawn from the well to be used at a distance, in bottles or other vessels in the mornings, payment must be made at the rate of one halfpenny for every Scots pint. Upon a proper certificate from any regular physician, surgeon, or apothecary of Edinburgh, the keeper shall supply poor persons with water at any time prescribed.' People had to bring their own 'proper glasses and cups' for drinking the water and 'retire immediately and walk about, or take other exercise for an interval of at least five minutes, both as a benefit to themselves, and to make way for other water drinkers.'

The well passed through various hands and in 1888 was purchased by William Nelson of the Edinburgh publishing firm Thomas Nelson & Sons. He had it restored and commissioned Thomas Bonnar to create a beautiful mosaic and marble design for the interior pump room. Those wishing to drink still had to pay, although by 1895 the charge was a flat one penny. The well then passed into the care of Edinburgh Council. In 1938 it was reported that the city council were considering 'a proposal is for the bottling of the waters of St Bernard's Well, Edinburgh, for sale not only in the city but throughout the country.' However, this did not go ahead. The well was shut for the Second World War and when it was reopened in 1956 the water was deemed unfit to drink.

The well remains in the ownership of Edinburgh City Council but is maintained by the Dean Village Association. Although it continues to be much visited and admired, the well's pump room is only open on special occasions, and the drinking of its once 'efficacious water' still prohibited.

INDUSTRIAL STOCKBRIDGE

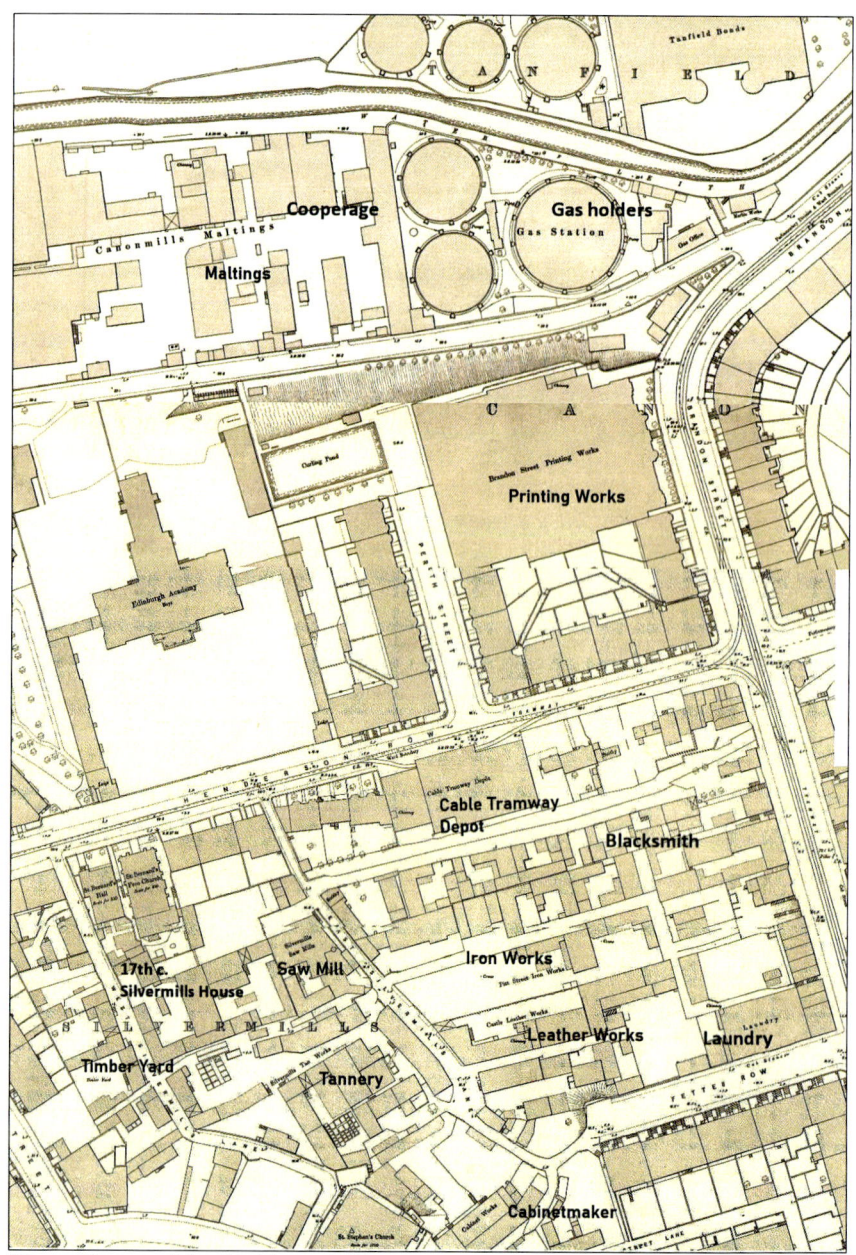

Silvermills area of Stockbridge, c.1890

The Water of Leith that runs from Pentland Hills into the Firth of Forth at Leith was a source of power from the 12th century onward. Weirs and mill lades were constructed to drive water-wheels for a range of industries including grinding grain, wood, spices and snuff, paper making, washing and waulking (fulling) cloth, tanning hides, and cutting timber and stone. The growth of industrial activity in Stockbridge began around 1750: Robert Raeburn expanded his yarn-boiling house; Stockbridge Mills was built on the south-east side of the bridge (behind today's Baker's Place) about 1760; and in 1780 James Haig built a large distillery on the south side of the Water of Leith – where the Colonies are today.

Four years after Haig's distillery opened it was attacked by a mob as there were food shortages and people heard the distillery was using potential food grain to make whisky. Their attempt to set fire to the distillery was beaten back by the army, with one rioter killed. Haig argued that the raw material being used was nothing humans would want to eat but in reality the grain could have helped. Haig was producing far more spirit than Scotland could possibly drink in an attempt to break into the English market where tax concessions resulting from the Treaty of Union gave them an advantage. In 1788 the Lowlands Licence Act prohibited the export of Scottish whisky to England for 12 months and Haig immediately went bust. The distillery was bought by John Stein and in 1825 returned to the ownership of the Haigs.

The distillery later changed production to brewery malting and in 1860 part of the site was sold for the building of the Stockbridge colonies while the remaining part was bought and expanded by the brewers William Younger. This firm began brewing in the 18th century and by 1830 had developed the Abbey Brewery near Holyrood, and expanded its business into international markets, during the Crimean War winning a lucrative government contract to supply beer to the army. Hence the need for larger premises: 'The great maltings and storehouses at Canonmills in which the bulk of the malt is prepared for the Abbey and Holyrood breweries occupy an area of nearly three acres. The buildings are remarkable for their strength and solidity, their cleanness and convenience of situations relatively to each other.' There had always been coopering on the site; this work was taken over by William Lindsay & Sons, who expanded the business, producing thousands of barrels for brewers. They were taken over by Scottish & Newcastle in the 1950s and by 1968 the use of metal casks had reduced demand for oak casks from the brewing industry so the whisky industry became the main clients. The business closed around 1970 and the site redeveloped.

In 1883 R & R Clark, book printers, built new premises on the corner of Glenogle Road and Brandon Street, opposite the cooperage, to expand its business. As well as large workshops, the firm built Dundas House on

1 A blacksmith & farrier in Canonmills, 1887 (photo - Thomas Begbie, Capital Collections)
2 Cask making at William Lindsay & Sons' cooperage, Glenogle Road, 1936 (still from the film, *Cooperage: The Craft of Cask Making*)
3 View of workshops and factories in Silvermills, c.1900
4 Bindery at R&R Clark, Glenogle Road, 1935
5 Thomas Hadden's workshop making the wrought iron gates for St Giles Cathedral, c.1910

Brandon Street, designed by John Chesser. Those entering the Dundas Street office were confronted with a sign: 'FRIEND! You stand on sacred ground! This is a printing office!' The firm was started by Robert Clark in 1864, who in 1871 trained the first woman compositor in Britain, Fanny MacPherson. She worked with the firm for over sixty years and trained more female compositors. The firm's print output included Robert Louis Stevenson's early work, *Travels with a Donkey* in 1879 and all Walter Scott's novels, in an edition known as *The Sixpenny Waverley*, each in an illustrated paper cover, that sold hundreds of thousands of copies. By the time of its move to Canonmills the firm was one of the leading printers in Edinburgh; a city regarded as Britain's main book printing centre. Clark's visitors' book includes the signatures of many great writers including Thomas Hardy, H. G. Wells, W. B. Yeats, Edith Sitwell and Bernard Shaw. In 1946, when Shaw was approached by Penguin for permission to publish a series of ten of his plays, Shaw stipulated one condition: 'Clarks of Edinburgh must do the printing.' One hundred thousand copies of each were produced in record time. The firm closed in 1978 and Standard Life bought the site, retaining Dundas House and building new offices behind.

In 1886 the Northern Cable Tramway erected a tram depot, designed by William Hamilton Beattie, in Henderson Row. It had a 'garage' for the tramcars and housed the pulley system that operated the underground cables. Later, Henderson Row Laundry was built alongside. When the cable cars were withdrawn it became a bus garage for a time. In 1991 the buildings were redeveloped as offices.

The Silvermills area housed a range of workshops, including an iron works, a sawmill, a brass foundry, a Venetian blind maker and, in the early 1900s the workshop of Thomas Hadden, a blacksmith specialising in wrought iron-work. He was a master craftsman and at his Silvermills workshop made a number of works designed by the architect Robert Lorimer, including the wrought iron screens for the Thistle Chapel in Edinburgh's St Giles Cathedral and the casket in the Scottish National War Memorial. Architectural commissions were a key area of his business - he made gates and railings but also more whimsical features including weather vanes, shop signs and boot-scrapers.

In the 1950s William Allan Smith & Co. of East Silvermills were commissioned to install an 'electric blanket' under the Mound to keep the road from freezing and in the 1960s it was announced that the firm had been contracted, 'to lay over 50 miles of cable which will be used to heat the roadway at the southern approaches to the Forth Road Bridge, where the toll booths will be situated.'

Over time the horses that had worked in the area and been stabled there, were replaced by motor vehicles, and as businesses closed or moved out, the buildings began to be demolished or converted for housing.

CHURCHES

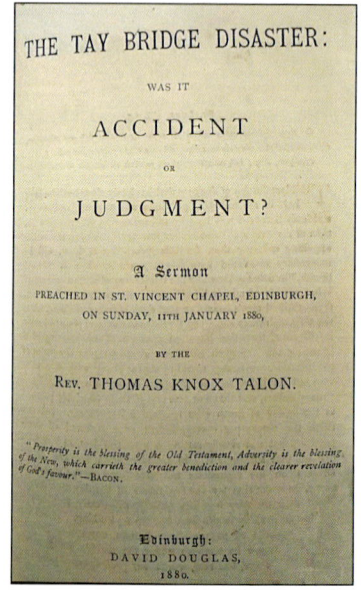

1 Former Dean Street United Presbyterian Church Mission Hall, 31 Dean Street, 2017 (photo – Peter Stubbs)
2 St Bernard's Free church, Henderson Row, opened 1854, demolished 1985
3 Stockbridge Free church, Deanhaugh Street, opened 1868, partly demolished in 1980s
4 Sermon, *Was it accident or judgement* by Thomas Knox Talon in reference to the Tay Bridge Disaster in 1880, preached in St Vincent's Chapel, St Stephen Street, 1880

On Sabbaths in the distant past, Stockbridge's worshippers would have walked up the steep Church Street/Lane (now Gloucester Street/Lane) to the West Kirk (St Cuthbert's), as until 1823 there was no church in Stockbridge. An essential part of a church's revenue came from annual charges for seats so it was not until the area had a sufficient well-to-do population that the first church was built. The Claremont Street Chapel designed by James Milne opened in Claremont Street (now Saxe-Coburg Terrace) in 1823. It was later renamed St Bernard's Church, Today it is Stockbridge Church and still used for religious services. In 1834 a concert of sacred music was held in the building; concerts and events continue to be regularly mounted there.

St Stephen's Church, designed by William Henry Playfair, opened in 1828 at the top of St Stephen Street. By the 1950s the congregation had declined and the building was remodelled with the gallery level floored over to become the church space and a large hall created below; today it is an arts venue. In the same year Dean Street Chapel (No. 30) designed by a Mr Ellison was built for members of the Relief Congregation, a non-conformist group, but within a short time became home to the United Presbyterian Church (UPC) and renamed St Bernard's Chapel, later Dean United Free Church. The UPC also had a hall across the road at No. 31. The chapel closed in 1915 and became a cinema for a time but during the 1950s housed the Elim Pentecostal Church.

The split in the Church of Scotland (the Disruption) in 1843 led to a flurry of new church building, as those who had left the established Church for the Free Church needed new places to worship. Thus in 1854 St Bernard's Free Church in Henderson Row designed by John Milne opened, and in 1868 Stockbridge Free Church in Deanhaugh Street, designed by Peddie & Kinnear, was built using material from Free St George's Church in Lothian Road that had to be demolished to make way for the railway's expansion. St Bernard's Free Church was demolished in 1985 and Stockbridge Free Church in 1980, although its tower survives. Similarly, a split in an episcopal congregation in Edinburgh in 1857 led to the building of Christ's English Episcopal Chapel (today, St Vincent's Chapel) opposite St Stephens Church. It was designed by the Hay Brothers of Liverpool.

Other buildings have been used for religious services. Around the 1860s signed deaf-led church services were held in St Stephen's School. The Wesleyan Methodists bought the Albion Halls in Hamilton Place, renaming it Wesley Hall, and held their services there through to around 1940; the building was then used for a time by the Jehovah's Witnesses. Today, Edinburgh North Church meets in the LifeCare Centre in Cheyne Street.

CHARITABLE INSTITUTIONS

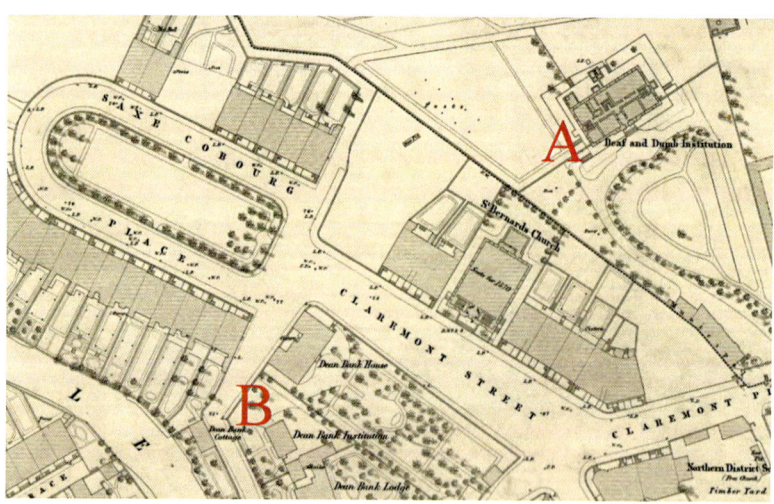

DEAF AND DUMB EXAMINATION.

THE ANNUAL MEETING of the Subscribers, and others friendly to the DEAF & DUMB INSTITUTION, will be held in the ASSEMBLY ROOMS, on MONDAY the 19th of JUNE, when the Pupils will be Examined, and the proceedings for the past year Reported.

The Chair will be taken at Two o'clock.
A COLLECTION will be made at the Doors in aid of the Funds of the Institution.
Edinburgh, 13th June 1843.

1 Ordnance Survey Map 1850 showing locations of A - Deaf and Dumb Institution & B - Dean Bank Institution (National Library of Scotland)
2 Deaf and Dumb Institution, c.1900
3 Advert, 1843
4 Women resident in the Dean Bank Institution for the Religious, Moral, and Industrial Training of Girls, c.1900

Thomas Braidwood opened the first British school for deaf children in Edinburgh in 1760 but moved it to London 20 years later. In 1810, one of his grandsons, John Braidwood, opened the Edinburgh Institution for the Deaf and Dumb in Rose Street and in 1824 it moved to a new building accommodating around 50 pupils and designed for free by the architect James Gillespie Graham on land between Saxe Coburg Street and Hamilton Academy. It had a large flower and vegetable garden, bleaching-green and playgrounds, and the interior spaces were described as 'admirably lighted'. On the first floor there were two interconnected classrooms, with the dormitories on the upper floors.

In 1837 Alexander Drysdale, who was himself deaf and dumb, opened a rival institution, the Deaf and Dumb Day School in St John Street that had a similar number of pupils. These two institutions merged in 1846 with Drysdale's 50 pupils moving to the Stockbridge building. In the 1890s additional wings were added, providing a swimming pool, gymnasium and additional classrooms.

Donaldson's Hospital, which opened in Wester Coates in 1850, was founded to be an asylum for destitute children, but it was decided that half of the accommodation would be for deaf children. In 1938 it merged with the Deaf and Dumb Institution as Donaldson's School for the Deaf. The Stockbridge building became the school's junior department, with Donaldson's Hospital now the senior department. In 2008 the school moved to a new campus in Linlithgow and the Stockbridge building was incorporated into the Edinburgh Academy.

The Dean Bank Institution for the Reformation of Female Juvenile Delinquents was established in Deanbank Lane in 1832. Its aim was to reform girls and young women who had been discharged from prison. In 1848 the Institution opened another establishment in Morningside. While the Morningside branch continued as a reformatory, Dean Bank became more preventative, taking in neglected, destitute or orphan girls and training them for domestic service; in 1870 its name changed to Dean Bank Institution for the Religious, Moral, and Industrial Training of Girls. The inmates were mainly occupied in washing and laundry work. The institution received an annual grant from local police funds but more had to be raised from donations and legacies. In 1870 it was reported: 'The number of girls at present in the Institution is 28, 15 of whom are above twelve years of age. 11 have been admitted during the year. Of those who left in the course of the year 6 have had situations procured for them as domestic servants, 5 have been removed by friends, 1 has absconded and 1 has been dismissed.'

In 1913 the building was acquired for Stockbridge School and the institution moved to newly built premises in Morningside.

SCHOOLS

EDINBURGH ACADEMY.

THE DIRECTORS hereby give notice, that the ACADEMY will be OPENED on FRIDAY the 1st of OCTOBER next, under the following arrangement of the Masters:—

Latin, Greek, and Geography,
First, or Junior Class........Mr CARMICHAEL.
Second Class.................Mr FERGUSON.
Third Class..................Mr MITCHELL.
Fourth Class.................Mr MARRIOTT.
Fifth and Sixth, or Rector's Classes } ......The Rev. JOHN WILLIAMS.
English Language and Literature, and Modern History.
Mr BARKER.
Arithmetic, Algebra, and Geometry,
Mr GLOAG.
Writing,
Mr GLOVER.

STOCKBRIDGE.

MR CAMERON will open a CLASS for BEGINNERS, on Monday the 3d of April. The PRIVATE CLASS for GEOGRAPHY is from 8 to 9 in the Morning.

Mr Cameron is to remove at Whitsunday, for the better accommodation of his pupils, to Malta House. The quietness and retirement of Malta House, and the advantage of play ground which it possesses, fit it admirably for the purposes of a private academy.

3, Johnston Place, March 24, 1826.

1 *Edinburgh Academy* engraving by Thomas Hosmer Shepherd, c.1830. The boy talking to the two men is holding a cricket bat.
2 Edinburgh Academy advert, 1828
3 Advert for Mr Cameron's private school, 1826

Before 1830 those in Stockbridge who wished to have their children educated had to pay as there were no free schools in the area. There were a number of private schools such as Maclaren's Academy in Hamilton Place (described in a later chapter) and Cameron's English Academy at No. 6 Raeburn Place. Both taught boys and girls, though not in mixed classes. In 1824 four daughters of James and Agatha Cullen who lived in Hermitage Place - Jane, Cordelia, Agatha and Matilda – all received 'a handsome silver medal and elegant book' from Mr Cameron in reward for 'their prowess in reading, spelling, recitation, grammar, history and geography'.

It is recounted that one day in the early 1820s, while walking in the Pentland Hills, Lord Cockburn, a judge, and Leonard Horner, a Scottish merchant, shared their concern at what they saw to be a decline of classical education in Scotland. Neither thought that the Town Council-run High School was providing the best education for the youth of the ever growing New Town of Edinburgh so resolved to establish a new school. They swiftly gained financial backing and support, including from the High School's star ex-pupil, Walter Scott, and in spite of fierce opposition from the Town Council, Edinburgh Academy opened in Henderson Row in 1824 in a building designed by William Burn.

The Academy was a boys' fee-paying day school and had around 500 pupils aged from 10 to 15. Many of the pupils came from overseas, where their fathers were serving in the forces or with the East India Company, and boarded in private houses nearby. Initially the staff consisted of the Rector (a minister), four Classical Masters (Greek and Latin), an English Master, a Writing Master, a French Master and a Mathematical & Arithmetical Master. The Academy's commitment to a classical education was even reflected in their janitor, John Howell, who wrote an *Essay on the War Galleys of the Ancients* and *A Life of Alexander Selkirk*, and built ingenious models, including a replica of Caesar's bridge over the Rhine. School hours were 9am to 3pm weekdays and, until 1850, additionally 9am to 11am on Saturdays.

In 1870 a hot lunch was provided whereas before pupils had to make do with a 'bap or equivalent bought from the Janitor's wife' or rush between lessons to nearby 'tuck shops', such as John Bowton's confectioners at No. 8 Hamilton Place. From the 1870s younger children were admitted and in the 1880s the school built its own boarding facilities. Later developments included a School Library, a Science Block, and a rifle range, opened in 1912.

The school greatly expanded after the Second World War with new campuses opening in different parts of the city. Recent additions include a new Science Centre (inspired by an alumnus of the school, mathematician and physicist James Clerk Maxwell) and the Salveson Performing Arts

1 Boys class at Stockbridge Primary School, 1900 (Capital Collections)
2 Girls class at Dean Street School, 1887 (Capital Collections)
3 Doorway at St Bernard's School, Dean Street, 2023

Centre. Girls were first admitted as members of the Sixth Form in the 1970s, but it was not until 2008 that the school became fully co-educational. It remains an independent fee-paying school and today caters for 2-18 year-olds with 600 in the Senior School, 400 in the Junior School and 100 in the Nursery.

Before the Education (Scotland) Act 1872 introduced universal education for all children aged from 5 to 13, those wishing to send their children to school but unable to pay fees were reliant on church schools. Two opened in the 1830s: St Stephen's School in St Stephen Street and Dean Street School next to St Bernard's Chapel. St Stephen's School was designed by George Smith and consisted of: 'three floors, each forming a spacious room for the accommodation of a separate class; the classes forming a boys' school, a girls' school, and an infant school, comprising about 400 children, belonging to the poorer classes of the parish.' Dean Street School was designed by Robert Wright. A third church school, the Northern District School, was opened in 1844 by St Bernard's Free Church alongside their newly built church in Henderson Row.

In 1624, George Heriot left a significant sum to found a 'hospital' (charitable school) to care for the "puire, fatherless bairnes" of burgesses of Edinburgh. By the mid-1840s only a minority of the pupils were orphans and the trustees used part of the funds to build free schools around the city. Although the trust built St Bernard's School at the top of Dean Street, on completion it was handed to the Edinburgh School Board. Designed by John Chesser and opened in 1877, it accommodated 600 pupils. In the same year Stockbridge School, built by the School Board and designed by Rowand Anderson, opened in Hamilton Place. It accommodated around 650 pupils. Attending its opening was Flora Stevenson, an active member of the local School Board. The 1872 Education Act establishing School Boards had given women the right to vote and to stand for election, the first opportunity for women to be elected to a public post. However, in the first election only 17 women were elected to the 5,650 places.

The church schools in Dean Street and Henderson Row closed in the 1870s but St Stephen's School continued to function independently until 1890, at which point Edinburgh School Board decided that there was no need for the school as sufficient accommodation existed elsewhere for all the pupils in the district. Yet in 1898 it was reported to the Edinburgh School Board that '200 children have been refused admission to Stockbridge School, and Dean and St Bernard's Schools are practically full.' In response the Board agreed to build a new school in Comely Bank Road; the Flora Stevenson school.

St Bernard's School closed in the 1970s but Stockbridge School continues as a nursery and primary school.

LIBRARIES

SOMERVILLE'S CIRCULATING LIBRARY,
STOCKBRIDGE.
The Best NEW BOOKS as Published. *Ask for a Catalogue.*
ROBERT SOMERVILLE,
STATIONER AND LIBRARIAN,
10 SPRING GARDENS, STOCKBRIDGE, EDINBURGH.

TERMS OF SUBSCRIPTION.
Commencing at any date.

SINGLE AND FAMILY SUBSCRIPTION.

	Six Months. £ s. d.	Twelve Months. £ s. d.
ONE VOLUME AT ONE TIME	0 12 0	1 1 0
FOUR DITTO DITTO	1 2 0	2 2 0
EIGHT DITTO DITTO	1 14 0	3 3 0

Subscribers are entitled to exchange their Books at pleasure—not oftener than once a-day.

The leading Periodicals may be obtained, one at a time, on the day of publication,—each being counted as one volume.

1 Advert for Robert Somerville's Circulating Library at No. 10 Spring Gradens, 1863
2 Circulating Library charges, c.1840
3 Stockbridge Library, 1915 (Capital Collections)

In the early 1800s books were expensive; the average three-volume novel cost a guinea that was roughly the equivalent of £100 today. Thus, private libraries opened - called subscription or circulating libraries - offering patrons access to more books than most could realistically afford. People paid an annual membership fee and then paid to borrow individual books. For many years these private libraries did not consider novels serious enough to be stocked, but the success of Walter Scott's novels, and women writers such as Jane Austen and Edinburgh's Mary Brunton began to change that view.

Robert Chambers, who features in a later chapter, opened his first 'Library of New Books' at No. 4 India Place in 1822. It moved to Hanover Street a few years later but from the 1850s Robert Somerville ran one at his stationers shop at No. 10 Spring Gardens.

When the philanthropist, Andrew Carnegie offered £25,000 to fund a public library for Edinburgh the owners of the many commercial subscription libraries blocked the idea through fear of losing business. It was only after Carnegie doubled his offer to £50,000 that the council finally agreed to go ahead and the Central Library opened in 1890.

Residents of Stockbridge soon began campaigning for a branch public library and after much debate the council agreed. The building in Hamilton Place, designed by Henry Ramsay Taylor, opened on 25 October 1900. A hall financed by the Nelson family was incorporated into the building. When Thomas Nelson junior, of the Nelson publishing firm, died in 1892, his will included a bequest for 'Shelter Halls' as 'places to which persons of the working class and others can go to sit, read, write, converse and otherwise occupy themselves.' *The Edinburgh Evening Despatch* reported on the new building: 'A handsome building, both externally and internally....The Nelson Hall is about 64ft. long by 50ft. wide, and is divided with two rows of double columns and arches carrying the roof.' The hall later was amalgamated into the library.

The Reading Room had newspapers and magazines etc.; in the early decades all references to horse racing were cut out of each newspaper at the start of the day to discourage gambling. In its first year Stockbridge Library issued 128,640 volumes. In those days books were not accessible to the public on the shelves, and a reader wanting a particular book had to consult the library catalogue for its reference number, and then check an indicator board that showed the book number with either a red or blue marker. Children were not entitled to use libraries until they were seven years old and everyone in the library, including staff, was discouraged from conversation – silence ruled! Today the library is more relaxed on use and among its many community activities are 'Bookbug' sessions; 'fun-filled times of stories, and rhymes for children aged 0 to 4 years and their parents or carers'.

LAUNDRIES

W. JOHNSTONE,
FAMILY LINEN BLEACHER,
Gets up in First Class Style all kinds of FAMILY, BED, and TABLE LINEN with nothing but the best soaps, pure water, and hand labour.
Bleach Work—PATRIOTHILL, STOCKBRIDGE.

FOWLER'S RAEBURN LAUNDRY
DEANBANK LANE, EDINBURGH
also
RAEBURN CLEANERS
For Quick Service Dry Cleaning
Regular Collections and Deliveries in all Districts
Receiving Offices — Telephone
31 Deanhaugh Street - 13 Deanbank Lane — DEAN 2274/5

1 Advert for Johnstone, bleacher, Patriot Hall, 1863
2 Advert for Fowler's Raeburn Laundry, 1956
3 Advert for Oxydol Washing Powder featuring the children of Mrs Notman of No. 16a Kemp Place, 1951
4 Henderson Road Public Laundry (The Steamie), c.1970s (Capital Collections)
5 Stockbridge Laundrette, No. 41 Raeburn Place, c.1960s

When Stockbridge was a village many women washed their laundry in the Water of Leith but as the water became polluted, this ceased to be an option, and washing had to done in the home. On laundry days the many that did not have piped in cold water had to collect what they needed from a nearby well. Once the water had been boiled over a fire, the clothes were put into the tub and stirred with a dolly (a wooden stick with what looks like a stool attached to the bottom), before being scrubbed. White and coloured clothes had to be washed separately so the process had to be repeated. Clothes then were put through a mangle turned by hand to squeeze out the water and the damp clothing dried in back gardens, drying greens or hung from windows or inside the house. For clothes requiring ironing, heavy metal irons were heated on a fire before use.

By the 1880s with more residents in Stockbridge able to afford to pay to have their laundry done and new equipment being introduced, commercial laundries began to be established. The Edinburgh & Northern Cooperative Society opened a large one at Patriothall, Hamilton Place: 'Ironers wanted, must be good hands at shirts. Patriothall, Stockbridge.' It continued through to the 1950s.

For many years a number of freelance washerwomen had worked in basements in Deanbank Lane and this developed into a small private laundry at Nos. 7-13. This was taken over in 1925 by Ben Gunn Fowler and named the Raeburn Laundry Company. Over the next two decades Fowler changed it to a steam laundry and continually modernised the business. One resident recalled: 'Vans went round and collected and delivered washing from and to hotels and private houses. At one time when I was small and we didn't have a washing machine, my mother sent our sheets there to be washed. The washing was always returned to us in a nice brown paper parcel. There were also what were called 'bag washes' where someone's clothes were handed in in a cloth bag and somehow kept together throughout the process. I remember that the boarders at the Edinburgh Academy sent bag washes.' Fowler died in 1948 but the laundry continued to operate until the early 1970s.

In 1903 Edinburgh Council opened the city's second public laundry washhouse in Allan Street. Colloquially known as 'The Steamie', the washhouse had 40 wash stalls and a crèche for the woman who used it. In 1908 it accommodated 30,000 washes. It was closed in 1928 when a new washhouse opened with a 200-foot high chimney at the far end of Henderson Row next to the former cable tram powerhouse. It had 80 tubs and 11 hydro extractors. It closed in 1977 in spite of local protest.

From the 1950s many people began to own washing machines but laundries and dry cleaners continued, and in the 1960s laundrettes, such as the Stockbridge Laundrette at No. 41 Raeburn Place opened. Today, Raeburn Place still has two dry cleaners and launderers.

COMMUNITY HALLS

 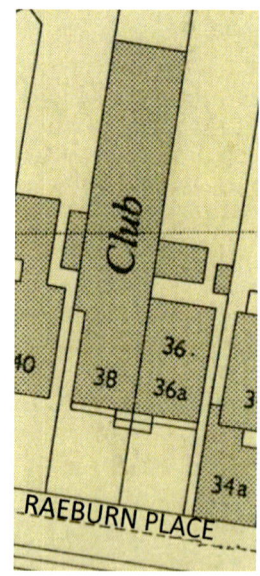

PRIMROSE LEAGUE — ST BERNARD HABITATION. — CONCERT TO-NIGHT, ALBION HALLS, HAMILTON PLACE, 8 P.M. Mrs COWIE, Misses MACDONALD, REID, and Messrs J. F. GRANT, SAWERS, MITCHELL, and J. O. SINCLAIR take part in Programme. RECITATIONS and VIOLIN SOLOS by Miss GERTRUDE SCOTT. ADDRESS by CHRISTOPHER N. JOHNSTON, Esq., Advocate.
K. J. HAY, Hon. Secy.

EDINBURGH Spiritualist Mission, 90 Raeburn Place. Sunday, at 11.30 and 6.30. Speaker—Mr Fulton, Clairvoyant. Monday and Tuesday as usual. Wednesday at 2 Leamington Terrace, at 3-8 p.m.—Mrs M'Quire, Clairvoyante.

1 Former Working Men's Institute, Brunswick Street (now 106 St Stephen Street), built 1867
2 Map extract showing site of Raeburn Place Hall/Club at No. 38 Raeburn Place, 1920
3 Advert for concert in the Albion Halls, Hamilton Place, 1891
4 Advert for the Edinburgh Spiritualist Mission that met regularly throughout the 1920s at No. 90 Raeburn Places, 1925

Stockbridge Parish Church, Edinburgh Academy, St Stephen's Church and LifeCare Centre are among the premises that today rent out spaces for weddings, concerts, theatre events, meetings, etc. but the specialist halls that once were peppered around Stockbridge have all disappeared or become used for other purposes.

Dance for All at No. 106 St Stephen Street is housed in the building erected as the Stockbridge Working Men's Institute. Here were presented lectures such as 'Rambles in Russia, illustrated by photographs of the public buildings in the cities of St Petersburg and Moscow, exhibited by the oxy-hydrogen light', and concerts. However, the club had a short life and became the hall of St Vincent's Chapel. Although primarily used for church activities, the hall was hired out for a range of activities. In 1879 the Stockbridge Conservative Association held its inaugural meeting in the hall, while in 1948 the relatively young Scottish National Party used it for a public meeting.

As part of the redevelopment of Hamilton Place in the 1880s, a hall seating 500 was created at No. 10. Named at various times, Webster's Hall, Hamilton Place Halls and Albion Halls, it housed a range of events including winter concerts; dance tuition; Sunday evening services by the Evangelist Serving Under Apostles congregation; the Edinburgh Northern District Ornithological Society's annual exhibition at which 150 birds were on show; the St Bernard's Football Club annual soiree; and meetings of all political shades. It was much used by the Wesleyan Methodists and eventually in 1904 its concern at, 'the association with boxing entertainments held there that recently have acquired unenviable notoriety' led the congregation to purchase the building and it was revamped as Wesley Hall: 'The commodious and efficient suite of buildings, admirably adapted for mission purposes, has been reduced from what was previously a bewildering collection of committee rooms of all sorts and sizes. An entirely new entrance leads through a crush corridor to the main hall, which will seat about 700 adults. The hall has been considerably altered, entirely re-seated, fitted with new ventilation, heating, and electric lighting. A smaller hall, seating about 300, has been made on the second floor for the Sunday School, Guild, and Band of Hope work.' While boxing no longer took place, it continued to house a wide range of events when not in use for church events. These included draughts competitions; rehearsals by the Edinburgh Amateur Orchestral Society; St Bernard's Ward Labour Association's meetings, (including a lantern lecture on the Russian five-year plan); and a cake and candy sale organised by the North Edinburgh Unionist Association. In 1939 the Jehovah's Witnesses took over the building and renamed it Kingdom Hall.

For a time it was used as a Territorial Drill Hall before becoming the Theatre Workshop in 1975. Established in 1965 by Catherine Robbins and

C. WOOD'S advanced classes, Tues., Thurs., Sats.; Mr Hardie's orchestra; splendid floor and lime-light effects.—Raeburn Hall, 38 Raeburn Place.

ST BERNARDS F.C.

MOVE TO FORM SUPPORTERS' CLUB.

"W. M." writes: The lowly position of St Bernards in the League is occasioning some anxiety to their supporters.

For some time past suggestions have been put forward with a view to forming a supporters' club, on the lines adopted by several Western organisations.

There is every possibility of this now materialising, and a public meeting is to be held on Wednesday first in the Wesley Halls, Stockbridge, when, it is hoped, a large attendance of supporters will be present.

EDINBURGH FILM AND THEATRE GUILD.
SUNDAY, 7.30, WESTFIELD HALL, GORGIE.
Sound Film of Russia's Red Army.
"IF WAR SHOULD COME."
ALBANIA NOW—WHAT NEXT?
Hear Rev. Percival-Prescott's Prophetic Sermon on Rome's Conquest. Buccleuch Ch., W. Crosscauseway, Sun., 11 a.m. Communion at close. All Invited.

REFUGEE CHILDREN OF SPAIN (Relief). GRAND CONCERT, LEITH S.S.S. PARTY and BASQUE GIRLS, THURSDAY, April 13, 7.30 p.m., MUSIC HALL. Admission Programme 2/, 1/-, 6d.—Matheson, 15 W. Maynield, 9, and at Door.

EDINBURGH BURGH LABOUR PARTY
WILL HOLD DEMONSTRATIONS,
On MOUND, SUNDAY, 9th, 7 p.m.
INTERNATIONAL SITUATION
PROMINENT SPEAKERS.

FILM AND LANTERN LECTURE.
SOVIET RUSSIA,
MONDAY, April 10, at 8 p.m.
INVERLEITH HALL, 90 RAEBURN PLACE.
ADMISSION FREE. COLLECTION.

PALAIS DE PLAISIR.
PREMIER SALON DE DANSE,
38 RAEBURN PLACE.

DANCING EVERY EVENING AND SATURDAY AFTEROON.

GRAND OPENING
CARNIVAL BALL,
FRIDAY, 2d SEPTEMBER,
8 p.m. to 1.30 a.m.
MUSIC BY RENOWNED
SAVILE ORCHESTRA.
Expert Instructresses and Instructors always in Attendance.
Admission: Gents, 3s; Ladies, 2s 6d.
Late 'Buses.
'Phone 25267 for Booking.

1 Advert for Professor Wood's dance classes at Raeburn Hall, 1905
2 Meeting in Wesley Halls on forming a St Bernard's F.C. Supporters' Club, 1920
3 Entrance to Wesley Hall in Hamilton Place - also shows new tenements being built, c.1900
4 Adverts linked to the tense International situation, including a lecture on Soviet Russia in the Inverleith Hall, April 1939
5 Advert for Palais de Plaisir at Raeburn Hall, 1927

Ros Clark, Theatre Workshop was Edinburgh's first arts and drama centre for children. As well as working with a wide range of local Stockbridge groups, the organisation toured small-scale plays and theatre-in-education projects across Scotland. After a revamping in 1990 the building was reopened with an event by Circus Archaos: 'Rather than cutting the ceremonial ribbon, they charged down Hamilton Place on unicycles and blasted it with fireballs.' Unfortunately funding issues led to the theatre's closure in 2010 and it has now become offices.

No. 90 Raeburn Place had a large space built as the photographic studio of T. P. Lugton in 1904 and when he moved away the studio was revamped as a hall and let for dances, weddings, whist drives and spiritualist meetings. Around 1930 the Independent Labour Party took the building as its ward headquarters and renamed it Inverleith Hall. In the 1940s it became home to the 27th Boys Brigade.

In 1904 the house at No. 38 Raeburn Place had a hall added at the back, which was rented by Charles Wood, a dance instructor until 1912 when he moved his dance academy to Leith. In 1911 Wood devised the popular Scottish dance, Pride of Erin Waltz. Alongside his regular classes in a variety of dance styles, Wood mounted dances, some being fancy dress balls –'costumes on hire'. By this time the tradition of marriages taking place in the home of the bride or groom was changing and halls began to be hired for weddings; the marriage of David Gellatly who lived along the street at No. 50 to Catherine Veitch took place there. For a brief time the hall became the Northern Roller Skating Rink - 'the ideal rink for beginners'- but closed when planning permission was given to Caledonian Electric Theatres for it and No. 36 to be 'converted into a 400 seat picture house'. However, the cinema plan did not progress and No. 38 reopened as the 'Palais de Plaisir, premier Salon de Dance', with a grand carnival ball, but closed a year or two later.

The hall then became the Edinburgh Academy Stockbridge Club, one of a number of boys' clubs opened in the city around that time. 'The annual pantomime of the Edinburgh Academy Stockbridge Boys' Club is always a joyous affair, but Bluebeard as presented in the Club Theatre, 38 Raeburn Place, last night, must rank as one of the best entertainments given by the boys. It was real pantomime, incorporating a wealth of popular songs, the majority of them delightfully parodied to suit the purposes of the story….. Other successful episodes were Bluebeard's Broadcast, a clever tap dance by A. Smith, and an alleged spiritualist séance.' In the early 1950s it was home to Edinburgh's Phoenix Youth Club that reputedly was the only club in Scotland specifically for young people with disability arising from polio paralysis, cerebral palsy and other conditions, and had around 100 members. However the club had to

1 The dancer Wayne Sleep promoting fund-raising for Stockbridge House, 1988 (photo - *The Scotsman*)
2 The Queen Mother opening Stockbridge House, July 1975
3 Judging of the Stockbridge Allotment Competition in Allan Street Hall, c.1950
4 Dance Ihayami, founded in 2003 by Priya Shrikumar, is Scotland's Indian dance company and based at Stockbridge House. The company create innovative contemporary dance works, and runs an extensive education and community engagement programme. (photo - danceihayami)

leave in 1957 as the property was sold. Together with No. 36 it was eventually demolished to make way for a Woolworths store.

Alongside the washing of clothes, public laundries were an important social meeting place for women and thus the closure in 1928 of Allan Street Washhouse behind Mary's Place would have been a double loss to many women. However, it found a new role in the life of the community as in 1933 the derelict building was revamped as The Stockbridge Mutual Service Club. In that year unemployment had reached 23% and the Edinburgh Community Service in Unemployment opened a number of clubs for those out of work. 'At Allan Street there are about 150 men on the roll, and they pay 1d a week each. In the chief room are a number of carpenters' benches and a ping-pong table. The men make various articles of household furniture and a room above is devoted to games. Cobbling is also one of the activities of the club.' The club later added drama, music, wireless, sports and talks to its offer and that year *The Scotsman* visited: 'There were sounds of revelry within the hall in Allan Street, where the Stockbridge Mutual Service Club has its headquarters. On one night the large hall is put by the men members at the disposal of the women, and a hundred or more were enjoying a social. No one was shy here. Mature matrons Palais-glided and Lambeth-walked with the best, all to the music of an accordion played by one of themselves. Every now and then there was a pause in the dance, filled in by someone singing a song, preferably a song with a chorus in which the others could join. There was no coming on to a platform or fuss of any sort. If you were going to sing, you sang where you stood or sat, the rest applauding when you'd done.' The Stockbridge Mutual Service Club closed at the start of the Second World War.

As part of the second redevelopment of Allan Street and Bedford Street a new community centre, Stockbridge House, designed by Robert Hurd & Partners, was opened in 1975 by The Queen Mother who, it was reputed, loved Stockbridge. The rumour was that she would have the royal chauffeurs detour via Ann Street on her way home to Holyrood Palace as 'the Queen Mother loved the feel of the elegant Georgian street, so reminiscent of the world of her youth. She liked to be driven along its stone setts – often with a young Prince Charles sitting beside her – soaking in the quiet and calm.' The primary role of Stockbridge House nowadays is as an old people's day centre run by the charity, LifeCare that was established in 1941 as the Edinburgh Old People's Welfare Council. Stockbridge House's many community initiatives have included St Bernard's Day Club for people living with dementia, launched in 1991, and local 'meals on wheels' service. The centre continues to be home to a wide range of community activities, including being the base for Dance Ihayami, Scotland's Indian dance company.

FIRE

1 Edinburgh Fire Brigade, 1866 (Capital Collections)
2 Advert for William Cook, Hairdresser, 1872
3 Hose tender outside Stockbridge Fire Station in Hamilton Place, c.1890
4 A three-horse-drawn Tullis Russell Steam Pump fire appliance galloping to a fire, 1913 (Capital Collections)

Even by 1821 there were still thatched buildings in the area and fires in these were common: 'On Monday evening a fire broke out in the small thatched building known by the name of The Grotto, at Stockbridge, which, for some time, has been occupied by Mr Edwards, bandage maker, and was totally destroyed.' This building was on the path to St Bernard's Well and *The Scotsman* was not sorry to see it gone: 'The road to the well has thus been greatly improved and visitors have been relieved of a grievous eye-sore.'

By the 1850s a fire station had been opened next to the police office in Hamilton Place. At that time there were 55 firemen in the city's fire service, of whom five were stationed in Stockbridge. Although the service had five horse-drawn engines, the Stockbridge station only had a handcart that contained two hoses. Later it became horse-drawn. Even by 1901, when William Cook's hairdressing shop at No. 20 Deanhaugh Street went on fire, there still was no local fire-engine: 'When the Stockbridge Fire Station hose tender arrived at the fire it was seen be a comparatively slight one, but the heat and density of the smoke caused great alarm among the occupants of the flats above the shop. The occupants in the second floor got very much alarmed, and in their despair, to escape crept out of the window to the parapet, which was only about 15 inches wide, and got out of danger by making their way to the window of the adjoining house at the same level, and though the two windows were only about six feet apart, there was considerable risk in the operation. However, John Simpson, his wife, two children, and two men who lodged in the house, were safely transferred from the one house the other.' Cook had operated there since 1860 and although his premises were completely burned out, his son soon had the hairdressers back in business; it operated through to 1926.

In 1898 Lieutenant Grinton and two men from Stockbridge Fire Station were summoned to a fire that had broken out on the ground floor of a house in Allan Street. On entering they found the bed clothes on two beds alight and once the blaze had been put out and the smoke cleared were distressed to see a partly charred corpse of a woman lying on one of the beds. It was with some relief that they discovered the fire had started in the middle of an Irish 'wake', and the body was that of the woman being mourned, around whom had been set the candles that had started the fire.

Fortunately, deaths in fires were uncommon. However, six people died and many were injured in an explosion at Stockbridge Mills in 1901. The mills (behind today's Baker's Place) were built around 1760 and had fires before without sustaining much damage. However, on this occasion engineers were replacing a gas engine and a combination of the men using a lantern with a naked flame and gas escaping caused a massive explosion and fire. One of the six people killed was the mill's manager, James Thomson who lived in Reid Place. 'The force of it in the confined space

1 Fire following the explosion at Stockbridge Mills, 1901
2 A motorised engine and fire crew leaving Saunders Street Fire Station, 1935 (Capital Collections)
3 Firemen outside the soon to be demolished Saunders Street Fire Station with an old Tullis Russell Steam Pump fire appliance, c.1967 (photo – John King)

caused the wall between the mill and Mr Bowie's shop to be blown out and the street was strewn with sugar, tins of beef and other groceries. A shopman across the street had a somewhat narrow escape, being missed by a tin of meat projected into the shop.' The fire brigade rushed to the resulting fire and although they managed to contain the blaze, there was substantial damage to the building and machinery.

It transpired that the Workmen's Compensation Act, which was designed to secure a reasonable provision for the dependants of workmen who were fatally injured at work, did not cover this disaster. So John Smith, a mill owner in Leith wrote to *The Scotsman:* 'There are five widows each with a family of young children, nearly all of whom are in destitute circumstances and I would suggest that a public subscription should be started.' His suggestion was taken up and the Lord Provost chaired the committee that raised money for the support of the deceased men's families.

Possibly as a result of this disaster, a new Fire and Police Station was opened in Saunders Street in 1907 and was the first in Edinburgh purpose-built to house a motorised fire engine that held 500 gallons of water. The crew at the new station was increased to eight, all of whom were housed above the engine house. In 1932 the adjoining Police Station was taken over by the Fire Brigade to cater for the increase in personnel required to man an increased number of fire engines. The prison cells were adapted as rest quarters by the simple method of removing the barred doors. This expansion was necessary as the number of fires attended by the Stockbridge service increased from 45 in 1907 to 990 in 1968. In 1969 the Saunders Street Fire Service moved to Crewe Toll, and the fire station was demolished as part of the redevelopment of Saunders Street.

It is not only when fighting fires that firefighters display their bravery. In 1942 Alexander MacConnell, a fireman at Stockbridge Fire Station, received the medal of the Royal Scottish Society for the Prevention of Cruelty to Animals for saving a dog from the Water Leith 'at a point between high banks where the animal was surrounded by ice and could not escape.'

Although fires still occur, modern technology often helps ensure the fire brigade arrive speedily and reduce the damage. In 1910 when fire broke out in a fish restaurant at No. 45 Dean Street, the fire service was alerted by 'a policeman calling at Stockbridge Fire Station' whereas when a fire started in Alba D'Oro fish and chip shop in Hamilton Place in 2023 the owner said: 'Thanks to our remotely monitored fire security system, the Scottish Fire and Rescue Service were immediately alerted and at the scene within minutes.'

LAW & ORDER

1 Fire House and Police House, Hamilton Place, 1890 (Capital Collections)
2 'Commit no nuisance' sign in Cheyne Street, 2023

One of the earliest reported punishments in Stockbridge for a crime was visited on Henry Raeburn's father. Previously a well-regarded tradesman in the village, Robert Raeburn's reputation was tarnished when he was found guilty of forging a signature on a financial document. His punishment was reported by the *Caledonian Mercury* on 7 January 1761: 'This forenoon, betwixt twelve and one o'clock; Robert Raeburn, yarn-washer at Stockbridge stood on the pillory at the Cross-well, pursuant to a sentence of the Lords of Council and Session, for making use of a false writ, in order to evade payment of a debt. As the mob owed him a grudge for some part of his former conduct, they were extremely liberal in rotten eggs, turnips, potatoes, dirt, stones, and every species of filth or rubbish they could collect together.'

As the area expanded, so did crime. In 1823 it was reported: 'Numerous depredations, chiefly in fruit gardens, have lately been committed at Stockbridge. As the protection afforded by the police does not extend to this fast increasing village, offenders often escape that punishment which their crimes deserve.' It was not only fruit at risk: 'The new chapel at Stockbridge has been twice broken into and the window blinds carried off.' In response, Stockbridge decided to create its own small police force paid for by a local tax. Yet crime continued to be a problem. In 1827 it was reported, 'The attempts at robbery in Stockbridge have of late been frequent and audacious.'

In addition to fighting crime, police oversaw the lighting and street cleaning, regulated hackney coaches, and controlled weights and measures. In 1832 the Edinburgh Police Bill proposed that the policing of Stockbridge, and other outlying areas, should become the responsibility of Edinburgh's police force. Stockbridge residents objected, pointing out that the tax they paid for their police force was less than that paid by Edinburgh residents: 'By means of a police of our own, established in virtue of our feu rights, we are as well-lighted, cleaned and protected as the town of Edinburgh and at an expense not exceeding sixpence in the pound.' However, the amalgamation went ahead as the city police pointed out, 'that offenders pursued by the Edinburgh Police find shelter in Stockbridge.' A positive aspect of becoming part of the Edinburgh police force was that a Police Office was opened at No. 5 Hamilton Place in the 1840s. Its cells were reputed the worst in the city. In 1910 the police station moved to a new building in Saunders Street that also housed the fire station, but was closed in 1932.

Violent incidents were common, more often than not fuelled by alcohol. In 1899 Francis Buchanan was charged with, 'assaulting a constable at Stockbridge Police Station by butting him, beating him with his fists and compressing his throat.' He pleaded guilty and the court heard he had nine previous convictions, mostly for assaulting the police. 'The accused asked

1 Edinburgh police constable, c.1870
2 Edinburgh police on patrol in Raeburn Place, c.2010
3 Police Box in Dean Terrace, c.1980s (Canmore)

for another chance for his old mother's sake, but the Sheriff sentenced him to sixty days' imprisonment with hard labour.' Many men were charged with assaulting their wives but domestic violence often was not taken very seriously. In 1879 David Grieg who assaulted his wife only received a £2 cautionary bond against 'future good behaviour' rather than a fine or imprisonment whereas three years earlier, when a Mrs Cox was found guilty of striking her husband's arm with a poker, she was sentenced to twenty days imprisonment. No doubt the more severe sentence was due to Mr Cox having told the court his wife drank heavily as the hypocritical view of the time was that female drunkenness was beyond the pale, while men's heavy drinking was more accepted.

The area has always had its thieves, although what is stolen changes. In the 1980s and 1990s theft from cars regularly filled the columns of *The Stockbridge & New Town Independent*, whereas in 2022 it was reported that the police were investigating the theft of a '£500 stash of sex toys stolen from a young woman's Stockbridge home'. In the 19th century the theft of clothing that had been hung out to dry was common. There are those today who believe harsher sentences by courts would deter criminals and yet severe punishment did not deter crime in the past. In 1852 Janet Campbell plead guilty to stealing two shirts, a table-cloth and a bed-gown from a green at St Bernard's Crescent and as she had a previous conviction for theft was sentenced to ten years transportation to Australia (in reality being sent there for life).

As well as dealing with the usual run of crimes, in earlier times policemen seemed to spend a significant amount of time checking up on pubs illegally serving drinks on Sundays or after closing time. Often they would pose as customers and enjoy a pint or two before charging the landlord for the breach of the law. Catching illegal gamblers in the days before off-line betting was legalised also often involved subterfuge. In 1904, 'Sergeant Allan went to a hairdresser's shop in Church Lane where gambling was suspected and gained entrance in a most effective disguise of a man of the labouring class'. Eight men were arrested.

Woman police constables were employed from around 1920 and police boxes also began to appear across Britain to assist the 'bobbies' who patrolled the street. Although a standard police box design – made famous by Doctor Who – was introduced in Britain in 1929, Edinburgh Council did not consider the design to be in keeping with the city's architecture and instead selected a neo-Classical design by the then City Architect, Ebenezer Macrae. Cast-iron versions were made by the Carron Foundry in Stirlingshire and around 140 were installed throughout the city, including one in Dean Terrace. These offered the police on the beat a place to hold arrested individuals while waiting on a police vehicle, but more importantly, somewhere for a quiet smoke or a cup of tea.

TRANSPORT

1 Quarry horse-carts, 1880 (Capital Collections)
2 St Cuthbert's Co-operative delivery wagon, 1910

Horses were central to the development of Stockbridge as they hauled the carts that brought in stone, timber, slates and other building materials. These heavy loads had to be towed over narrow, rough roads in all weathers, so life expectancy for most cart horses was as low as three years. The city's expansion led to many more commercial horse-drawn vehicles including small carts and vans delivering goods to local shops and houses; wagons ferrying coal, funeral coaches, fire engines, etc.

Unlike the New Town where many mews with coach-houses and stables were built, few were erected in Stockbridge. Dean Park Mews was not built until the 1880s and it was created in response to the development of the Dean. Mews buildings usually contained a coach 'garage', a stable for one or two horses and living accommodation above for a coachman. Many residents would have walked to the New Town, as Raeburn did each day, while those requiring transport in the early days would have hired a hackney cab. By the 1850s Robert Atkinson's horse-drawn hackney cab company at No. 8 North West Circus Place was one of the city's largest.

At that time the fare from Stockbridge to the city centre was 1s6d and to Newington, 2s6d. About 1760 a toll gate was erected at Stockbridge (in today's Kerr Street) by the Road Trustees to take money for road upkeep; all vehicles travelling to Edinburgh had to pay to pass through, including hired cabs: 'The existence of a toll in Stockbridge is the occasion of a vast deal of inconvenience and annoyance. If one has occasion to hire a coach, twenty-five per cent needs added to the fare and there is the inconvenience of waiting at the toll bar on a cold winter night until the toll-man can be aroused from his slumbers.' Around 1830 the toll gate was moved to the north side of the bridge, at the end of Dean Street and although there were constant calls for the toll gate to be removed, it was not until 1853 that the Stockbridge toll was removed and one built at Comely Bank instead.

In 1874 a meeting of 200 cabmen was held near St Stephen's Church to demand a minimum weekly wage and one Sunday off in two. Twenty years earlier the Church of Scotland had called for cabmen to be banned from working any Sunday: 'The cabmen state that their average time on watch and work, from Monday morning to Saturday night, is seventeen hours a day, and on Sabbath are on the stand from nine in the morning till nine at night. Their toil has nothing intellectual about it, nothing to excite their faculties; but very much to weary, to deaden, to degrade, and to drive to unlawful stimulants. They are chained to their stand in the summer's heat and the winter's cold. They are banished from their own homes - from their wives and families. They are deprived the usual opportunities of intellectual and spiritual improvement. They hear the Sabbath-bell; but they cannot join in the Sabbath song.' There were some who argued it was the horses that really deserved one day's rest.

1 Horse Omnibus, c.1890
2 Cable Car in Raeburn Place, c.1900
3 Number 24 electric tram coming down Kerr Street, c.1930s
4 Edinburgh Corporation Motor Bus outside Henderson Row bus garage (former Cable Car depot), 1919

In 1839 Thomas Thorburn, a draper who lived at No. 44 Ann Street, established the first horse-drawn omnibus service between Stockbridge and Newington. He had two horse-drawn omnibuses that ran between Raeburn Place and Clerk Street on the half-hour from 8.30am until 9pm. Due to the steepness of the hills the omnibuses were pulled by three horses. In 1843 William Scott set up in competition, running buses on the same route, and drivers' competition for passengers led to accidents: 'Robert Wilson was charged with driving three horses attached to an omnibus in a furious and reckless manner down North West Circus Place to Stockbridge. A girl who was standing with a number of other children was knocked down and only escaped death by a kind of miracle.' She was lucky, as many other children were killed in similar incidents. There were also numerous instances of bus drivers being charged with cruelly maltreating the horses. On one occasion, Scott's bus was travelling to Newington when Thorburn's bus passed it at St Patrick Square going the other way. To the alarm of his passengers, the driver of Scott's bus turned his bus and began racing Thorburn's bus back up Clerk Street. Unsurprisingly, complaints from passengers were many as were those from residents about, 'the ear-piercing and discordant noises from the conductors blowing on their trumpets.'

In 1882 it was reported, 'Gentlemen resident in the Stockbridge district of the city who are dissatisfied with the omnibus service have formed a company for the purpose of laying and working two cable tramway lines.' Cable trams had been introduced in Glasgow but given Edinburgh's steep inclines it was the success of the cable car system in San Francisco, invented in the 1870s by Andrew Hallidie, a Scottish engineer, that inspired the Edinburgh model. The first cable tram line opened in early 1888, running from Trinity via Canonmills to Princes Street. The second line, from Comely Bank through Stockbridge to Princes Street, opened two years later. The cables were powered from a pulley unit in a building in Henderson Row. Cable cars set off every 5 minutes on both lines. They were painted dark blue and cream, with an initial fare of 3d (first class) on the inside or 2d upstairs on the outside.

Motor buses began to appear around 1910 but the early vehicles were unpopular due to the vibrations from their hard tyres on Edinburgh's cobbled streets. However, as tyres and suspension improved bus use increased. In 1922 Edinburgh Corporation decided to convert the entire cable system to overhead electric powered trams and the number 24 tram rattled through Stockbridge for three decades. The conversion from cable meant that the old powerhouse in Henderson Row became one of two bus garages in the city and housed 45 vehicles. The Stockbridge trams were discontinued as part of the city-wide switch to buses in the 1950s.

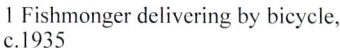

1 Fishmonger delivering by bicycle, c.1935
2 St Stephen's Motor & Cycle Depot, Hamilton Place, c.1920
3 Malta Green Cottage converted into W. Stein Motor Engineers, c.1930
4 No. 28 bus in Raeburn Place, 1992
5 Croall & Croall, Volkswagen dealers, Silvermills, 1966
6 Horse-drawn milk float in Leslie Place, 1980

Early bicycles were expensive and the large-front-wheel 'penny farthing' bicycles difficult to ride on Edinburgh's steep cobbled streets, so it was not until the 1880s when the easier to ride 'safety bicycle' (similar to today's model) was introduced that cycling became more common. Delivery boys on bikes became a common sight in the streets of Stockbridge. More women began to cycle in spite of claims that women cyclists could suffer from the medical condition, 'bicycle face' described as 'usually flushed, but sometimes pale, and the beginning of dark shadows under the eyes, and always with an expression of weariness.' Deliveries by cyclists would have been a common sight in Stockbridge until the 1950s, and after many decades they are again, with hot meals being ferried around.

Horse transport began to be replaced by motorised vehicles, although some horse-drawn carts, particularly milk floats, continued into the early 1980s. Many cabmen began to swap their horse-cabs for motor taxis and as driving tests did not start until 1935, dangerous driving was common. In 1924 Charles Marr, who lived in St Stephen Street, was arrested for drunk driving. The charge was not hard to prove as while he was driving along Princes Street, one of his front wheels came off. Unaware or undeterred, Marr drove another 100 yards or more before stopping and being arrested.

Jack & Renwick at No. 99 St Stephen Street who had been in the horse business moved into the motor-car business early and in 1910 were one of the first in the city to advertise motor cars for hire. 'Shopping and Town calling in luxurious Landaulettes (open-topped models) at very low rates'. They later moved premises to Silverburn. Mr Nelson who owned the St Stephens Motor and Cycle Depot in Hamilton Place became treasurer of 'the law-abiding but dynamic new youth movement, The Road Vigilants'. The group formed in response to a local motorist deciding to go to prison rather than pay the £2 fine imposed on him for breaking the 20 mph speed limit. As those with money began to buy cars, coach houses in mews were converted into 'motor car houses' and garages such as the Raeburn Motor Works in Raeburn Mews, opened. In the 1960s Croall & Croall, who had begun as coach builders, had a garage and a showroom selling Volkswagen 'Beetles' in Silvermills.

In the 1960s the view of the Water of Leith from Hamilton Place was blighted by a large car scrapyard between Haugh Street and the river - where Haugh House now stands – and another car-related eyesore was Forth Car Hire's conversion of Malta Green Cottage into a garage that included a petrol pump forecourt where the house's garden had stood. While these blots are long gone, Stockbridge's village ambience continues to be adversely affected by the volume of motor vehicles. In April 2023, following a young girl being knocked down, fellow pupils of Stockbridge School launched the campaign, 'Safe, Slow, Stockbridge'.

EDINBURGH ACADEMY SPORTS GROUND

1 Edinburgh Accies cricket team, 1880
2 The world's first international rugby match between Scotland and England, 1871
3 The Calcutta Cup
4 First Calcutta Cup match between Scotland and England, 1879

From its opening in 1824 the Edinburgh Academy in Henderson Row was keen for its boys to be fit and employed a drill sergeant to oversee pupils' exercise. The pupils also played a primitive form of rugby named 'the muddle' that had no rules. Injuries were common as the players wore iron-toed and heeled boots. Cricket was played on Bruntsfield Links and in 1854 the Academy opened its sports ground at Raeburn Place, the oldest purpose-built sports ground in Scotland. The first match played there was between the Academy and the High School, in June 1855: 'On Saturday the pupils of the Fourth Classes in these two institutions played a match on the Edinburgh Academy cricket ground. The Academy went first to the wicket, and notwithstanding the very unfavourable state of the weather, the match was played out. At the conclusion, the score stood as follows: Fourth Class, Academy - 1st inning - 26, 2d innings - 24, total 50. Fourth Class, High School - 1st innings - 50; the High School thus winning by an innings.' The Edinburgh Academical Cricket Club, was founded the following year.

Rugby also began to be played at the ground and the Academical (Rugby) Football Club (the Accies) was founded in 1858; the first rugby club in Scotland and the second oldest in the world. The first match was arranged between the Accies and students from Edinburgh University, and it was decided to play until the best of seven 'goals' (a try allowing a kick at goal) had been scored. Thus, although the game 'kicked off' on 26 December 1857 it did not finish until three weeks later - with a win for the Accies.

The annual Edinburgh Academy Club Foot Races that 'embraced foot-races and other athletic sports' were first held in the ground in 1858: 'The field presented a brilliant and animated appearance - the knoll on the north side being crowded with ladies, notwithstanding the unpropitious aspect of the weather during the forenoon. The field was tastefully decorated with flags, and the band of the Royal Sussex Militia contributed to enliven the proceedings by the performance of a variety of pleasing airs.' The ground also hosted many other sporting events. In 1863 the ninth Scottish National Archery meeting was held there, with archers competing for the gold medal: 'Both the Misses Edmonstone of Edinburgh, who have now become so famous in archery competitions, carried off prizes.'

The world's first international rugby match was played between Scotland and England at the Academy's ground on 27 March 1871. It arose from a challenge issued in the sporting journal *Bell's Weekly* inviting any team 'selected from the whole of England' to a 20-a-side game. The game was watched by 4,000 spectators and Scotland beat England by two tries and a goal to England's single try. Eight years later the two countries played for the Calcutta Cup, a fixture that has been played annually ever since. The Cup was crafted by Indian silversmiths from melted-down

1 Edinburgh Accies playing Edinburgh University in 1930, photo captioned 'An effective tackle at Raeburn Place' – a tackle that would get a red card today!
2 Women's Scottish Hockey team, 1951
3 Scotland v Ireland Women's International rugby match, 1993
4 New stand designed by Michael Laird Architects (photo - Michael Laird Architects

silver rupees which were the balance of the funds of the Calcutta Football Club on its disbandment in 1878 and is the oldest trophy in world rugby.

In 1888 Robert Mackenzie was appointed as rector of the Academy and he made cricket and football compulsory throughout the school. He wrote, 'If were asked what was the most dangerous occupation for a boy's hour of leisure, I should at once name loafing,'

The First World War interrupted sport for many: 'A. S. Pringle, the Edinburgh. Academical Rugby player, has received his commission in the Sportsman's Battalion of the 3rd Royal Fusiliers (City of London)'. And many who had played at the ground lost their lives: 'Died on board H.M.S. Hawke, Surgeon J. H. D. Watson, the well-known Edinburgh Academical Rugby player. For four seasons he was one of the stalwarts at Raeburn Place, and he was captain in 1912-13. He gained honours as an all-round athlete and was a good cricketer.' The Second World War also brought the loss of great players: 'Major George H. Gallie of the Royal Artillery has been reported dead (1944). He was awarded the M.C. last August for gallantry in the Middle East. He was a member of Edinburgh Academicals Rugby team and represented Scotland against Wales in 1939.'

In 1951 the ground hosted the hockey international between Scotland and Holland, the first time a continental club played in Scotland. This also was the first time an international had been played on a Sunday and the Sabbatarians must have been delighted that the match was played in a 'steady drizzle and a cold, raw wind that kept the attendance down to a few hundred sturdy souls huddled up in rugs.'

The centenary of the field was celebrated in 1954 with a cricket week, including a two-day match between the Academicals and Marylebone Cricket Club. In 2008 Accies Rugby Club commemorated its 150th birthday by welcoming the famous Barbarians Football Club to Raeburn Place, at which a sell-out crowd of 3,000 enjoyed an entertaining game, even though the Accies lost 0-43.

The first Scottish Women's Rugby International was played at Raeburn Place on 14 February 1993, with the Scots beating Ireland by 10-0. Two years later Anna Boast, who had played in that first international, was playing for Aberdeen University against Edinburgh Academicals at the ground when she became the first woman to be sent off during a match. Perhaps her red carded kicking of an opposing player came from frustration as Aberdeen lost 69-0. In 1994 the ground was used for the final of the first Women's World Rugby Cup in which England beat the United States 38-23.

In 2020 a new 2,500 seated stand, designed by Michael Laird Architects, opened at the Raeburn Place end, providing an improved spectator experience along with up-to-date changing, training and gym facilities, thus equipping the ground for even greater success in the future.

GRANGE CRICKET CLUB

1 Original Grange Cricket Club Pavilion, on the right the Score Box and a stable, c.1880
2 Donald Bradman being cheered off the ground, 1948
3 Ticket for Scotland v Australians cricket match, 1926
4 Advert for Richardson's 'Penny farthing' bicycles
5 Tennis match with the 'Tin Pavilion' behind, c.1920
6 Grange Cricket Pavilion, rebuilt 1893, 2022

In 1872 the Grange Cricket Club, founded forty years earlier, moved to Raeburn Place and the new ground was inaugurated by 'a Grand Match between Edinburgh and Glasgow'. The following year around 2,000 people crammed into the ground to watch 'Eighteen Gentleman of Edinburgh and District versus the United South of England eleven.' The big draw was the celebrated English player, W.G. Grace and the crowd were not disappointed, as Grace reportedly made the biggest hit of his career; a full blooded drive that measured 140 yards. Grace returned to the ground in 1895 to play in a match to mark the opening of the club's stylish pavilion that included a 'Long Room' modelled on the one of the same name at Lord's Cricket Ground in London.

For many years the Grange Club acted as the governing body of cricket in Scotland but by 1900 there were calls for change. National responsibility passed to the Scottish Cricket Union in 1908, although the Grange continued to be influential in Scottish cricket's development. The ground has hosted many international matches. On 13 September 1948, Don Bradman, another of cricket's legends, was in the Australian side that played Scotland there over two days. This was Bradman's last tour so the match drew a particularly large crowd. Although 'continuous rain ruled out any possibility of play before lunch', it did not dampen the crowd's spirits and when Bradman went out to have a look at the sodden pitch he received an ovation. The match got underway later in the day. Bradman was bowled out for only 27, but the Australian side won. A few days later both teams travelled to Balmoral to meet George VI and the Royal family.

The invention of vulcanisation meant that tennis could now be played outdoors on grass and an early version of modern tennis evolved. In 1875 James Patten (later Scotland's Registrar General) invited some lawyer friends to try out the new version at the Grange Cricket ground. They went on to found the Edinburgh Lawn Tennis Company, building two indoor grass courts in a building - known as 'the tin temple' - that sat between the cricket ground and Raeburn Place, plus four adjoining open-air courts. Patten recounted those early days: 'The game as played in the covered courts was considerably different from the game of the present day. It was more like real tennis or racquets, and it was part of the game to play the ball after it had hit the wall.' In 1878 the first Scottish Championships were held at the Grange, just one year after the first tournament at Wimbledon. In 1902 the 'tin temple' was demolished to make way for the Grange Cricket Club's pavilion, but not before being used for a 'Cycle Riding School' providing lessons in riding the 'penny farthing' bicycle. The Edinburgh Lawn Tennis Company evolved into the Grange Dyvours club that continues today and it is the only club in Scotland to boast four grass tennis courts.

STOCKBRIDGE PARK

OSBORNE ATHLETIC v. VIRGINIANS.
SEMI-FINAL OF THE KING BADGES.

The Osborne Athletic journeyed to Stockbridge Park on Saturday to decide their tie in the semi-final. A great many followers went to witness this match. The Osborne lost the toss and had to play up the hill and against a strong wind in the first half. The "Virgins" pressed, but Lawrie relieved. Bee took the ball well up the field and centred, but the backs cleared. Bruce on the left wing was ever prominent for the Virginians. The "Virgins" tried hard to score, but the grand defence of Lawrie, Mayer, and Holligan was too good. M'Kinlay now had a run on the right, but the backs were always there and the ball was soon returned. The "Virgins" tried very hard to score and the ball was sent through. A foul was claimed and the goal was disallowed. The ball was "thrown up" and Bruce scored the first goal for the Abbeyhill boys. This reverse made the Athletic play up and Bee getting on the ball had a good run and passed to Cairns, who sent

MUSIC IN THE PARKS. — The band of the Q.E.R.V.B. (C. Laubach, bandmaster) will play in Stockbridge Park at seven o'clock this evening. The following is the programme :—
March................"Livorno".............*Conradi.*
Overture..........."Bannockburn"..........*Edwards.*
Valse..............."Im Lager"..............*Bucalah.*
Polka.............."Kutschke"..............*Stiasny.*
Lancers............"Trial by Jury"..........*Sullivan.*
March ...."Mary of Argyle"......... *Scotch.*
Galop..............."Storm"..............*Burrasca.*

1 St Bernard's Football Club team after winning the Scottish Cup, 1895
2 Map showing location of Stockbridge Park, 1890
3 Extract from football report in *Portobello Advertiser*, 1890
4 Advert for Music in the Parks, 1891

In the early 1850s James Crighton, an Edinburgh councillor, campaigned for a local Stockbridge park and eventually the land that would later become Grange Cricket Club was leased. When the small park opened it was announced that 'games allowed to be played are cricket, football, quoits and running. No swearing or improper language, or fighting, or quarrelling, or betting, or playing for money will be permitted.' In 1858 a larger area between Ann Street and Comely Bank belonging to the estate of Sir John Hope was leased and the park moved there and was called Stockbridge Park (or John Hope's Park). Cricket, football and shinty matches took place there, while Stockbridge Golf Club was permitted to use the park in the early mornings. Other users of the park were sheep, employed to keep the grass down.

A correspondent to *The Scotsman* in 1876 did not think much of the park: 'At present there is no healthy open ground for recreation at all. The bit of bare and damp green called "Stockbridge Park" is not worthy of the name.' Yet it served sports well enough. In 1878 a local Stockbridge football team, St Bernard's FC, was formed and the following year played Waverley FC in the park, winning by six goals to one. In 1882 football was banned from the park and Crighton expressed outrage: 'There now is not a single square yard in Edinburgh where young men can kick a football.' The Chairman replied that with the Parks Committee of the Town Council having closed the Meadows for football, 'The whole town will come to our park and interfere with the rights and liberties of Stockbridge residents'. The ban was lifted and football returned. St Bernard's FC moved to play at Powderhall and by the 1890s was one of the three main Edinburgh teams; in 1895 they won the Scottish Cup. The club folded in 1940.

In 1885 the traditional New Year's match by 'members of the Edinburgh Shinty Club was played at Stockbridge Park yesterday. The players, of whom there were ten each side, wore kilts, and after a spirited match the secretary's team defeated the chieftain's team by four hails to one.' The year before the Royal Highland Society held its annual show in Dean Park and Stockbridge Park. The park also hosted regular concerts: 'Arrangements have been made by Edinburgh Town Council for entertaining the public during the summer months with open air concerts. The band of the Gordon Highlanders will give concerts on Thursday evenings in Stockbridge Park.'

In the late 1880s the council acquired Inverleith Park and Stockbridge Park was sold to the builder, Sir James Steel to develop as the Comeley Bank/Learmonth estate. So in March 1892 Bonnyrigg Rangers played Cheyne Athletic in the last football match to take place at Stockbridge Park, with Cheyne Athletic winning by 2 goals to 1, 'the Rangers not being used to such a short pitch'.

OTHER SPORTS VENUES

1 Football match at Inverleith Park, 1960
2 Early golf, c.1880
3 Model yachts being sailed on Inverleith Pond, 1966
4 Coates Curling Club medal, 1855
5 Curlers, c.1900

Around 1850 Duddingston Curling Club (established in 1795) became the Coates Curling Club and bought land at the side of Arboretum Avenue to build a permanent curling pond. 'A brief quotation from the manifesto which led to its formation will show the high ideal of its founders "Resolved, that the sole object of this institution is the enjoyment of the game of curling, which, while it adds vigour to the body, contributes to vivacity of mind and the promotion of social and generous feelings."' In the 1930s the curling pond was converted into a bowling green and putting green by the Tanfield Bowling and Putting Club. Another curling pond and bowling green was opened in 1879 in Perth Street by the Northern Bowling Club but had to move ten years later when the land was sold for house-building.

The 54 acres on which Inverleith Park was developed had been the South Inverleith Mains Farm, part of the estate owned by the Rocheid family. The park opened in 1889 and the sports played at Stockbridge Park moved there. A nine hole golf course was also created for the Raeburn Short Hole Club. As there were a number of short-hole courses in Edinburgh, a league was formed and in 1904 Raeburn played its first inter-club match against Bruntsfield Short Hole Golf Club on the Inverleith course. The course had one unusual obstacle, as in 1905 it was reported: 'The (army) volunteers came to drill on the park, and much to the disgust of the golfers began exercising in the centre of the course until it was hardly possible to strike a ball without coming into contact with the legs of some of the volunteers.'

Inverleith Pond was constructed as a model boating pond in the 1890s and the Edinburgh & Leith Model Club were among those who raced their model yachts there. This was appropriate, for Henry Raeburn built model boats and sailed his on Warriston Pond. Powered model boats began to appear in the 1920s and in June 1939, on the eve of the Second World War, a large crowd watched models of warships made by the East of Scotland Model Marine Engineers Club being sailed. The ducks usually stayed well out of the way but in 1944 during a model yacht regatta, 'one of the competing vessels attracted the attention of a duck family. After some preliminary investigations, the six junior members of the family decided on boarding operations, and spectators were rewarded with the glorious sight of the stately yacht cleaving the main with six dauntless ducklings working their passage to distant shores.' On particularly cold winters, as in 1929, ice-skaters were able to skate on Inverleith Pond and in 1910 a small roller-skating rink opened briefly at 38 Raeburn Place: 'Admission free; skates 6d.'

In the late 1890s the lack of washing facilities inside many houses led to the building of a number of communal baths and swimming baths. As Saxe-Coburg Place had not been fully completed due to the builder's bankruptcy, there was an empty site above Glenogle Road and Glenogle

Congratulations are due to the Boys' Brigade Roxburgh Shield Swimming team at Glenogle Baths, Edinburgh, on Saturday night. They met and defeated Edinburgh and Dundee, thus qualifying to again represent Scotland at Liverpool sometime next month. The contest was of the most exciting nature throughout, and the winners only got home with a small margin of two points. The local boys were successful in the following items:—Graceful swimming in which Private R. Martin excelled himself and gave an almost perfect display. The local boys also gained full points with J. Fulton winning the 100 yards event. In the other events they secured second place to Dundee in the diving. Team race also went to Dundee with the local boys second, and they secured third place in life saving. After the competition the visiting teams and officials were entertained to tea by the Edinburgh Battalion, returning home about 9.45. To Mr Joyce and Mr Martin the thanks of the boys are due for so willingly putting their cars at the disposal of the boys. The team was in charge of Lieuts. J. Addie and T. Prentice.

LIST OF FIXTURES
Note—All Runs subject to alteration.

Date	EVENT	Meet
1935		
Sept. 28	Inter-Club Run (E.H., E.S.H., H.C.C.C., E.E.H., E.R.S., and P.H.)—Open	Portobello Baths
Oct. 5	Club Run	Portobello Baths
,, 12	Novice Championship (Mitchell Medal)	Musselburgh
,, 19	Club Run	Portobello Baths
,, 26	Inter-Club Run (Maryhill Harriers)	Glasgow
Nov. 2	N.C.C.U. Novice Championship	
,, 2	Club Run	Dr Guthrie's Sc.
,, 9	League Race	Portobello Baths
,, 16	2½ Miles Handicap	Musselburgh
,, 23	Club Run	Dalkeith
,, 30	Eastern Relay Championship	Kirkcaldy
Dec. 7	5 Miles Handicap (Almond Medal)	Musselburgh
,, 14	Club Run	Dr Guthrie's Sc.
,, 21	Club Run—Open	Glenogle Baths
,, 28	Northern Yuletide Handicap	Glenogle Baths

BILLIARDS.
PALACE SPORTS, LTD.
3 ST BERNARD'S ROW, STOCKBRIDGE
25 BILLIARD TABLES by JOHN TAYLOR & SON, Ltd. All Ivory Balls Used.
A PUBLIC BILLIARD HANDICAP will Start on 18th October. Entries should be lodged at once with the Manager.
TWO EXTRA RIFLE RANGES, making eight ranges in all, have been added for shootings under conditions approved by Lord Roberts. Those wishing to join St Bernard's Rifle Club should apply to the Secretary, c/o Palace Sports, Ltd.
FOUR SKITTLE ALLEYS, the First and Best in Edinburgh. No Matting used. Special Laid Rink Wood, which gives an accurate game. Anyone wishing to become members of the Edinburgh Trotters Skittle Club should apply to the Secretary, c/o Palace Sports, Ltd.

1 Newspaper report, August 1929
2 Winner of the Allan Street Badminton Club Singles Competition, T. Macintosh receiving the cup from Mrs Gilbert, 1957
3 A police swimming team, 1910
4 Edinburgh Northern Harriers Fixture list, 1935
5 Advert for Palace Sports in St Bernard's Row, 1919

Baths, designed by Robert Morham, was built there. The baths opened in 1900 and were immediately well used: 'Last Sunday being the anniversary of the opening of the baths, D. Watt, the general superintendent, has supplied the following details: Admissions from September, 1900, to September, 1901 - males, 53,730; females, 4229; total of 57.959, the total receipts being £647. Mr Watt adds that ladies have only the use of the Baths one afternoon and evening per week (Thursday), and that the above figures compare favourably with the other city baths.' Swimming baths such as Glenogle encouraged recreational, and competitive, swimming. By 1903 the St Bernard's Amateur Swimming Club had been formed and that year a large audience attended a lecture on 'life saving and resuscitation, illustrated with limelight views, and a detachment of the city police gave a practical demonstration of life saving and the modes of restoring life.' The baths also became regularly used for swimming competitions - 'graceful swimming' often featured - and later water polo. By 2000 the building was in a poor state of repair and under threat of closure. Fortunately, a campaign to save the baths led to substantial investment from Edinburgh Council and others, and in 2019 the baths reopened after a £5.7 million revamp. Before the Second World War Edinburgh Harriers often began their runs from Glenogle Swimming Baths: 'The Harriers started a mid-week section and tomorrow hold their first Wednesday afternoon run. Meeting at Glenogle Baths at 3 o'clock.'

For those wishing a less athletic sport in the early 1900s, Stockbridge briefly had two large billiard halls: St Bernard's Billiard Hall in Haugh Street and the Palace Sports Club in St Bernard's Row. As well as 26 billiard tables, the latter contained two rifle ranges, four carpet bowl rinks and four skittle alleys. Others enjoyed a game of chess or draughts. James Rose of Deanbank House was an early member of Edinburgh Chess Club, which was established in 1822, but it was not until the 1920s that a Stockbridge Chess Club came into being. One of its skilled young players was Robert Davidson Dykes; he became club secretary in 1927 and the club flourished under his direction. It acquired rooms of its own in Fettes Row and a healthy membership of good playing strength. In 1937 the club hosted an attempt by Georges Koltanowski, a Belgian, to break the world record for playing simultaneous games blindfolded. 'Koltanowski played 34 games simultaneously, without seeing a single board. Although not blindfolded, he faced away from the boards, and as officials passed round the 34 tables, Koltanowski called out his move. The opponent's reply was then called back to him. He gained the record, winning 24 games and losing 10 over a period of 13 hours, and it was not until the 21st century that his feat was bettered. In 1938 the chess club won the Spens Cup, defeating Glasgow's Jewish Chess Club. In 2011 the 118th Scottish chess championship took place at the LifeCare Centre in Cheyne Street and over

1 Georges Koltanowski playing 34 chess games simultaneously, 1937
2 Grand-master, Ketevan Arakhamia-Grant, winner of the 2011 Scottish Chess Championships, in play at LifeCare Centre in Cheyne Street, 2011
3 Draughts players, 1900
4 Edinburgh Academy Sports Hub Climbing Wall

a tense nine days Edinburgh-based Ukrainian-born grand-master, Ketevan Arakhamia-Grant won the £1,200 first prize.

In the 1940s and 50s a number of the Stockbridge Chess Club members 'felt the need for a more exuberant form of activity than chess and so it was their wont to finish the chess session early enough to get in some table tennis before departing for home.' They formed the Gambit Table Tennis Club that in the 1940s and 1950s was one of the leading clubs in Scotland, helped by Dykes' marriage to Helen Elliott, whose successes included winning 13 consecutive Scottish Open women's singles titles from 1946 and becoming table tennis world champion in 1949. In the 1950s the converted washhouse in Allan Street became a centre for badminton and table tennis: 'The popularity of the annual competitions for the Edinburgh League combined singles and doubles championships was again shown when an entry of 76 for the singles and 27 pairs for the doubles were forward when the preliminary ties were played off at the Allan Street Club on Saturday. The standard of play was generally good and there were one or two surprises.'

Draughts was considered a working-class game and often played for money. In 1838 Edinburgh saw the first of five much-publicised matches between James Wylie, who was born at Piershill Cavalry Barracks in Edinburgh, and Andrew Anderson, a stocking weaver who established the game's rules and was considered the best draughts player in Scotland. The two men played five matches for significant stakes, of which Anderson won four. The Stockbridge Draughts Club was formed around 1900 and Sir Lewis McIver, MP for West Edinburgh presented the club with the McIver Medal, a silver medal inscribed with a draughts board, 'that is well known as the leading draughts trophy in Edinburgh.' It was played for annually. In 1902 the Edinburgh and District Draughts Association was formed and the first League match was played at Stockbridge between the Stockbridge club and West End Draughts Club in the Nelson Hall attached to Stockbridge Library. The club appears to have disbanded in the mid-1930s.

A recent addition to Stockbridge's sports venues has been Edinburgh Academy's New Town Sports Club: 'Set amongst the huge green spaces of our Arboretum Road site in the heart of Stockbridge, our Sports Hub offers everything from rock climbing and badminton to hockey and lacrosse. The Hub is based around our Sports Centre, with a newly-refurbished main hall, studio, fully equipped gym, squash courts and climbing wall. Step outside the Sports Centre onto our immaculately-maintained grounds, offering the best surfaces for the ultimate sporting experience. With two full sized rugby pitches, perfect for training and club matches, and astro pitches that can host up to four hockey games at once or 16 tennis courts, there's plenty of room to keep everyone happy'.

ENTERTAINMENTS

1 Postcard advertising *Cinderella* at the Grand Theatre, St Stephen Street with Miss May Marton as Cinderella, Miss Millie Engler as Prince Rupert, and Little Zola as Buttons. Caption Reads: "That's your little game, Buttons! I'll call again tomorrow", 1904
2 Advert for the Grand Reopening of St Bernard's Picture Palace, 1928
3 Tudor Cinema, St Bernard's Row, c.1960
4 Advert for Pavilion cinema, Dean Street, 1924
5 Advert for Grand cinema, St Stephen Street, 1926
6 Bingo session, early 1960s

While a variety of entertainments took place in Stockbridge's community halls throughout the 1900s, it was not until 1901 that the area gained a dedicated theatre. A huge hall, measuring 190 feet long by 79 feet wide and about 45 feet high had been built in upper St Stephen Street as an ice rink, but the rink never materialised. For a few months it housed fun-fair rides and then was converted into the Tivoli Theatre by Weldon Watts, who owned theatres across England. The theatre opened in November 1901: 'Watts slated a popular piece for the set-off, and the furious fun of "Swiss Express" kept up almost a continuous flow of merriment. The theatre itself is a commodious and comfortable building, plainly but yet tastefully decorated. There is sitting accommodation for about 2,000 persons.' The shows presented at The Tivoli were diverse. In March 1902 the Osmond Tearle Shakespearean Company performed a different Shakespeare play each evening for a week, but mostly the theatre presented evenings of variety: 'The principal attraction at the Tivoli Theatre this week is a party of six lady international wrestlers. The programme concludes with an exhibition of animated pictures depicting scenes at Hampton Park races.'

The theatre changed hands and renamed The Grand, but continued its eclectic programming. Over the 1904/5 festive season the theatre presented *Cinderella* and then: 'From the frivolity of the pantomime to *Uncle Tom's Cabin* in which the elements of tragedy, pathos, and humour, are mixed, is a great change, and there was a large house at the Grand Theatre last night to welcome the production of the play based on Mrs Beecher Stowe's great work. A touch of realism is given by the employment of several negroes and the play keeps strictly to the beaten track.' However, audiences were mixed and the theatre closed in 1906. The building became the Grand Picture House in 1920. By then two other cinemas had opened in Stockbridge. In 1911 the Palace Sports Club in St Bernard's Row became a cinema. It changed names twice - the Savoy and Tudor Cinema. The chapel at No. 30 Dean Street was converted into the Pavilion Cinema and began showing films from 1917. Later renamed the Dean Street Cinema, it closed in 1936.

In 1960 the Betting and Gaming Act legalised commercial bingo and like many cinemas, the films at the Tudor Cinema and the Grand Picture House were replaced by calls of 'legs eleven' and 'a monkey's cousin' (dozen) as they became Bingo Halls. By 1963 more than 14 million people had become members of commercial bingo clubs around the UK, and like other such clubs, Stockbridge's two bingo halls served as a meeting place and social hub for the community. However, the media resorted to moralisation, condescension and in some cases outright vilification of bingo. *The Times* derided the game as a 'cretinous pastime', denouncing

1 Poster for Little Richard concerts at the Pentland Club, St Stephen Street, 1966
2 Tiffanys Club, St Stephen Street, c.1975
3 The famous Stockbridge Duck Race, 2010 (photo – Richard Findlay)

female players who (allegedly) sent their children 'after a hasty tea to hold their mother's places in the queue'.

The bingo clubs closed in the mid-1960s and while the St Bernard's Row building was demolished to build flats, the St Stephen Street building became a music venue, the Pentland Club. National and international acts performed there including, in December 1966 for ten nights, the flamboyant US rock & roll star, Little Richard. Given his stage persona involved a pompadour hairstyle, androgynous makeup and glitzy clothes, one wonders what any older Stockbridge residents thought who happened to see the outrageous, flamboyantly dressed, gay American strolling through the streets. In the early 1970s the club changed to Tiffany's and featured punk, reggae and new-wave music, including Iggy Pop, Elvis Costello and Aswad, and in the 1980s Simple Minds, Siouxsie & The Banshees and the Police.

Around 1980 it was renamed Cinderella Rockerfellas and continued as a music venue and discothèque. One of the disk jockeys was John Leslie, who later found fame as a presenter of the children's TV programme, Blue Peter. However, in May 1991 the building burned down, bringing to an end its colourful 90 years, and the site was redeveloped as flats.

Through the 1990s there was an annual summer Stockbridge Festival that included concerts, exhibitions, poetry readings and such. While that ended, local venues began to be used for Festival Fringe events in August. In 2001 Wolfgang Hoffmann, a dancer, director and producer from former East Germany, launched Aurora Nova, named after the Russian battleship that fired the first shot in the October Revolution, in St Stephen's Church. For seven years the venue hosted some of the finest physical theatre in the world to Edinburgh. 'This festival-within-a-festival is a must for those seeking out the most adventurous Fringe programming.' In 2017 the church was bought by Peter Schaufuss, founder of the English National Ballet School, and in 2022 he presented a version of *Hamlet* starring Ian McKellen.

Stockbridge Church and St Vincent's Chapel are still religious centres but also provide space for arts events. Both regularly house Edinburgh Fringe events and in 2023 those at Stockbridge Church included the Haggis Ceilidh and the Soft Shoe Skiffle Band. St Vincent's Chapel has been the venue for a variety of musical events – from concerts marking Record Store Day, mounted by Darren Yeats who runs Vox Pop Records in St Stephen Street, to the Edinburgh Sacred Music Festival. Also it is used for book launches by Golden Hare Books.

One of the area's most famous events is the annual Stockbridge duck race. Started in 1988 by Susie Gregor, the occasion involves hundreds of intrepid yellow plastic ducks plunging into the Water of Leith from the main bridge and racing to be first to reach Falshaw Bridge.

FIRST & SECOND WORLD WARS

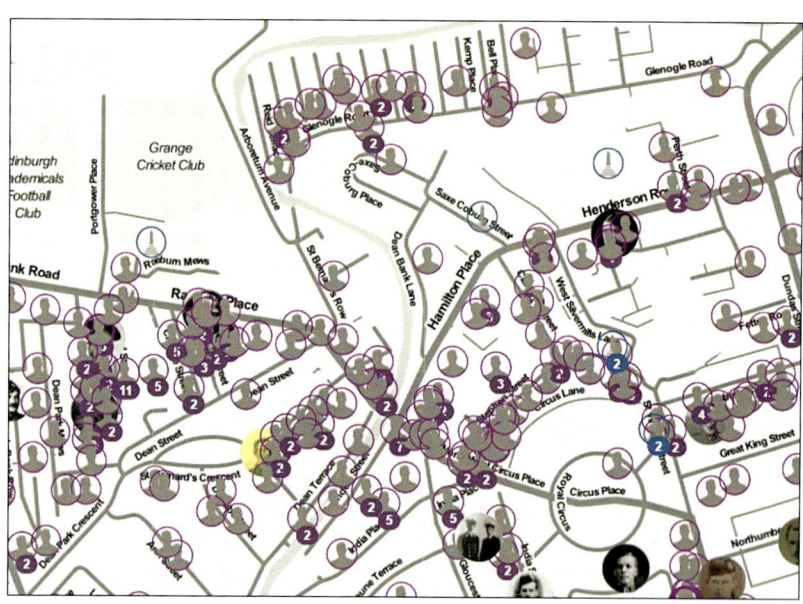

1 Section of website, A Street Near You, mapping soldiers who died in the First World War on to Stockbridge map
2 James Gatheral
3 Frank Tillie's war medals: British War Medal - Silver issue, Inter-allied Victory Medal and Territorial Force War Medal

Within days of Britain declaring war on Germany on 4 August 1914, thousands of men flocked to join the armed forces. With so many servicemen being killed, in 1916 the Military Service Act imposed conscription on all single men aged between 18 and 41. The map opposite detailing those from Stockbridge who died highlights the appalling impact of the war on the community.

Among the many who died were Alexander White (32), a Writer to the Signet (solicitor) who was living at No. 22 Ann Street with his wife and new son when war was declared. For many years he had been a Captain in the Queen's Edinburgh Rifles Volunteers so was immediately assigned to the 5th Royal Scots and promoted to major. In August 1915 while leading men at the landing at Suvla Bay he was seriously wounded and died later. He was educated at Edinburgh Academy; one of 1,024 former pupils who died in the war. Another casualty was James Gatheral, who lived with his parents in Raeburn Place and was a cub reporter with the *Edinburgh Evening News* before joining the 7th Queens Own Cameron Highlanders. On 25 September 1915 he took part in the Battle of Loos, the first large scale engagement of the war, and died within hours.

Others survived. Frank Tillie, who lived with his family in Deanhaugh Street and worked for Edinburgh Tramways, joined up and became a driver with the Army Service Corps. He served in France, where he drove a horse-drawn supply wagon moving food, equipment and ammunition. Many drivers were killed as were their animals: around eight million horses, donkeys and mules died in the war, three-quarters of them from the extreme conditions they worked in. Tillie returned to work with Edinburgh Tramways and lived to be 85. Henry Fairley also worked for Edinburgh Tramways and also survived and returned to live with his family at No. 18 Dean Park Street. However, he died in May 1919, aged 24, from injuries sustained in the war, one of many who survived but died later or continued to suffer from physical and mental disabilities as a result of the war.

The large number of men required by the war meant that Stockbridge's businesses found themselves depleted of experienced male employees. As well as this sudden shortage of staff, shops experienced a scarcity of many items and by late 1917 official food rationing was phased in. Food shortages led to land being brought into use for growing fruit and vegetables, and in March 1918 the council made over part of Inverleith Park for 250 allotments, erecting a fence to keep out the sheep that grazed in the park. In spite of later attempts to return the land to public park use, the allotments remained.

Countless women were widowed, and so many men died that numerous younger women never had the chance to marry. One positive outcome was that the shortage of labour meant that women were employed in many jobs

A PATRIOTIC EDINBURGH FAMILY.

The tenth member of the family of Mrs M'Gravie, 10 India Place, Edinburgh, passed through the recruiting office at 1 North-West Circus Place, yesterday. Five of the family are already at the front.

1 Article, 10 Dec 1915. Sadly four of the ten who went to fight died in the war
2 Rationing - Sugar Ticket for the Coop, Hamilton Place, 1917
3 Humorous postcard about the creation of allotments, c.1917
4 Advert for Edinburgh Zoo mentioning air raid shelters, 1941
5 Rationing – sign on greengrocer's stall, 1943
6 Queue for gas masks in Edinburgh, 1939

that previously had been closed to them; between 1914 and 1918, an estimated two million women replaced men in employment. This led to the Representation of the People Act in February 1918 giving women a vote for the first time. While the Act granted the vote to all men over 21, only women over the age of 30 were given the same privilege. Yet for the women eligible to vote, the election on 14 December 1918 was a significant event: 'Suggestions of apathy on the part of the women voters were not supported by the evidence of the polling booths, for everywhere they showed a determination to record their votes. This feature was especially noticeable in the towns. Women of all social positions took their part in the election. The working man's wife often carrying the youngest child was much in evidence at many polling booths.'

In the run up to the Second World War in 1939 there was fear of German bombing and gas attacks. Air raid shelters were built, gas masks issued and children evacuated out of the cities. There were six bomb shelters in Stockbridge as well as personal ones built in residents' gardens. In December 1939 The Edinburgh Academy advertised: 'The Preparatory School will be re-opened at Henderson Row. Adequate Air Raid Shelters are available. The part of the School evacuated to Hartree, Biggar will continue there as at present.' Fortunately, the feared gas attacks did not materialise and no German bombs fell on Stockbridge.

In the summer of 1939 a pamphlet, Advice to Animal Owners appeared: 'If at all possible, send or take your household animals into the country in advance of an emergency. If you cannot place them in the care of neighbours, it really is kindest to have them destroyed.' Although vets and animal protection organisations were incensed, and appealed to owners not to put down their pets, in one day in early September Broughton Dog and Cat Home put down 200 dogs and cats.

Rationing was introduced in January 1940, with everyone given an allowance for basic foodstuffs. Although fruit and vegetables were never rationed, they were in short supply and many grew their own. *The Scotsman* announced in June 1940: 'Rabbits raised in gardens and allotments can now be sold by retail without a licence from the local Food Office.' Due to petrol rationing horse-drawn vehicles returned to the streets. It was not until the early 1950s that rationing came to an end.

While the number of men and women from Stockbridge who died in the Second World War was far less than in the First, still many lost loved ones. Two sons of Mr and Mrs Mason who lived at No. 9 St Stephen Place died. Andrew (19) was killed in the fighting at Arnhem in May 1944 while serving with the Airborne Division of the Kings Own Scottish Borderers and John (29), who was serving with the Royal Naval Patrol Service on board HMS Ebor Wyke, perished when it was sunk by a German submarine in May 1945.

DRUGS & DRINK

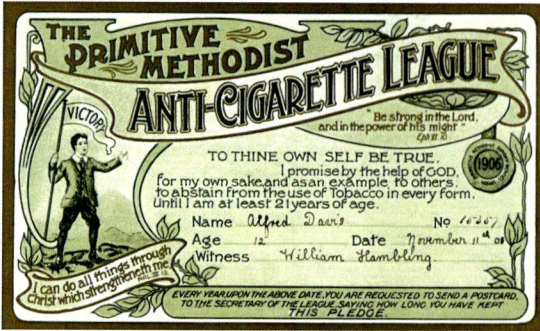

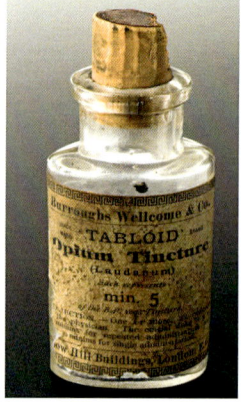

1 Elizabeth Hodge's tobacconist and confectioner shop at No. 1 Spring Gardens, 1968 - today, No. 32 N. W. Circus Place (photo – S. G. Jackman, Capital Collections)
2 Portrait of Thomas de Quincey by John Watson-Gordon, 1845
3 Anti-Cigarette League Membership Card, 1902 (Wellcome Collection)
4 Bottle of Laudanum (British Museum)
5 Poster for Leap, c.2010

In earlier times, the better off consumed their tobacco as snuff, although from around 1815 cigars became fashionable, while the majority smoked a pipe; clay pipes were given away for free by publicans. However, it was the introduction of cheap cigarettes in the 1880s, allied to mass marketing, that led to smoking becoming common among both men and women. By 1950 80% of men and 40% of women smoked. Workplaces, entertainment venues, transport and pubs were generally shrouded in tobacco smoke in spite of negative reports of the impact on non-smokers. In 1925 the *Edinburgh Evening News* wrote: 'Nothing is more characteristic of our civilisation than the abandon with which one section of mankind blows its tobacco smoke in the face of the other.' In spite of the dangers to health of smoking and the passive ingesting of cigarette smoke, when the Scottish Government introduced the ban on smoking in enclosed public spaces in 2006, many smokers attacked the legislation as an affront to their liberty.

Mary Gordon's memoir of her childhood at No. 29 Ann Street recounts that Thomas de Quincey, author of *Confessions of an English Opium-Eater*, stayed with her parents for a few months in 1829. 'An ounce of laudanum per diem prostrated animal life in the early part of the day. It was no infrequent sight to find him in his room lying upon the rug in front of the fire, his head resting upon a book, with his arms crossed over his breast, in profound slumber. For several hours he would lie in this state, till the torpor passed away.' Laudanum was an alcoholic herbal mixture containing 10% opium and often called the 'aspirin of the nineteenth century', as it was a popular and relatively cheap painkiller and relaxant. It could be bought at any chemists and was recommended for all sorts of ailments including coughs, rheumatism, 'women's troubles' and, most disturbingly, as a soporific for babies and young children. While the upper-class accepted drug-taking among their equals as an acceptable idiosyncrasy, they regarded the use of laudanum by the working class as a symptom of low morals.

During the First World War restrictions were placed on the possession of some drugs and the 1920 Dangerous Drugs Act prohibited the possession and unlicensed import or export of opium, heroin and cocaine. In the 1950s and 60s the use of drugs became increasingly associated with new subcultures, and reporting on drug-taking often had racist overtones as the rise was blamed on immigration; somewhat hypocritically as in the past Britain had profited substantially from selling opium to China. Eventually all drugs were made illegal in 1971, though this has done little to limit drug use. To help tackle drug (and drink) addiction, in 2008 the Lothians and Edinburgh Abstinence Programme (Leap) was established in Malta House, then owned by the Church of Scotland, and opened by Princess Anne. This joint initiative of NHS Lothian and Edinburgh City Council offered small groups of addicts a three-month treatment and

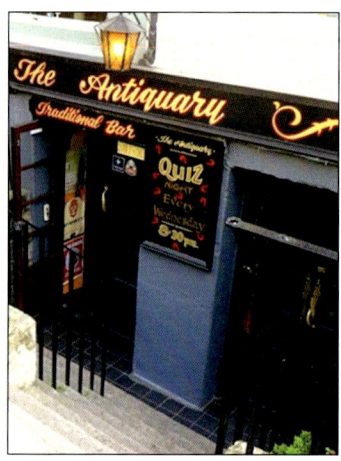

1 The Antiquary, 72-78 St Stephen Street, opened around 1990
2 The Bailie, Nos. 2-4 St Stephen Street, 2020
3 The Odd Spot Bar on corner of Church Street & India Place (demolished), c.1960
4 The Territorial Arms, Nos. 47 & 49 Deanhaugh Street, 1910 (Capital Collections)
5 Advert for sale of The Brief Encounter pub, 1995
6 Advert for The Odd Spot Bar, 1953

rehabilitation programme, with those becoming substance-free helped to find housing, further education, training or work. In spite of the project's success in assisting over 300 addicts, the project had to close in 2012 as the Church of Scotland's financial pressures forced it to sell Malta House.

From 1756 local councils were given responsibility for licensing the sale of alcohol and this applied to spirit merchants (pubs) and wine and spirit merchants (licensed grocers or off-licences). The premises in St Stephen Street that now house The Bailie has been a pub since 1825. Its long life is recounted in full in *The History of St Stephen Street*. For a long time it was called The Grand Bar. Other renamed pubs are Hectors at Nos. 47-49 Deanhaugh Street (The Territorial Bar); the Stockbridge Tap at Nos 2-6 Raeburn Place (Bert's Bar and Raeburn Bar); and St Bernard's Bar at No. 10 Raeburn Place (The VAT, John's Bar and Brief Encounter).

While drinking to excess is not limited to the poorer classes, instances of drink-related violence, abuse and anti-social behaviour were more common in the past among the disadvantaged sections of society. So from the 1850s concern about alcohol abuse and its adverse effects resulted in a widespread temperance movement. Ebenezer Murray who lived at No. 38 St Stephen Street was President of the Edinburgh Total Abstinence Society. This powerful temperance lobby found an ally in the MP Forbes Mackenzie, a tee-totaller who, in 1853, drove the Local Burgh's Police Bill through Parliament. This established pub closing times at 11pm from Monday to Saturday and complete closure on Sundays. In the 1880s the closing time was further reduced to 10pm and this stayed in place until 1977. The temperance movement continued to be strong and its campaigning led to the introduction of the Temperance (Scotland) Act 1913 that enabled voters in local areas to vote on whether their area should remain 'wet' or go 'dry'. The Anti-Prohibition Lobby held a meeting in the Grand Cinema in St Stephen Street. Over 1,300 electors of St Stephen's Ward attended, perhaps attracted by the free musical programme rather than the various speeches, and Stockbridge's wards voted to stay 'wet'

A common role for the police was checking that licensed premises did not breach closing-time rules. Mrs Jane Cuthbert who had a grocer's shop at No. 36 St Stephen Street lost her licence in 1861 after the police found she had sold spirits on a Sunday. While the 1853 Act closed pubs on Sundays, hotels were allowed to serve alcohol with food to 'bona fide' travellers, but until relatively recently Stockbridge had no hotels. There still is only one, the stylish boutique hotel, The Raeburn at No. 112 Raeburn Place; a conversion of the villa, Somerset Cottage. Whether one is a 'bona-fide traveller' or not, its award-winning bar - judged best in the Scottish Hotel Awards 2018 – will be happy to provide a drink.

SHOPS

1 Mrs Young, fishmonger, photographed on her Golden Wedding anniversary, 1912
2 Entrance to Stockbridge Market, c.1900
3 William Gardiner, Baker & Confectioner, No. 43 Dean Street - lived at 6 Hermitage Place, 1900 (Capital Collections)
4 Robert McPherson, Confectioner & Fruiterer, Nos. 118 & 120 St Stephen Street - lived above the shop, 1917 (photo - Steve Salvini)

Although the proprietors of Stockbridge's shops and the goods sold have changed over time, the majority of occupations are unchanged: bakers, dairies, butchers, greengrocers, confectioners, stationers, newsagents, chemists, pubs, off-licences, booksellers, laundries, tobacconists, shoemakers, grocers, clothes shops, etc. Many shops come and go, although a few endure. For over 50 years from the 1860s, locals bought their fish from the stall run by Mrs Young in Stockbridge Market while over the last 70 years Armstrong's at No. 80 Raeburn Place has been the place to find the best products from the sea. Across the road at No.75 is another long-established shop; George Bowers, a specialist game butcher whose products range from venison from the Highlands to kangaroo meat from down under.

For most of the 19th century the majority of shops were clustered around the bridge in Deanhaugh Street, Hamilton Place, Kerr Street (demolished) and St Stephen Street (then Brunswick Street). In 1826 Stockbridge Market opened on a site between Hamilton Place and Brunswick Street. It was developed by a retired soldier, Captain David Carnegie who commissioned a design based on Liverpool market: 'On Saturday the splendid New Town markets at Brunswick Street were opened, and visited by thousands of the citizens, who crowded to them from an early hour in the morning. When we look not only to the comfort and cleanliness everywhere displayed in these markets, but to the extreme elegance of their structure and reflect that they have been projected and executed at the sole expense and risk of patriotic citizens, we cannot omit this opportunity of expressing our high opinion of Captain Carnegie's public spirited exertions.' The market was divided into two sections. The smaller northern part was open and exclusively for the sale of fish, while the larger part that was on two storeys with a roof had stalls selling flesh, poultry, vegetables, fruit, &c. 'The whole is planned and executed with great taste, and has the commodious and elegance we would expect to find in a Fancy Bazaar.' Yet, the market was not the commercial success Carnegie and his investors had hoped. There were complaints about ventilation and a planned expansion never happened. In the 1850s part of the market was moved to allow new houses to be constructed and some of the trade moved away, although a few butchers continued to trade until it finally closed in 1900.

By the 1890s Raeburn Place had begun to evolve into the shopping street it is today. In 1899 it was reported: 'twenty new shops in Raeburn Place have been readily taken up by a good class of shopkeepers.' A number of the gardens of villas in the street were built over as shops, including No. 44 that was purchased around 1904 by Mr Grieg. The first occupant was his son-in-law, Thomas Polson Lugton, a photographer who had his photographic studio and a photography supplies outlet there.

1 William Hill Pawnbrokers above Raeburn Bar, No. 8 Raeburn Place, c.1950s
2 Illustration of new St Cuthbert's Co-operative store, Hamilton Place, 1908
3 St Cuthbert's Co-operative butcher's shop, 1900

In 1902 the first purpose-built large store in the area was opened at Nos. 56-60 Hamilton Place by the Edinburgh & Northern District Co-operative Society (ENDCS), which had originated in a small shop in Brunswick Street. In 1859 workmen in the south-west of Edinburgh set up St Cuthbert's Co-operative Association, owned and controlled by its members, all of whom received a dividend from any profits. It opened a grocery shop in Fountainbridge and, in 1863, a second shop in Brunswick Street. Although the latter closed in 1866, a number of local Stockbridge members, including John Dawson, a bell hanger and Venetian blind maker in Silvermills, decided to set up their own co-op - the ENDCS - and re-opened the shop. After a few difficult years trade began to improve and during a public holiday the committee members enlarged the shop, with those who were not joiners or masons acting as labourers. By 1875 the society operated a bakehouse, and stocked a wider selection of items, including coal, and boots and shoes. In 1880 the cooperative was able to purchase the whole tenement in which the store was housed and a few years later purchased the adjoining shop to enlarge their drapery department and add a tailoring and dressmaking section. In 1894 the Co-op built a large bakery and laundry in Patriot Hall and moved its Brunswick Street operation to the newly built store in Hamilton Place that is still a Coop today.

One common trade in the past was pawnbroking. The first to open in Stockbridge was John White at No. 4 Dean Street in 1855. Later based in St Stephen Street and on North West Circus Place, and renamed the Stockbridge Equitable Loan Company, it operated through to the 1960s. William Hill Brothers, pawnbrokers and jewellers, had a number of branches in the city and opened one at No. 8 Raeburn Place. There was never any shortage of local customers, for pawning items was the only way many could make ends meet. It was common for people to pledge their best Sunday church clothes on a Monday and redeem them on the Friday or Saturday when they had been paid. Of course, the cash lent was significantly less than an item's value. Varying rates of high interest were charged – between 15% and 30% - and there was the option of a fee for special storage, such as hanging clothes to prevent creasing. Items under ten shillings value not redeemed within the specified time became the pawnbroker's property, while more expensive unredeemed pledges were sold by public auction. In 1912 one auction of items forfeited at the St Bernard's Pawnbrokers Office in Kerr Street comprised 'Tailor-made Suits, Trousers and Vests, Topcoats, Dresses, Capes, Underclothing, Bed and Table Napery, Blankets, Boots, Shoes, &c.' Stolen goods often were pawned: 'Susan Colville, a woman of no fixed residence, was sent to prison for ten days for stealing a tweed waistcoat from off a clothes line in North West Circus Place. 'The item was missed and afterwards pledged in

1 & 2 View across bridge to Deanhaugh Street, before and after building of the Edinburgh Savings Bank in 1900
3 James Cochrane, draper, Nos. 8, 9 & 10 Baker's Place, c.1900
4 Deanhaugh Street - Pestle & Mortar sign above chemist shop at No.7 and early Natural Wholefoods shop at No. 9, 1985 (photo David Anderson, Capital Collections)
5 David Elmslie, Grocer, Hugh Miller Cottage, Glenogle Road, c.1900

a pawnbroker's in St Stephen Street by the accused, who got drunk on the proceeds.'

The first pharmacy shop was opened in 1828 by Robert Jamieson at No. 4 Deanhaugh Street and traded through to the early 1850s. Pharmacists made up medications specifically for customers - many still based on old herbal remedies - and also sold proprietary brands: 'Lungular Complaints are the prevailing Diseases of the English climate, and the thousands who are now suffering from Asthma, Coughs, Incipient Consumption, and other Pulmonary maladies, would at once be relieved, and by perseverance entirely cured, by adopting Keatings Cough Lozenges.' Deanhaugh Street has housed many chemists' shops, and the traditional pharmacy Pestle & Mortar sign still sits above No. 7 that was Boots in past years and is now Lloyds Pharmacy.

In the late 1890s the tenancy of William Smith's chemists shop at No. 1 Deanhaugh Street came to an end when the property was sold to Edinburgh Savings Bank. The bank was looking to open its sixth branch in the city and had decided that this should be in Stockbridge. The existing building was rather plain so the bank had it demolished and commissioned a new building from the architects, David MacGibbon and Thomas Ross who recently had published a five volume series, *The castellated and domestic architecture of Scotland*, a comprehensive survey of Scottish architecture prior to the Restoration. Their building for the bank was strongly influenced by the historic architecture they admired, such as Edinburgh's Tolbooth; it opened in December 1900, and is one of Stockbridge's most admired buildings.

In 1895 the shop at No. 28 Raeburn Place was constructed over the existing garden of the villa and leased by Otto Goll, a men's hairdresser. Today, it is the longest continuous business in Stockbridge. In the same year new tenements built at the western end of Raeburn Place incorporated shops on the ground floor and William Corson opened an ironmongery shop at No. 62. This family business operated until 2022, though by then called a hardware shop. That the shop survived so long is a wonder, for Eric Corson, the third generation to run it, gained a widespread reputation for grumpiness and unhelpfulness. Locals had a multitude of stories of his crabbiness and reluctance to sell goods that clearly were on display. One person blamed his contrariness on the simple fact he had inherited the shop from his father and never wanted to run a hardware shop.

Fortunately, Mr Corson's approach to service is uncommon in Stockbridge. In 2020 Scottish Post Office customers voted Stockbridge's Post Office at No. 70 Raeburn Place best for its commitment and friendliness. It was opened in 2002 by Mohammed Akram and his daughter, Waheeda was appointed postmistress. Mohammed Akram came

1 Corson Hardware, No. 62 Raeburn Place, c.2000
2 Opening of the Post Office at No. 70 Raeburn Place in 2002. Mark Lazarowicz, MP for Edinburgh & North Leith, Mohammed Akram with his son, Shafkat Akram, and Postmistress Waheeda Akram
3 Ping On Chinese Restaurant, Nos. 26-32 Deanhaugh Street, c.1990
4 Remo Mancini outside his café at No. 23 Raeburn Place, c.1960
5 Advert for Dog Foods Edinburgh. No. 26 Raeburn Place, 1954
6 Advert for Refreshment Rooms in Glanville Place, 1854

to Britain from Pakistan in 1961 aged 20 and for 11 years worked in a weaving factory in Huddersfield. In 1972 he, his wife, Sherifan and their eight children moved to Edinburgh and lived at No. 44 Raeburn Place. Akram purchased No. 72 and opened a newsagents and greengrocers shop, and later also bought No. 70. For 41 years until his retirement Mohammed Akram provided exemplary service to his customers and was a popular 'weel kent' face in Stockbridge. Waheeda recounts, 'My father always said that to succeed in life you had to put your heart and soul into your business. He also said, when dealing with the public. "they are always right!" Well, not always but you just have to pretend they are sometimes!!

Like Mr Akram who moved to Britain to make a new life, Kenny Mak arrived in Edinburgh from his native Hong Kong in 1965 and after working for a few years as a waiter introduced Stockbridge locals to Chinese food when he opened Ping On at No. 28 Deanhaugh Street in 1968. However, like other Chinese restaurants at that time, Mak had to adjust the menu to align with local taste and alongside more authentic Chinese dishes, served chips and curries. Kenny and his wife Fiona had five children and lived at No. 30 Raeburn Place. One of the earliest eateries was 'Refreshment Rooms for the Working Classes' in Glanville Place in the 1850s. In 1972 Bell's Diner in St Stephen Street brought American-style burgers to the area and in 1975 newly-weds Filippo and Maria-Celeste Crolla brought a taste of their beloved hometown of Picinisco, Italy to Stockbridge when they opened L'Alba D'Oro at No.5 Henderson Row. This almost certainly was the first fast-food takeaway in the world to sell Cloudy Bay Sauvignon Blanc, Cristal Champagne and Louis XIII Cognac alongside fish suppers. Little surprise that in 2014 *The Times* named it the No.1 Fish and Chip Shop in the UK. Today Stockbridge is home to a wide range of cuisines, from Thai to Scottish.

From the 1890s to the 1930s those wealthier Stockbridge residents wishing to entertain at home in style were able to have their dinner parties catered by J. Ramage & Son, at Nos. 1-4 Albert Place (N.W. Circus Place), a bakery and confectioner firm that also had tearooms elsewhere in the city. Stockbridge has always been fond of a cake or three. In 1835 William Thomson at No. 1 India Place advertised 'High-class fruitcakes' while by the 1950s 'fancies' could be bought at the splendidly named Preacher's Patisserie Perfection at No. 38 Raeburn Place. Today Stockbridge cake lovers are spoilt for choice, as are coffee and tea aficionados. The earliest coffee house was the New Slaughter Coffee House and Tavern at No. 4 Hamilton Place, opened by Charles Presgrave in 1838: 'C.P. omitted to mention in his last advertisement that either a party or a single gentleman can be accommodated with a private room, not inferior to any in the metropolis, at the same moderate charges as in the splendid Coffee Room.'

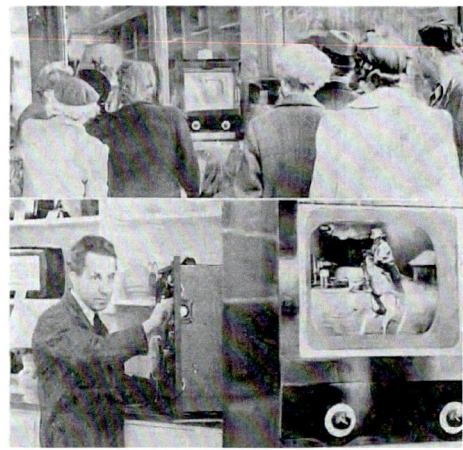

1 Preview of television in window of Cavendish Radio & Electricals, No. 44 Raeburn Place by back-projecting film on to a dummy TV set, August 1951 – TV broadcasting in Scotland began in March 1952
2 Golden Hare Books, No. 68 St Stephen Street, 2020
3 Thomas Pulson Lugton, Photographer, No. 44 Raeburn Place, 1906
4 Radio Supplies, No. 30b Raeburn Place, 1931
5 Children rushing to buy sweets at end of sugar rationing, 1953
6 John Wilson, Plumber, No. 62 Dean Street/St Bernard's Crescent c.1960 (building demolished)

However, it was short-lived. The 1950s saw the rise of Italian cafes throughout the city, including Dalessio's Café at Nos. 10-13 India Place and Remo's Café at No. 23 Raeburn Place. The latter was a firm favourite with trendy youngsters as it had a jukebox and songs such as *Volare* boomed down Raeburn Place.

In June 1939 the first 'Self Service Store' opened at No. 106a Raeburn Place selling groceries and provisions: 'All plainly marked at unheard-of prices. Just walk in! Serve yourself!' In 1964 two houses, including Raeburn Hall, were demolished to make way for a Woolworths store; a shopping arrival that no doubt excited many but depressed others. The store closed in 2008.

There have always been a few specialist shops. In 1862 D. Willoughby, who was employed by Edinburgh Academy to teach cricket, opened a shop at No. 8 Market Place (now St Stephen Place) where he sold: 'seasoned cricket bats, scoring sheets and every article connected with the noble game.' Today that shop is part of Treen, a stylish clothes shop offering, 'a killer wardrobe without killing the planet.' The main clothing shop in Stockbridge from the 1850s through to the Second World War was the draper's shop on the corner of Baker's Place (where Starbucks is today). It was opened in 1850 by James Munro and sold clothes, materials for dressmaking - 'New London prints will be to hand in a few days, the newest designs, beginning at 2s6d up to 4s6d per Dress, fast colours' and 'hosiery, gloves, ribbons, laces, umbrellas, trimmings, underclothing, etc.' By the 1930s it was one of four Barnets stores in Edinburgh selling clothing and bed linen.

The first book shop in Stockbridge was opened by Robert Chambers in 1822 as part of his Subscription Library in India Place, although he soon moved to the New Town. For around 40 years from 1860 Robert Somerville ran a stationers and bookshop at No. 10 Spring Gardens (now N W Circus Place) and it was he who published Cumberland Hill's *Reminiscences of Stockbridge*. In the 1950s Edina Book Emporium was at No. 13 India Place and in the 1980s there was a branch of Bobbies Bookshop in Raeburn Place; particularly popular for its wide range of comics. In recent years, in spite of small independent bookshops appearing to be under threat, three have opened in Stockbridge: Golden Hare Books at No. 68 Stephen Street and across from it at No. 51, Ginger & Pickles Children's Bookshop; Rare Birds, specialising in women's writing, at No. 13a Raeburn Place; and along from it at No. 25 is Oxfam's specialist second-hand bookshop.

Shops in Raeburn Place have reflected changing technology. Radio Supplies at No. 26 advertised in 1932: 'Radio Supplies, the only firm in town which guarantees 18 months' free service and free installation of any receiver; cash or credit. 1933 Marconi 2volt to rent 2s/6d weekly. Aerial

1 Advert for The Astrology Centre, No. 60 St Stephen Street, c.1983
2 Bill Purves outside his Lamp Emporium, No. 9 St Stephen Street, 1991
3 Bric-a-brac on sale on steps at No. 8 St Stephen Street, c.1980
4 Mary Portas in Mary's Living & Giving Shop for Save the Children, No. 34a Raeburn Place, c.2010
5 I. J. Mellis, Cheesemonnger, No. 6 Baker's Place, 2023
6 Stall at the Sunday Stockbridge Market, 2023

system erected free.' In 1951, the year before television came to Scotland, one ingenious Raeburn Place shop owner set up a dummy television set in his window with back-projected film to show people how TV would look, although it was the 1953 Coronation that led to a flurry of sales of television sets. For children (and confectioners) the main excitement of 1953 was the ending of sweet rationing in February, and the 1950s also brought youngsters thrilling new toys: 'Just arrived – Walkie-Talkie Doll 63s. Mobo Scooter 19s. Triang Jeep £5.19.6. Hosts of exciting toys at Stephens of Stockbridge, 54 Raeburn Place.'

The decline of St Stephen Street and potential threat of redevelopment meant that by the 1960s many shops were vacant. A number of young entrepreneurs, part of the 'Swinging Sixties' youth-driven cultural revolution that had emerged in London, took the opportunity to open businesses in the street at low cost. When consideration was being given to demolishing the street, this was noted by the city planners and was a factor in the street's survival: 'St Stephen Street contains many small specialist shops which bear no direct relationship to the shopping in the rest of the area. These have grown up due to the availability of low-rateable-value property which has enabled small shops to start with a low capital investment. In some cases the traders display their wares on the stairs in front of their shops.' By 1983, alongside the street's half-a-dozen antique and bric-brac shops, shoppers could buy Latin American folk art at Azteca (No. 12); fashionable second-hand clothes at Old Habits Die Hard (No. 53); microbiotic foods at East West Centre (No. 12); designer clothes at Tommy Rot (No. 60); and even learn their fortune at the Astrology Center (No. 60). In 2020 a tourism website commented: 'St Stephen Street is perhaps Edinburgh's best-known street for independent shops. It's a peaceful spot but filled with local businesses that make it worth a visit.'

In the 1980s in Stockbridge as elsewhere, the rise of supermarkets and an economic downturn led to many shop premises becoming vacant. To help avoid shopping street blight, the Government introduced significant incentives for charity shops and a number opened in Stockbridge. Today many of these have evolved in response to more up-market shops opening in the area. In 2009 TV retail advisor and Save the Children Ambassador, Mary Portas chose Stockbridge for one of the charity's boutique style shops. 'We want to create a real buzz around second hand shopping and make the old fashioned charity shop a thing of the past'.

Stockbridge's draw as a shopping destination was enhanced in 2011 when the Sunday Market opened in Jubilee Gardens on the corner of Kerr Street and Saunders Street. This popular food and crafts market is, appropriately, just a short walk from the location of Captain Carnegie's long-gone Stockbridge Market.

PART TWO
50 PORTRAIT SKETCHES

Allan Street - Christian Wilson	108
Ann Street - Flora & Rosaline Masson	110
Avondale Place - Hepburn Leitch	112
Baker's Place - William Hannah	114
Balmoral Place - Veronica Cassie	116
Bell Place - David Valentine	118
Brunswick Street - Hugh Nelson	120
Carlton Street - Henry Glegg	122
Cheyne Street - Jessie King	124
Claremont Street - Alexander Brown	126
Clarence Street - Alison Dunlop	128
Collins Place - Patrick Macnamara	130
Colville Place - William Crawford	132
Danube Street - Dora Noyce	134
Dean Bank Lane - Elmslie Dallas	136
Dean Bank Lane Mews - John Swanson	138
Deanhaugh Street - James Young Simpson	140
Dean Park Crescent - Phoebe Traquair	142
Dean Park Street - Otto Goll	144
Dean Street - Andrew Raven	146
Dean Terrace - Nancy Loudon	148
Dunrobin Place - James Gillies	150
Glenogle House - Margaret Maxton	152
Hamilton Place - James Maclaren	154
Henderson Row - William Macao	156
Hermitage Place - Cumberland Hill	158
Hugh Miller Place - Kenneth Vyner	160
India Place - Robert Chambers	162
Kemp Place - James Colville	164
Kerr Street - James Crighton	166
Leslie Place - David Nelson	168
Mackenzie Place - Emma Stirling	170
Malta Green - William Cushnie	172
Malta Terrace - Kenneth Macleay	174

Mary's Place - Alexander Edgar	176
North West Circus Place - Barclay Todd	178
Perth Street - Sadie Aitken	180
Portgower Place - Thomas & Francis Collinson	182
Raeburn Place - James Simpson	184
Reid Terrace - John Thomson	186
Rintoul Place - James Caw	188
St Bernard's Crescent - William Mowat-Thomson	190
St Bernard's Row - Mary Jameson	192
Saunders Street - George Kemp	194
Saxe-Coburg Place - William Hole	196
Silvermills - Lauder family	198
Spring Gardens - William Brodie	200
Teviotdale Place - Rachel Hazell	202
Upper Dean Terrace - Helen Marshall	204
Veitch's Square - Helen Whitelaw	206

Phoebe Anna Traquair, artist & Ramsay Heatley Traquair, palaeontologist, No. 8 Dean Park Crescent

(photo of Ramsay Traquair by Hugh Ritchie - Manuscript Collection of William Carmichael McIntosh, St Andrews University)

ALLAN STREET - CHRISTIAN WILSON

1 *Playmates* by Alexander Burr, engraved by Lumb Stocks, 1867 (Wellcome Collection)
2 Post Office Directory street listing, 1851. Although there were over 45 tenants living in Allan Street at this time, only these four were listed in the Street Directory and both cowfeeders had cow byres in the street
3 A Victorian midwife

In 1825 Christian (Potter) married Hugh Wilson, a mason, and they rented a two room flat at No. 13 Allan Street. In 1845, when Christian had recently given birth - at least the tenth child she had borne - Hugh died, leaving Christian, then 45 years old, widowed with six children under the age of ten. While her older children were working, Christian needed to earn additional money and began advertising as a midwife; a role she performed into her sixties.

It was not until the 1940s that births in hospital began to become standard, and in Victorian times most home births were attended by a midwife, as they cost far less than a general practitioner or a specialist obstetrician. Although there were early courses for midwives, it is unlikely that Wilson would have had any training. For some years previously she had worked as a home 'nurse' assisting experienced midwives at births and she would have learnt from them. In addition she had her own extensive personal experience of childbirth. Standards among midwives varied but Wilson must have had a good reputation because she then worked in that capacity for around 20 years. Also, living for so many years in Allan Street would have made her part of the local community and quite likely similar to the local midwife described by Flora Thomson in *Lark Rise to Candleford*: 'She was a decent, intelligent old body, clean in her person and methods and very kind ... She was no superior person coming into the house to strain its resources... but a neighbour ... who would make do with what there was, or if not, knew where to send to borrow it.' Midwives also were valued by women as they could be consulted on reproduction and other confidential matters relating to the female body.

At this time pregnancy was a period of considerable vulnerability, particularly in the cramped and often insanitary tenements in Stockbridge's poorer streets. Indeed, few pregnant women, of whatever class, did not worry about injury during delivery or death in childbirth. Many sadly did die, often from puerperal fever, a highly contagious disease, and as large families were the norm, the constant succession of pregnancies increased the risk. Stillbirths and infant deaths were common, and midwives often must have provided sympathetic support to women and families who experienced such losses.

Mothers generally stayed in bed for at least 10 days after the birth, during which time the midwife or 'nurse' assistant took care of household chores and looked after any other children. So childbirth was a costly event for poor families, as they also had to provide necessities for the infant. Some received assistance from the Edinburgh Lying-In Institution established in 1824, which offered 'poor married women every requisite attendance, either by a Medical Gentleman or a Midwife' and provided necessary medicines and the temporary use of bed linen, etc.'

ANN STREET - FLORA & ROSALINE MASSON

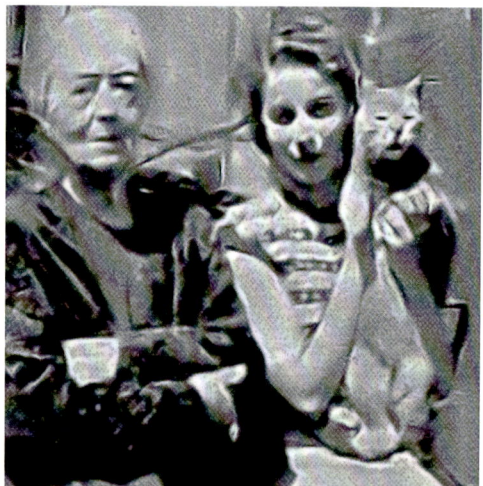
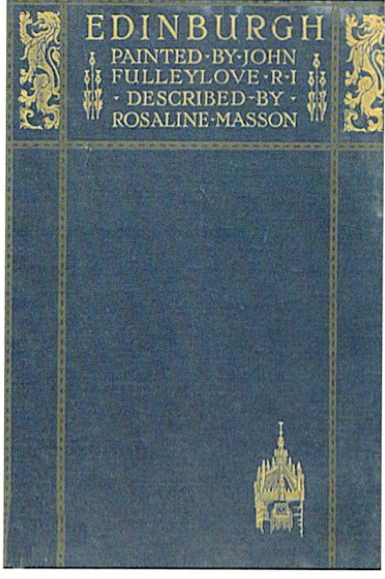

1 Flora Masson
2 Rosaline Masson and unknown woman holding Turbineus
3 Letter of reference for Flora Masson, written by Florence Nightingale to the Radcliffe Infirmary, Oxford, 1891 (University of Leeds)
4 *Edinburgh* by Rosaline Masson, published 1904

In July 1909 *The Standard* published a letter that began: 'Sir, In your header on "Suffragette Activity" you state "we should welcome suggestions from the saner half of the female sex as to to the right way of dealing with the intractable maid, matron or widow when she takes it into her head that the right of voting may be won by muscular exertion." May we suggest that the right way of dealing with them would be to grant the parliamentary franchise to women who possess the same qualifications as our men voters?' The letter was signed by Flora and Rosaline Masson who lived at No. 38 Ann Street. They were daughters of David Masson, Professor of Rhetoric and Literature at Edinburgh University and Emily Orme, secretary of the Edinburgh National Society for Women's Suffrage; they had moved with their mother to Ann Street in 1907, following the death of their father. At the time of writing the letter Flora was in her early fifties and Rosaline ten years younger.

They had been brought up to view women as equals in a home visited by many great writers, including Elizabeth Barrett Browning, Thomas Carlyle and James Barrie. Rosaline's unique hobby when young was collecting kisses from the famous visitors. Both were active in the women's suffrage movement with their mother, a policy that their father also supported, speaking out when many men remained sceptical. Flora wrote about women's right to vote in *The Parliamentary Franchise for Women* published in the *Ladies Edinburgh Journal* in 1876.

Flora trained in England as a nurse and became close friends with Florence Nightingale. During the First World War she was matron of a Red Cross hospital and awarded the Royal Red Cross 1st class 'in recognition of valuable services'. After returning to Edinburgh she edited two of her father's works, and published several biographies, including *Florence Nightingale, by one who knew her* (1910) and *The Brontes* (1912).

Rosaline remained at home and also wrote. Her books included biographies of William Wordsworth and Robert Louis Stevenson; a writing guide, *Use and Abuse of English* (1899); novels and much else. She was an early conservationist and lover of Edinburgh, and an active member of the Cockburn Association. Her book, *Edinburgh* ends: 'At any other season Edinburgh is a hospitable city, and it is growing every day a more cosmopolitan one. English residents have altered national ways; ruthless hands are tearing down our beautiful old stone houses, and building tenements in their places; and soon - too soon - all Scottish traits will be lost. But the Castle Rock cannot be levelled. It was there, in the mist and the rain, before Edinburgh began; and it will be there, in the mist and the rain, when Edinburgh has ceased to be.'

After Flora's death in 1937 Rosaline lived on in Ann Street with her much-loved cat, named Turbineus in reference to its tail, and died in 1949.

AVONDALE PLACE - HEPBURN LEITCH

1 Valuation Roll for 1885 listing Hepburn Leitch at No. 26 Avondale Place
2 Advert, 1892
3 Airbnb listing for No. 28 Avondale Place, 2022

The original idea of Airbnbs was that residents would let a room or two as bed and breakfast accommodation, although the majority now are whole properties let for short periods. One recently advertised in Avondale Place was listed as, 'a 2-bedroom holiday home with a living room, a fully equipped kitchen and one bathroom'. A reviewer described it as, 'very cosy'. From around 1878 the house next door, No. 26, was the equivalent of the original concept of an Airbnb as Mrs Hepburn Leitch lived in the house and let space to two lodgers. Since her four sons were also living there, the term 'very cosy' would have had a different meaning.

Hepburn Woodcock was born in 1840 in Dundee, where her father worked as an upholsterer, but the family later moved to Edinburgh. In 1860 she married Robert Leitch, the son of a fishmonger. He worked as a baker and by the 1870s had a baker's shop at No. 5 Johnson Place (today St Bernard's Bar in Raeburn Place). In the early years of their marriage Robert and Hepburn lived in Haugh Street with Robert's father and sister. Their first child, a daughter, died when an infant but their later four sons all survived into adulthood. Around 1870 Robert purchased No. 26 Avondale Place. It is likely that he would have paid a deposit and taken out a loan for the balance.

In 1877 Robert died, aged just 54, and Hepburn was widowed with four sons, aged 2 to 12, and the house loan to repay. With four young sons to look after, employment possibilities would have been limited. Although she may have taken ad-hoc work, her main source of income came from squeezing lodgers into the house. Over time her sons moved into work: William for a bell hanging firm, Adam and James as print compositors, and Alexander as a tailor. That she retained the house and brought up her sons is evidence of her resolve.

By 1893, with at least two sons having moved out, Leitch, describing herself as a lodging house keeper, advertised a larger space: 'Comfortable parlour and bedroom, piano, suit 1 or 2; very moderate.' Hopefully only lodgers with musical aptitude took advantage of the piano on offer. Lodging housekeepers had to deal with a range of issues, including troublesome tenants, but the most upsetting - and one that was relatively common - was the death of a lodger. In 1903 Archibald Stewart, an 82 year old retired shoemaker died in the house. His death certificate states that he died at 2.30am so Leitch must have had the distressing task of calling a doctor in the middle of the night to register the death. She then would have had to contact any relations and given his age, possibly had a hand in arranging his funeral.

Hepburn Leitch continued to let rooms until at least 1905 and died at Avondale Place in 1908. Her eldest son, Adam married and in 1901 was living in Balmoral Place with his wife and three children, and they too rented a room to a lodger.

BAKER'S PLACE - WILLIAM HANNAH

WILLIAM HANNAH, SURGEON DENTIST *(Upwards of Twenty Years Assistant to Mr NASMYTH, Charlotte Square),* respectfully intimates that he has commenced PRACTICE in the above PROFESSION at 10 BAKER'S PLACE, STOCKBRIDGE, and from long practical experience in a First-Class Practice, he is enabled to supply the Best ARTIFICIAL TEETH on the most approved principles, and at the most moderate Prices.
EXTRACTIONS carefully performed.
TEETH Scaled and Stopped.
CHILDREN'S Teeth regulated.

LYON & TURNBULL, 51 GEORGE STREET, EDINBURGH.
Respectfully announce the following Sales:—
Within 67 NORTHUMBERLAND STREET (Main-door),
THIS DAY (FRIDAY), at Eleven o'clock,
EXCELLENT HOUSEHOLD FURNITURE,
PAINTINGS, ENGRAVINGS, BOOKS,
PIANOFORTE, &c.,
Which belonged to the late Mr WILLIAM HANNAH, Dentist.

1 Advert, 1870
2 Victorian Dentist's Surgery (Victorian Museum, University of Liverpool)
3 Advert for the sale of William Hannah's belongings following his death, 1899
4 Robert Nasmyth, c.1850

William Hannah was born in Glasgow in 1827. It is likely he had medical training, as in 1850 he was appointed as an assistant to the surgeon-dentist Robert Nasmyth who had set up in practice in Edinburgh in the 1820s. Nasmyth was a recognised leader in the field - often called 'the father of Scottish dentistry' - and appointed surgeon-dentist to the Queen. He pioneered many new procedures, including gaining a reputation for his technique of gold fillings for dental cavities. Working as an assistant to a surgeon-dentist was the only available form of training until 1856, when the first dentistry course for medical students in Edinburgh was established. Nasmyth was involved in the founding of the Edinburgh Dental Dispensary at No. 1 Drummond Street in 1860 that provided for those in need of dental care and to give clinical instruction in dentistry.

The 1878 Dentists Act legislated that only those who had undergone recognised training could call themselves 'dentist' or 'dental surgeon', whereas before dentistry in Scotland was completely unregulated. The majority of people with toothache went to druggists and apothecaries for remedies such as oil of cloves or laudanum. Other cures were advertised: 'Toothache. No cure for this distressing complaint has been found half as efficacious as the Chinese Toothache Essence. It gives immediate ease to the most excruciating toothache; and by its corrosive influence on the nerve renders the recurrence of the pain extremely improbable. It is sold in bottles with directions. Price 7½d'. However, the only answer to badly decaying teeth, a common problem, was extraction, and for most this was undertaken without any form of anaesthetic, usually by barbers. False teeth were often made by craftsmen such as jewellers and watch-repairers. Teeth from the deceased, including soldiers who died in the Battle of Waterloo, were removed and used in dentures; although other materials were beginning to be used by the 1860s, barrels of teeth from those who died in the American Civil War were shipped to Britain.

In 1869 when Nasmyth closed his practice - he died the following year, aged 79 – Hannah moved to Stockbridge to begin his own practice. He had married Eliza Ritchie in 1855 and they and six children first lived in Rintoul Place but within a year moved to a flat in 10 Baker's Place. There Hannah established his dentist's surgery, the first in Stockbridge. It was around this time that nitrous oxide ('laughing gas') began to be used as an anaesthetic for tooth extraction.

Hannah later moved to Northumberland Street and died there in 1893. Two of his sons became dentists. Robert Nasmyth, named in honour of his father's earlier employer, set up his practice in Howe Street while his brother Thomas emigrated to Brisbane, Australia. 'Robert Hannah, an Edinburgh dentist, is now supplying his brother, Thomas Hannah, Brisbane, with Artificial Teeth of all qualities, so that he has the advantage of supplying teeth cheaper than other dentists in Queensland.'

BALMORAL PLACE - VERONICA CASSIE

1 VE Day Street party at the Stockbridge Colonies, 8 May 1945 (Capital Collections)
2 Cakes for the Queen Elizabeth Diamond Jubilee party at the Stockbridge Colonies, June 2012

In July 1956 the *Edinburgh Evening News* reported: 'The housewives of Balmoral Place and Collins Place have special reason to hope that the weather will favour their activities to-morrow evening, for streets in Stockbridge's colonies will be transformed into a veritable open-air market and tea-garden with perhaps, one is told, a little light entertainment thrown in. A Bring and Buy Sale has been organised by Mrs Veronica Cassie of Balmoral Place, and the neighbours in the two streets have rallied wholeheartedly to help with the scheme. There will be a grocery stall, a "cake and candy", a "white elephant," and even a fish stall, as well as the teas and the entertainment, and proceeds (which Mrs Cassie hopes will exceed £20) will go to help with the care of spastic children. This Stockbridge cul-de-sac has been the scene of several happy and successful outdoor events. There was the Victory party, the Coronation party, and one to celebrate a visit by the Queen a few years ago. Nor is Mrs Cassie the only member of her family to organise charity events, for during the war her daughter organised several successful concerts in their own home. What if it rains to-morrow evening? That, too, has been provided for as if the weather does break down the organisers will hold the sale in a huge marquee.'

Veronica Cassie clearly enjoyed organising community events and others were reported in local papers. In 1942 she and her two teenage daughters held a children's concert in their small house, 'attended by neighbours and friends' in aid of the Russian War Comforts Fund and raised £5.5s. In the following year, 'a sale of work in aid of the Red Cross (Prisoners of War) Fund was held by the children of Collins Place and Balmoral Place. The sum of £5 was raised, the sale being organised by Veronica Cassie.'

Veronica was working as a printer machinist when she met Richard Cassie, who worked as a butler at the Caledonian United Services Club in Shandwick Place. They married in 1928 and set up home in Teviotdale Place where she gave birth to their two daughters: Veronica and Irene. By the start of the Second World War the family had moved to No. 21 Balmoral Place. In 1978 Richard and Veronica were still living there and no doubt the celebration of their Golden Wedding Anniversary would have been a grand event. Their daughter, Veronica lived on in the house until 1999 when it was put on the market for 'offers over £150,000'.

The community spirit of Veronica Cassie has lived on in the Stockbridge Colonies. For the Queen's Jubilee in 2011 residents held a street celebration and in 2015, to mark the 70th anniversary of the end of the Second World War, the BBC One Show worked with residents in Bell Place and Kemp Place to recreate a party mounted by Cassie and other Colonies' residents to mark VE (Victory in Europe) day in May 1945.

BELL PLACE - DAVID VALENTINE

1 David Valentine & family, 1914
2 Leith Burgh Police, 1906

Many policemen chose to live in the Stockbridge Colonies, including David Valentine. He was born in St Andrews in 1877, one of eight children, and his father and elder brothers worked as agricultural labourers. However, after marrying Rachel Mentiply in 1890, Valentine moved to Edinburgh to join the Leith police force that at the time had around 120 officers. His family of four daughters and two sons, together with Valentine's elderly father for a few years, lived in the small ground floor house at No. 17 Bell Place.

Being a policeman in Leith would have been a tough job. The ratio of one constable for every 918 inhabitants was far lower than elsewhere and like all dock areas, crime was high. In addition to patrolling the streets, attending incidents and making arrests, the police had other roles, including checking that pubs did not breach their opening hours and controlling illegal street gambling. Drunkenness was common and often led to violent domestic disputes and street fights. In dealing with these, policemen often were assaulted. In 1901, while trying to arrest two men, Valentine was punched in the face and the accompanying constable kicked to the ground. It was reported the 'constables were obliged to use their batons' and one of the assailants appeared in court, 'his head swathed with bandages'. In 1924 Valentine was commended and received a guinea for being one of a number of policemen on duty at a Territorial Army march past in Princes Street who managed to bring under control two horses that bolted while drawing a general service wagon.

In 1902 the Leith policemen began agitating for more men and reduced hours: '95 out of 101 constables have signed the petition to the Council explaining that there are 16 men doing day duty whose combined working hours for the year are 3,480, which, if compared with Edinburgh, with only 2,880, makes a difference in hours of 800, which, at the rate of 8 hours per day, is equal to 100 days extra labour for each Leith constable.' Eventually their hours were aligned to those in Edinburgh.

Valentine was a keen sportsman. He was a member of both the Edinburgh City Police Bowling Association and Edinburgh Police Golf Club. In 1911 Valentine was one of eight Edinburgh police golfers that played the Glasgow Police Golf Club, 'in fine weather on the course of the Glasgow North-Western Club at Ruchill, Glasgow.' He won both his singles and doubles matches, thus helping the Edinburgh team win by a single match.

Valentine was promoted to a sergeant before retiring. The 1921 census records all the children as still living at home. Betsy was working as a tailor, Margaret as a shop assistant at Lumley's Sports Outfitter, William (15) as an apprentice cabinetmaker, and James (14) as a message boy, while Rachel (12) and Elizabeth (10) were still at school. David and his family later moved to live in Comely Bank Place.

BRUNSWICK STREET - SIR HUGH NELSON

DEATH OF SIR HUGH NELSON.

Sir Hugh Nelson, Lieutenant-Governor of Queensland, a former Premier, died at Toowoomba on Monday morning. His death leaves vacant the Presidency of the Queensland Legislative Council.

The son of the Rev. W. L. Nelson, LL.D., Sir Hugh was born at Kilmarnock, Scotland, on December 31, 1835. Educated at the High School, Edinburgh, and at Edinburgh University, he came to Queensland in 1853, where he engaged in pastoral pursuit. In 1883 he was elected to the Legislative Assembly as the representative of Northern Downs, and sat for that constituency until 1888, when he was returned for Murilla and accepted the post of Secretary for Railways in the M'Ilwraith Ministry. He retained that portfolio when the Administration was reconstructed under Mr. B. D. Morshead, and went out of office with his colleagues in 1890. Two years later Sir Hugh was Colonial Treasurer, holding that office until 1893, and in the same year the Premiership fell to him, and he ruled the political destinies of Queensland until 1898.

In that year he quitted the activity of the Lower Chamber and occupied the office of the President of the Legislative Council. He was created K.C.M.G. in 1896, P.C. in 1897, and was Lieutenant-Governor since 1903. In 1897 the hon. degree of D.C.L. was conferred upon him by Oxford University.

PRESENTATION.—On Tuesday evening, at a soiree given upon the occasion, the Rev. W. L. Nelson, of North Esk Church, Musselburgh, formerly Head Master of St Stephen's Parish School, Edinburgh, was presented by his old pupils with a handsome writing-desk, as a mark of their respect and esteem for him. The Rev. Dr Muir, St Stephen's, presided, and the meeting was addressed by the Rev. Mr Muir of Dalmeny, Rev. Mr Playfair of Abercorn, &c. &c. The desk was presented to Mr Nelson by Mr A. Henderson (an old scholar and teacher in St Stephen's), on behalf of his fellow-scholars; and altogether the evening was spent in the most harmonious and agreeable manner.

1 Hugh Nelson Obituary, *Australia Town & Country Journal*, 3 January 1906
2 Hugh Nelson, 11th Premier of Queensland, Australia, c.1893
3 Article, 1850

In 1897 Sir Hugh Nelson, Premier of Queensland, Australia, travelled to Britain to represent Queensland at the Queen Victoria Diamond Jubilee celebrations in London. While in the country he travelled to Edinburgh and was a guest at a reception in the City Chambers, along with a number of former pupils of St Stephen's School in St Stephen Street, as that was where he was first educated.

In 1839, at the age of five, Hugh Nelson moved from Glasgow with his family into one of the eight flats at No. 50 Brunswick Street (later St Stephen Street). His father, William, although 30 and with a young family, had decided to study divinity at Edinburgh University and to support his study took the post of Headmaster at St Stephen's School. The school had been built by St Stephen's Church three years earlier to provide free education for local children. William was assisted by one teacher, 20-year-old David Muir, who lodged with the family. It must have been a hard time for all the family as the flat was small and William had to combine running the school with his university studies.

All four Nelson children attended St Stephen's School, which consisted of: 'three floors, each forming a spacious room for the accommodation of a separate class; the classes forming a boys' school, a girls' school, and an infant school, comprising about 400 children, belonging to the poorer classes of the parish.' In 1844, Hugh, the eldest son, moved to Edinburgh's Royal High School on Calton Hill, one of the three pre-eminent private schools for boys.

In 1849 William, having completed his divinity studies and been ordained, was appointed minister of Northesk Church in Musselburgh and the family moved there. In 1851 Hugh entered Edinburgh University to study under Sir William Hamilton, professor of civil history. However, two years later, Hugh's life dramatically changed when his father accepted an offer from the Sydney Presbytery in Australia to take charge of the Presbyterians in the district of Ipswich, Queensland. All the family agreed to emigrate and in late April 1853 boarded the Elora, a ship that mainly carried goods but had 'a large and roomy cabin, fitted up for twenty passengers.' They arrived in New South Wales in August but then had another lengthy sea journey to Queensland.

While the port of Ipswich was expanding, at the time they arrived it only had around 1,200 residents. Thus job opportunities for Hugh were slim. He took a job as a storekeeper's clerk and then as a station-hand. It was later said of him that he was most at home with herds and flocks, and in time his expertise and business acumen saw him acquire a 40,000-acre property, where he developed a prize-winning and lucrative stud, and wool-producing flock. In 1892 he sold his property and entered politics, and after serving in a range of roles, in 1893 was elected Premier of Queensland. He died in 1906.

CARLTON STREET - CAPTAIN HENRY GLEGG

1 East India Company Army recruiting advert, c.1850
2 *Portrait of Captain Henry Glegg* by unknown artist, c.1830s
3&4 Extracts from Henry Glegg's journal (National Library of Scotland)

In 1839 Henry Glegg, a captain in the army of the East India Company (EIC) based in Bengal, was appointed Recruiting Officer for the EIC army in Edinburgh. Scotland supplied many men for the EIC in India and rising tensions within India made the need for more soldiers acute. Glegg sailed to Scotland in May and in a notebook he kept (now in the collection of the National Library of Scotland) recorded that he had travelled 55,000 miles in sea voyages, and in India, 6,000 miles on land and 3,000 by river; listed the 'equipment (on the most moderate scale) required for a Lady and Gentleman during a 16 week passage to India'; made a calculation on the pension he might expect on retirement; and jotted down assorted random facts about geography and other subjects.

On his return to Scotland he married Mary Anderson and they set up home in Gayfield Square, where five children were born; Charles (1840), Henry (1841). Cecilia (1844), Mary (1845) and Harriet (1846). In 1847 he purchased No. 8 Carlton Street and two further children were born there; Patrick (1847) and James (1851).

Glegg, whose father also had been a captain in the EIC army, was born in Calcutta in 1796. Tragically both his parents died of fever within weeks of each other in 1804. In 1814 Glegg joined the EIC army as a cadet and two years later was appointed a Lieutenant of the 19th Bengal Native Infantry Regiment. The recruitment of Indians into the British Indian Army began in 1776 and those recruited mostly came from the upper-castes. A regiment usually consisted of around 900 Indian soldiers and 26 British commissioned officers. Regiments were commanded by a lieutenant-colonel and divided into 10 companies, each assigned 2 British officers and 2 native officers. Each regiment was assigned an adjutant, an interpreter and a quartermaster.

Glegg was fortunate to be posted to Scotland, for in 1857 the Indian Rebellion (known on the British side as the Indian Mutiny) erupted. This major uprising was against the rule of the EIC which functioned as a sovereign power on behalf of the British Crown. Large numbers of EIC soldiers and British civilians, and many more Indians, died. As a result the British Government brought an end to EIC rule in India and the role of the Native Infantry Regiments was reduced. The EIC European regiments were amalgamated with the British Army and Glegg's post was discontinued.

Henry died in 1874 but Mary lived on in the house until her death in 1894. In the past it was common for sons of EIC officers to follow their father into the EIC army, but none of the Glegg sons, all of whom attended Edinburgh Academy, did. Charles became a civil engineer and emigrated to New Zealand; Henry also emigrated to New Zealand and worked for the National Bank; Patrick became a Chartered Accountant in London; while James worked for Scottish Widows in Edinburgh.

CHEYNE STREET - JESSIE KING

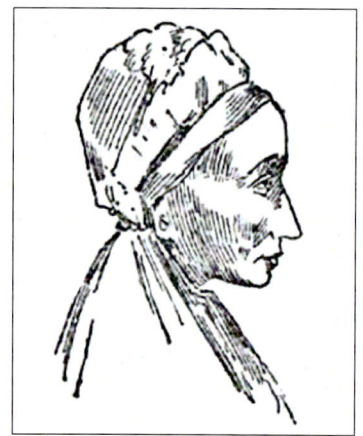

A WOMAN HANGED AT EDINBURGH.

This morning Jessie King was hanged at Calton Gaol, Edinburgh, for the murder of two children which she had undertaken to rear. After a quiet night, the wretched woman rose at five o'clock and partook of breakfast. She was attended last night and from an early hour this morning by Canon Donlevy. The magistrates proceeded to the condemned cell two minutes before eight. The condemned woman, who seemed thoroughly resigned to her fate, received them calmly, and the magistrates having signed the receipt took possession of the unfortunate woman. The procession was then formed by the city officers, with halberds leading. Canon Donlevy continued reading the Litany, and King responded till the noose was adjusted by the executioner, Berry. Not a second was lost; the lever was drawn; and the culprit died without a struggle. A drop of 6 ft. 6 in. was allowed. The murderess left behind her a confession implicating another person in the crime. A large crowd awaited the hoisting of the black flag outside the gaol.

1 Still from *Baby Killer? Sgeulachd Jessie King*, a BBC Alba documentary about the case, transmitted January 2015
2 Newspaper drawing of Jessie King, 1888
3 Report of the execution in the *St James's Gazette*, 11 March 1889
4 *Calton Jail* engraved by W.Tombleson after a picture by Thomas Hosmer Shepherd, 1831

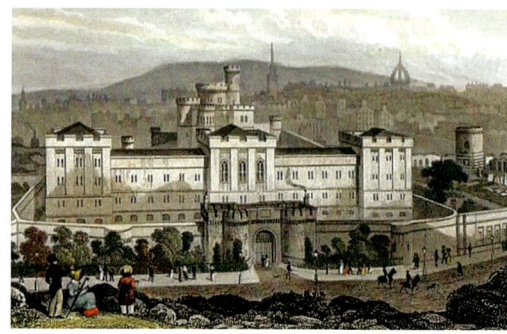

In October 1888 children discovered a dead baby wrapped in paper in a backyard of Cheyne Street and alerted the police. The baby was found to have been strangled and a few days later the police arrived at the house in Cheyne Street where Jessie King and Thomas Pearson, later described as King's 'alleged paramour', lived. On searching the premises they discovered the dead body of another strangled baby in the coal cupboard.

The lurid coverage of the case brought to light the scandal of 'baby-farming'. The term was coined during the Victorian era to describe the practice of women who had given birth and then been abandoned by the father, or were unable to care for a child, paying a fee to someone to take custody of their child. Essentially, a baby farm was a for-profit orphanage long before adoption was put on a formal basis, Most women assumed that their child would be properly cared for although some must have suspected that would not be the case. Using the alias of Mrs Macfarlane, King took at least three unwanted babies in exchange for payment of a small amount of money, and then killed them. Infanticide was not uncommon. At the time this case was going to court *The Scotsman* reported: 'a male child found wrapped in a parcel in Surrey Street, Glasgow has shown that the infant was strangled.' However, society wished to turn a blind eye to the fate of unwanted babies and instead vented their ire on Jessie King, who was tried on two counts of murder.

In the press King was portrayed as evil, although it is possible the 27-year-old woman had a mental health problem and was certainly under the malign influence of Pearson. At the time of her arrest, she was herself pregnant by a man who had falsely offered to marry her so was vulnerable and penniless. In desperation she had taken up with the much older Thomas Pearson who had abandoned his wife and family, and was drinking himself towards destitution. During the trial Jessie claimed he knew nothing of the babies' deaths, and although the remains of one of the victims were found on a shelf that was too high for King to reach and another child was found wrapped in Pearson's coat, Pearson was given immunity from prosecution after he turned Queen's evidence.

While the judge indicated that the parents of the babies must bear at least some moral responsibility, he advised that if the jury accepted the evidence, it was enough to convict. After an absence of just six minutes, they unanimously found King guilty of murder on both charges and she was sentenced to hang. Her Roman Catholic confessor wrote pleading for her life to the Secretary for State: 'To save Pearson she made the statement which has done her so much injury. She now declares that he in one of the cases did the deed and in the other two, he stood near directing and guiding her.' The appeal was refused. On the night of 10 March 1889, King was parted from her recently born baby and hanged in Calton Prison the next day. She was the last woman to be executed in Edinburgh.

CLAREMONT STREET - REV ALEXANDER BROWN

APPLICATION FOR ADMISSION BY MR A. W. BROWN.

The MODERATOR read the following documents —one a petition from Mr Brown, and the other a certificate from the Free Presbytery :—

"Unto the Reverend the Edinburgh Presbytery of the Church of Scotland, the petition of the Rev. Alexander W. Brown

"Humbly Sheweth,—That your petitioner was ordained by the reverend the Presbytery of Edinburgh to the pastoral charge of St Bernard's in 1841 ; and that from May 1843 to June 1863 he was minister of Free St Bernard's.

"That, while your petitioner felt it to be his duty in 1843 to leave the Established Church, he has also felt it to be his duty, in consequence of certain recent events, seriously to reconsider his position.

"That with the views which your petitioner entertains—first, with regard to the principle of 'a national recognition and a national support of the Christian religion ;' and next, with regard to the freedom of the Christian ministry—these events have led him to look back upon his secession with a feeling of regret.

"That your petitioner has no hesitation in expressing to your reverend Court his regret at having taken such a step ; that he has cordially rejoined the communion of the Established Church ; and that he now respectfully asks to be readmitted as an ordained minister within its pale.

"May it therefore please your reverend Court to take this petition into consideration, and your petitioner will ever pray.

"ALEXANDER W. BROWN.

"Edinburgh, 26th April 1864."

1 Edinburgh Presbytery, Rev Alexander W Brown second standing from left, c.1845 (photo - Robert Adamson & David Octavius Hill)
2 Rev Alexander W Brown, c.1845 (photo - Robert Adamson & David Octavius Hill)
3 Brown's application for readmission to Church of Scotland, 1864

For a number of years many in the Church of Scotland had been arguing that the Church should be independent of the state, as parish landowners still had the right to appoint the minister. Those challenging the status quo were termed 'evangelicals' and the dispute came to a head on 18 May 1843, the first day of the General Assembly. The retiring Moderator read out a lengthy protest charging the British state with encroaching on the spiritual independence of the Church of Scotland, and then walked out, followed by all the other Evangelical ministers and elders. They processed 'through an unbroken mass of cheering people and beneath innumerable handkerchiefs waving from the windows.' The Disruption, as it became called, was on a remarkable scale: around 40% of the ministry and a third of congregations left and formed the Free Protesting Church of Scotland.

One of those who left the established church was Rev Alexander Brown, minister of St Bernard's Church in Claremont Street (now Saxe-Coburg Street). He was born in Musselburgh in 1811 and studied theology at Edinburgh University. His first ministerial position was in Portobello, where he was clearly popular as on leaving in 1840 the ladies of the congregation presented him with a 'handsome gold watch in testimony of their regard for his personal character and the high esteem in which he was held as a minister of the gospel.'

He was ordained minister of St Bernard's in 1841, married Eliza Lockhart the following year and they lived at the manse at No.7 Claremont Street. As the established church still owned the churches, Brown and those in the congregation who split with him now had to leave St Bernard's. For a time they worshipped at Tanfield Hall, Howard Place (now demolished); a significant building in the history of the Free Church as it was there in May 1843 that its first assembly was held. On a personal level it was disruptive for the church also owned the manse and the Browns moved to Dean Bank Lodge in Dean Bank Lane. While the split was upsetting in communities, it was a godsend for architects as it led to a flurry of church building by the Free Church. Brown's congregation commissioned the architect John Milne to build St Bernard's United Free Church in Henderson Row (now demolished) and it opened in 1854. Brown also opened a primary school next to the church.

In June 1863 it was reported that, 'The Rev. Alexander W. Brown, minister of St Bernard's Free Church, Edinburgh, did not appear on Sabbath last to conduct divine service as usual.' It transpired that Brown was in dispute about his stipend and he resigned soon after. The following year he applied to be readmitted to the established Church of Scotland: 'Your petitioner has no hesitation in expressing his regret at having left the Established Church and he now respectfully asks to be readmitted as an ordained minister within its pale.' He was readmitted and appointed minister of the Church of Scotland in Aberdeen. He died in 1895.

CLARENCE STREET - ALISON DUNLOP

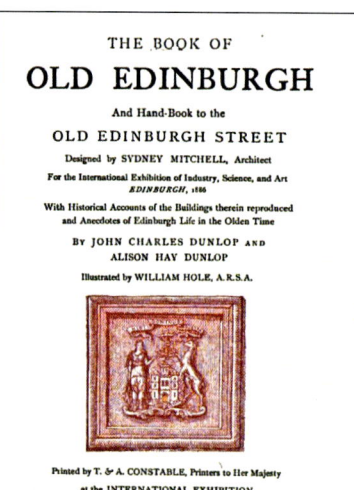

1 Frontispiece to *The Book of Old Edinburgh* by John & Alison Dunlop
2 Alison Dunlop, c.1870
3 Dedication by John & Alison Dunlop in flyleaf of *The Book of Old Edinburgh* presented to Andrew Carnegie
4 East Gate piers, Inverleith Park, Arboretum Place - erected in memory of Alison Dunlop, 1890

Alison Hay Dunlop was born in 1836 and grew up at No. 29 Brunswick (St Stephen) Street. Her father, Charles, was a cabinetmaker and in the year she was born had helped establish St Stephen's School to provide local children with free education. Alison attended the school along with her two brothers, John and James. It is likely that all three had additional private schooling as they became keen antiquarians in later life, and Alison could read and converse freely in several foreign languages.

John joined his father's cabinetmaking business, which diversified into new areas including estate agency, undertaking and antique dealing, while James studied divinity and became a minister in the United Presbyterian church. Alison began working as a governess but as the family business grew, joined the firm to manage the administration. In 1863 she became friendly with a young minister and poet, Thomas Davidson. He travelled widely for the church and later became an invalid, living in Jedburgh, so the two barely met but exchanged weekly letters until his death in 1870. Alison remained unmarried. While working in the family firm, she was able to study thanks to a scheme established by The Edinburgh Ladies' Educational Association to provide higher education for women. Her main study was creative writing and she won first prize for English Literature.

She was an early advocate for city conservation and at a time when many ancient buildings in the Old Town were being demolished, rummaged among the debris, saving distinctive fragments. She also began researching and recording vignettes of Edinburgh's past life and a number were published in *The Scotsman*. In 1886 the *International Exhibition of Industry, Science and Art* was held in Edinburgh in an enormous 120-foot tall pavilion built on the Meadows. Her brother John, at the time a member of Edinburgh Town Council, oversaw the creation of a section in the exhibition entitled *An Old Edinburgh Street* in which a number of medieval buildings that had been demolished in the past were reconstructed, including the Netherbow Port and the West Bow Assembly Rooms. A catalogue for this section had been planned but instead Alison and John wrote *The Book of Old Edinburgh*, published to coincide with the exhibition. A review said: 'The authors enter with spirit into a recital of some of the more romantic legends of the old city, historic scenes and the humours of social life in past generation are not forgotten. He must indeed be a cold-hearted Scot whose enthusiasm is not vivified by such a story.'

In 1887 John and Alison moved to No. 32 Clarence Street, where Alison died the following year. Her brothers published a selection of her writings in 1889 as *Anent Old Edinburgh and some of the worthies who walked its streets* and also paid for the Inverleith Park's East Gate piers opposite the entrance to the Botanic Gardens to be erected in her memory.

COLLINS PLACE - PATRICK MACNAMARA

1 British soldiers, part of the Black Mountains Expedition, 1868
2 Uniforms of the Volunteer Rifle Battalion of the Royal Lothian Scots
3 India General Service Medal, clasp North West Frontier

On Wednesday 22 September 1915 the daily routine of the Stockbridge Colonies paused in respect for what must have been one of the most impressive funerals ever to take place in the area. The previous Sunday 81 year-old Patrick Macnamara had died at No. 17 Collins Place and as a former soldier, a full military funeral was arranged. On the day of the funeral, soldiers from the Royal Field Artillery carefully carried Macnamara's coffin down the steep stairs from the house and placed it on a gun carriage positioned in the road. Standing in silence in Glenogle Road was the band of the 4th Argyll and Sutherland Highlanders and as the soldiers began pulling the gun carriage out into the main road, the Drum Major raised his mace and the massed pipes and drums rumbled into life. As Macnamara had been born in Ireland, perhaps they began with the Irish tune, Londonderry Air that five years earlier had the now famous 'Danny Boy' lyrics added by an English lawyer, Frederic Weatherly. The band and gun carriage, followed by the many mourners, processed to Comely Bank Cemetery. On the way shopkeepers, customers and passers-by would have stopped to pay their respects, especially as the stirring military funeral would have had special resonance for those who had already lost sons, brothers and husbands, while others feared for the safety of their loved ones still fighting in the war,

Patrick Macnamara was born in Limerick, Ireland in 1836 and moved to England. In 1853 he joined the Royal Warwickshire Regiment and in 1857 his infantry regiment, the 6th Foot, was dispatched to India to help quell the major uprising that had erupted against the rule of the British East India Company. The rebellion – known in Britain as the Indian Mutiny – was a bloody affair that lasted two years. The regiment then returned to England and in 1862 Patrick married Elizabeth Docherty from Cork .They had eight sons and their birthplaces reflect their father's roving army career: England, the Channel Islands, Ireland, India and Scotland.

In 1868 Macnamara's regiment was dispatched back to India to fight the local North West Frontier tribes, a campaign named the Black Mountain Expedition. In one battle Macnamara saved the life of his commanding officer and was awarded the India General Service Medal. In 1877 the family moved to Edinburgh when he was appointed instructor to the 4th Volunteer Rifle Battalion of the Royal Lothian Scots Regiment and the family moved into No. 17 Collins Place. The 1881 census records that living in the house were Patrick, Elizabeth and their eight sons, three of whom were now working. Macnamara retired from the army in 1887.

The youngest son, Robert, who had married Jane Burgess in 1911 and had a young daughter, missed his father's funeral as he was fighting in France. Fortunately he survived and on his return, moved into No. 17 with his family to look after his mother. She died in 1927, aged 88, and Robert lived on in the house until his death there in 1965.

COLVILLE PLACE - WILLIAM CRAWFORD

1 Glenogle Road Baths, c.1900
2 Children in Stockbridge Colonies, 1902 (Capital Collections)

When William Crawford was growing up in Colville Place in the 1880s sheep still grazed directly across from the road in a field between Glenogle Road and Saxe-Coburg Place. He was born at No. 7 Dunrobin Place in 1884, one of the five children of William and Charlotte Crawford, and when he was three the family moved to No. 24 Colville Place. William's father was a joiner and one of the tradesmen who built the Stockbridge Colonies. Like many of those he bought one of the completed houses in Dunrobin Place. He later also bought the Colville Place house and let the other for income.

In 1896 word spread that the Council were planning to displace the sheep and build a swimming pool and baths on the site. Swimming clubs and bath houses were established following the 1846 Act to Encourage the Establishment of Public Baths and Wash-houses, designed to improve general public health with access for all classes of citizen. Work began on building Glenogle Baths in 1899 and William, like most 14 year olds, went to observe the digging operations.

He later recounted that one of the men asked him if he could get him the loan of a saw and William's father was happy to oblige. His mother then began to have young William deliver pitchers of water with oatmeal added to the thirsty builders. 'I took this along with a tin mug and handed it to one of the navvies. I continued doing this all the time the work was going on. Always on the Saturday I got one or two shillings, which I handed over to my mother. How she used to make a fuss of me!'

By the time the work was finished William was well known to the building team and they told him the pool was about to be filled with water for testing. Determined to be the first to swim in the pool William and five of his friends, 'clubbed together to buy a pint of whisky to bribe the watchman to allow us into the baths. We all got in the pond, which had all sorts of rubbish — shavings, sawdust, planks of wood —floating about. One of my friends dived into the pond and struck his forehead on a plank of wood. It was not much, but it bled a great deal. The watchman appeared on the scene, and, whether because the water had a pinkish colour or the blood on my friend's forehead I do not know, but he ordered us out of the pond.'

However, William and his mates no doubt proudly recounted that they had been first to swim in the new pool. Once it was formally opened William swam almost every day through his teenage years. If his sister was as keen, she had to make do with the one afternoon and evening per week when females were allowed to use the baths, as mixed bathing was not introduced until 1956.

On leaving school at 15, William Crawford became a warehouseman in a printing company.

DANUBE STREET - DORA NOYCE

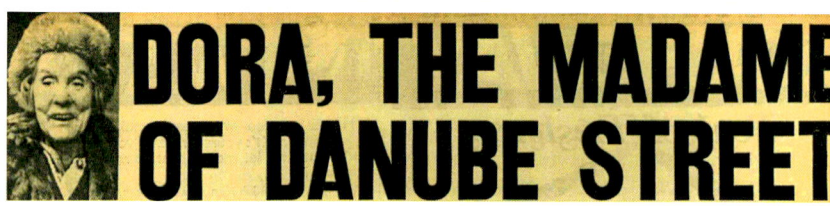

1 Dora Noyce, c.1970 (photo -Jack Crombie)
2 Headline in a 1973 *Daily Mirror* article by Paula James that began: 'A bust of Churchill glowers behind a cut-glass vase filled with autumn chrysanthemums. We sit in the elegant first-floor drawing room taking afternoon tea. "My dear, I do so hate the word brothel. Just say I run a house of ill-repute. So much nicer, don't you think?" says my hostess, in the plummy accent of an old girl from one of our best public schools. Mrs. Dora Noyce, 73 is probably the best known madame in Britain.'
3 Newspaper report, September 1960

Edinburgh woman fined £100

A 60 - year - old Edinburgh woman, Mrs Dora Rae or Hunter or Noyce, 17 Danube Street, was fined a total of £100 at Edinburgh Sheriff Court to-day, when she admitted four charges of keeping brothels at three houses in the city.
She admitted eleven previous convictions, dating from 1934.

In 1966 *The People* newspaper wrote: 'It was with a feeling of genuine regret that Mrs. Dora Noyce saw the last of the visitors leave the fair city of Edinburgh after this year's famous festival of the arts. Now she looks forward to next year's festival. Mrs. Noyce is not particularly artistically inclined. The joys of Marlowe and Mahler leave her comparatively unmoved. Her interest in the festival is a strange one. It seems that for even the most serious devotees of the arts a daily diet of poetry reading and classical music can sometimes pall. When this happens some of the male visitors indulge in a little divertissement which is definitely not on the festival programme. They go to a certain house in fashionable Danube Street - No. 17. It is the home of Mrs. Noyce and it is no more than a blatant house of vice.' Indeed it was, as there for 30 years Dora Noyce ran Edinburgh's most legendary brothel.

Born Georgie Hunter Rae in Rose Street in 1900 Noyce became a prostitute at an early age, and by 1945 established what she described as 'a house of leisure and pleasure', or on one occasion, 'a YMCA with extras'. She was the image of respectability, dressing in twinset and pearls, and when out and about in the winter, swathed in a fur coat. Around 15 young women were resident prostitutes and at busy periods other women would arrive by taxi. It is said that when ships docked at Leith, queues of sailors formed down Danube Street. She ensured that all her prostitutes had regular health checks in line with the Criminal Justice (Scotland) Act 1949, which legislated that 'habitual prostitutes' should be checked for sexually transmitted diseases.

Running a brothel was illegal but Noyce evolved a working relationship with the local police. In exchange for supplying them with any information about the criminal underworld that came her way, they limited their raids on the premises to about twice a year. On each occasion she was charged and thus was fined 47 times for living off immoral earnings, and in 1972 imprisoned for four months for running the brothel.

Noyce was always polite and courteous, and known for her wit as shown by her quips such as, 'I do my best business during the General Assembly of the Church of Scotland'. She became a much-loved character among the press as she provided salacious stories for copy, and after her court appearances would hold court for reporters in Deacon Brodie's. She was a canny self-advertiser: 'Just remember to get the name and address right,' she would say to the eager journalists. 'There's no such thing as bad publicity in my profession.'

Many neighbours constantly complained, and although they failed to have the brothel closed, the council gave them a reduction in rates. Others liked her and accepted the situation. Following her death in 1977 one neighbour wrote: 'I confess to having felt something of affection for Dora Noyce.'

DEAN BANK LANE - ELMSLIE DALLAS

1 Elmslie Dallas, self-portrait photograph, 1860s
2 *Interior of a Monastery in Italy* by Elmslie Dallas, 1853
3 Photograph of Dr James Young Simpson by Elmslie Dallas, 1860s

In 1859 Elmslie William Dallas (50) married Jane Rose (26) and they set up home in Hanover Street. He was a well-regarded painter and a teacher at the Edinburgh School of Design. He studied at the Royal Academy in London and his first painting, the interior of a Roman convent, was exhibited at the Royal Academy in 1838. In 1840 he assisted Ludwig Grüner in the decoration of the garden pavilion at Buckingham Palace, painting a series of views linked to the writings of Walter Scott, and two years later exhibited for the first time at the Royal Scottish Academy. His major pictures were highly studied interiors and medieval subjects. In 1851 he was elected a Fellow of the Royal Society of Edinburgh, before which body he read several valuable papers including ones on crystallogenesis and the optical mathematics of lenses.

Jane's grandfather, James Rose, a Writer to the Signet (solicitor) and for many years Depute Clerk of Session in Edinburgh, had Deanbank House built and in 1800 advertised the house for sale: 'A villa at Dean Bank below Stockbridge with offices, and a piece of ground, partly laid out in garden, and partly in shrubbery.' However, it did not sell and instead was let. In 1820 Rose feued parts of the house's gardens and other land around the house for building: 'A new place, to be called Saxe-Coburg Place has just been begun on Mr Rose's property of Dean Bank, the plan of which combines elegance and convenience in no ordinary degree.' Both of his brothers became significantly engaged in the slave trade and through nefarious dealings made large fortunes before returning to live in Scotland. One of Rose's two daughters married Colin Campbell of Demerara (Guyana) and his other died unmarried while visiting Demerara.

James Rose died the following year and Deanbank House was inherited by his son, also James and also a Writer to the Signet. He continued to rent Deanbank House but on his death in 1864 his sister Jane inherited the house, and she and Elmslie moved there with their four children. By this time Elmslie had given up teaching and switched from painting to photography, working from a studio in Princes Street. He mainly took portrait photographs and an early one was of his father-in-law: 'E.W. Dallas's portrait of Mr Rose, WS, is exceedingly good.' Dallas won a number of awards for his photographic portraits and other works: 'Mr Dallas has successfully shown the varied purposes to which photography may be applied.'

Elmslie Dallas died at Deanbank House in 1879 and Jane lived on there until her death in 1927. It was then occupied by two of their children, both unmarried: Brigadier General James Dallas of the Royal Engineers who during the First World War had been Director General of Military Works in India and Evelyn Dallas. James died in 1937 and when Evelyn died in 1942 the house was sold.

DEAN BANK LANE MEWS - JOHN SWANSON

1 Coachman John Swanson, senior, driving carriage at Boghead House c.1890
2 Chauffeur, 1910

Thomas Durham who owned Boghead House near Bathgate, employed a coachman, John Swanson and when Swanson retired his son, also John, took over. Durham died unmarried in 1899, and his relation, James Robertson, a chartered accountant, inherited Boghead House and re-titled himself James Robertson-Durham. He retained his Edinburgh house in Buckingham Terrace, and he and his wife, Minnie, lived between the two properties. To house his carriage and horse when in Edinburgh, Robertson-Durham purchased No. 25 Dean Park Mews. Like most of the properties in the mews it comprised a coach house and stable with living accommodation above. When John Swanson, junior married Janet Brown, a domestic servant working at Boghead House, in 1907 they lived in the mews house and their one child, a boy, was born there.

Robertson-Durham died suddenly in 1909: 'The death took place, yesterday, with tragic suddenness of Mr. James Alexander Robertson-Durham, head of the firm of A. and J. Robertson, chartered accountants, Edinburgh. He was on the telephone informing his office he would arrive later when he suddenly expired, death being due to heart failure. He was 61 years of age.' Minnie Robertson-Durham retained John as coachman but in 1912 decided to modernise and replaced her carriage with a motor car. John now became her chauffeur. The term originated in the late 19th century from the French word 'chaufer' meaning 'stoker' as the earliest petrol powered motor cars required pre-heating and were ignited – 'stoked' - by 'hot tubes' in the cylinder head.

At this time there was no driving test, so Swanson simply switched from the horse-carriage to the motor-car, and instead of having to look after the horse, would have had to become a mechanic as cars at that time were prone to breakdown and punctures.

Unfortunately, in 1915 he had an accident and was sacked by Minnie: 'John Swanson, motor car driver, was charged with two offences - first, with being drunk in charge of a car; and, secondly, with having driven it recklessly and negligently to the danger the public near Milton of Campsie. Accused pleaded guilty to both charges, and explained that he had had no food on the day in question, and did not think all the drink he took in Kirkintilloch would do him any harm. He had lost his job through the affair. The court heard that the vehicle narrowly missed running down a cyclist. The car was swerving all over the road and latterly crashed through a hedge and fell over an embankment. He and his passenger who was thrown through the wind screen of the car had to be extricated from underneath the vehicle by some men who were passing along the road at the time. The car was considerably damaged. He was fined £5 and the accused's licence was endorsed.'

Having lost his job Swanson and his family had to leave the house at Dean Park Mews. What became of them is not known.

DEANHAUGH STREET - SIR JAMES YOUNG SIMPSON

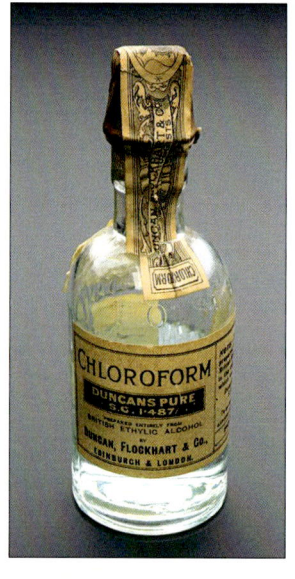

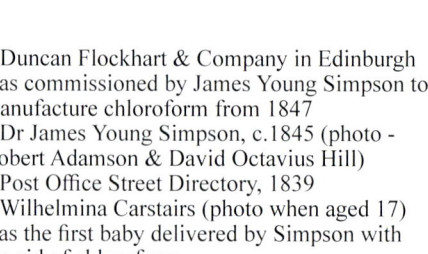

1 Duncan Flockhart & Company in Edinburgh was commissioned by James Young Simpson to manufacture chloroform from 1847
2 Dr James Young Simpson, c.1845 (photo - Robert Adamson & David Octavius Hill)
3 Post Office Street Directory, 1839
4 Wilhelmina Carstairs (photo when aged 17) was the first baby delivered by Simpson with the aid of chloroform

In the early 19th century those who studied medicine were almost all sons of professional men. That James Young Simpson, the seventh son of a baker, managed to graduate from medical school was remarkable and underlined his intellectual capacity. However, his lack of contacts among Edinburgh's upper-class was a disadvantage when he began practising, as all doctors needed to charge fees that only the better-off could afford. Those with less income accepted pain and discomfort as part of life to be endured with stoicism, and their source of medical help usually was the local druggist for medicine and advice.

With limited means Simpson opened his first surgery in low-cost premises at No. 2 Deanhaugh Street in 1837, and lived with his brother who ran a bakery at No. 1 Raeburn Place. Simpson had begun to specialise in obstetrics, and his skill and care quickly gained him a reputation and a growing clientele. In 1839 he decided to apply for the post of Professor of Midwifery at Edinburgh University but was informed that a single man would never be appointed, so quickly married Janet (Jessie) Grindlay. In spite of his reputation in the field, some on the appointment committee felt that the son of a poor baker was not suitable material for a professor's post, but by a single vote Simpson was appointed. He and Jessie moved to No. 1 Dean Street and Simpson's sister readied the house for the newly married couple, leaving a note: 'How do you like your ain house? Every visitor from Edinburgh brings us word of your prosperity, or rather of your industry and its reward.'

The following year the Simpsons moved to the New Town. In November 1847, only six days after administering chloroform to ease the pain for some minor procedures, Simpson successfully used it to ease the childbirth of Jane Carstairs at No. 19 Albany Street. Simpson later recounted that when Mrs Carstairs came to, her baby was brought in by the nurse from the adjoining room and 'it was a matter of no small difficulty to convince the mother that the labour was entirely over and that the child presented to her was really "her own living infant"'.

Although chloroform was a god-send to women giving birth, many - almost all men - argued against its use, asserting that women were destined by the 'curse of Eve' to experience pain during childbirth. Most opposition fell away when Queen Victoria had Simpson assist with the birth of her eighth child and commented: 'that blessed chloroform soothing and delightful beyond measure'.

Simpson was elected President of the Royal College of Physicians of Edinburgh and, made a Baronet in 1866. When he died in 1870, at the age of 58, the day of his funeral was declared a holiday in Scotland, and more than 100,000 people lined the streets of Edinburgh to see the funeral cortege pass by on its way to the family grave at Warriston Cemetery.

DEAN PARK CRESCENT - PHOEBE TRAQUAIR

1 Phoebe Ann Traquair at work
2 Murals in the Catholic Apostolic Church, now Mansfield Traquair Centre, Mansfield Place
3 Detail from *Red Cross Knight*, embroidered panel by Phoebe Anna Traquair, 1907 (Museum of Scotland)

A 1903 article in *Queen Magazine* profiling Phoebe Traquair stated: 'As a girl, brought up in a quiet country place, her talents lay unsuspected even by herself until one eventful day she was taken to Dublin to see an exhibition, and the beauty woke her instincts. She asked, and was allowed to study at the School of Design of the Royal Dublin Society but, alas! that very common hindrance to a woman's career, marriage, followed quickly and for years following her "light was hidden under a bushel."'

Although marriage in 1873 to Ramsay Traquair, a palaeontologist and the first Keeper of the Natural History Collections at the Museum of Science and Art, postponed her artistic career, Phoebe was content to focus on bringing up their three children at No. 8 Dean Park Crescent. While she found time for embroidery and other creative pursuits, it was not until the 1880s that she began to exhibit work. In 1882 she exhibited a number of palaeontological drawings related to her husband's research on fossil fish at the International Fisheries Exhibition in Edinburgh, and also began to show her embroideries, jewellery and other decorative craft work to friends. The inventiveness and quality of her work was swiftly recognised and in 1885 the Edinburgh Social Union offered Traquair her first professional commission: to decorate a coalhouse that was being converted to a mortuary chapel of the Royal Hospital for Sick Children. The building was small, but the hospital ladies committee hoped that it could become 'a suitable place where the bodies can be left reverently and lovingly for the parents before the burials.' As a mother, Traquair was delighted to accept the commission.

This work led to a larger commission in 1888 to paint murals for the song school of St Mary's Episcopal Cathedral and these gained Traquair national recognition: 'Mrs Phoebe Traquair, the well-known decorative and mural painter, whom Mr Ruskin is said to regard as an artist of rare genius.' From 1893 to 1901 she created her best-known work; murals for the interior of the former Catholic Apostolic Church on Mansfield Place (now called the Mansfield Traquair Centre). This achievement has been described as 'Edinburgh's Sistine Chapel'. Although by 1901 she had an international reputation – 'We may regard Mrs Traquair as one of the leading symbolists, for the feeling for the hidden life is observable in all and every kind of her work' - it is telling that in the occupation column of the census for that year her entry is 'wife'.

Phoebe Traquair became a leading member of the Arts and Crafts movement and as well as her acclaimed murals, produced watercolours, embroidered panels, illuminated manuscripts, book illustrations, enamelling and jewellery. She was invited to exhibit at the World's Fair in Chicago in 1893 and in 1920 was elected the first female member of the Royal Scottish Academy. In 1905 the Traquair family moved to Colinton, where she died in 1936.

DEAN PARK STREET - OTTO GOLL

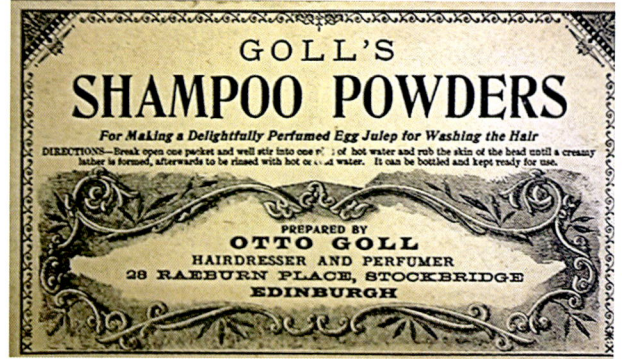

1 Otto Goll (centre) outside his hairdressing saloon, 28 Raeburn Place, c.1910
2 Marriage announcement in *The Scotsman*, June 1901
3 Advert for Goll's Shampoo Powder, c.1920

In 1895 two shops were erected over the garden of No. 28 Raeburn Place and one was rented by a men's hairdresser, Otto Goll who lived at No. 19 Deanpark Street. All that is known of Goll's early life is that he was born in Germany in 1871. There were a significant number of Germans in Edinburgh and a German Church designed by the architect, James Wemyss, was opened in Bellevue 1881. However, the Free Gardeners Hall in Picardy Place in 1901 was the venue for Goll's marriage to Barbara Cooper, then living in Jamaica Street. They had a son, Ernest, in 1903 and a daughter, Elizabeth in 1907. The family later lived at No. 68 Raeburn Place and around 1930 Goll purchased No, 28.

When the First World War was declared the Aliens Restriction Act was passed requiring anyone born in Germany to register with the police and later, many were interred. Paradoxically, Goll was interred in Germany as at the outbreak of the war he was there on a visit and like all British nationals living, working or on holiday in Germany was taken to Ruhleben Prison Camp, previously a horse racecourse. The camp was guarded by police rather than the military as the inmates were classified as Enemy Aliens rather than Prisoners of War.

Over time the men came to organise most of the running of the camp. A range of social and sporting activities were organised, and it is possible that Goll worked as a barber as many inmates plied their trade. Mail was allowed to be sent and in 1914, 25 Scottish prisoners, including Goll, signed a Christmas Card that was sent to the Lord Provost of Edinburgh: 'The compliments of the season to the Lord Provost, Council, and citizens of Edinburgh from the civil prisoners of war at Ruhleben.' Others who signed the Christmas card included William Lindsay, an Edinburgh-born pianist and operatic singer, who, in January 1915, played piano at a Burns Night celebration that took place in the camp, and Letham White, the son of an Edinburgh Councillor. White had been on holiday in Germany in order to learn the language, as he planned to become an engineer and that required passing a German exam. Undaunted, he arranged to sit the German exam set by the London Matriculation Examination in the camp in December 1916.

In late 1918 the Scottish prisoners sailed home and when their ship arrived at Leith they were met by a huge crowd and given a rapturous reception. Amid the relief and joy of Goll having returned safely, it must have been strange for the young children who had not seen their father for four years.

Otto returned to cutting men's hair and his son Ernest later took over. He was followed in turn by his son, John. Otto Goll died in 1941. In 2008, John sold the business to his assistant who had worked for him for a number of years and the men's hairdressers continues today, its frontage unchanged since 1895.

DEAN STREET - ANDREW RAVEN OBE

Deer numbers

I welcome debate about deer matters, but the letters from Iain Thornber (24 January) and Peter Fraser (29 January) do not give the whole picture. Determining numbers of wild animals is self-evidently difficult; unless and until distance sampling technology develops, it is generally acknowledged that Deer Commission counts of open range red deer are the best available.

But the scale of the task is such that we can only aspire to count areas on a rolling seven-year cycle, increasingly in partnership with local deer management groups. Thus there can currently be no single snapshot of overall numbers, which anyway are only meaningful when considered as discrete populations alongside local conditions and habitat quality.

What our open range census results do demonstrate is that, despite great effort and record culls, numbers have continued to rise in many areas.
ANDREW RAVEN
Chairman
Deer Commission for Scotland

1 Andrew Raven, c.1999
2 Ardtornish House
3 Letter in *The Scotsman*, January 2001

In earlier times there have been Stockbridge residents with family estates in Scotland, but possibly the only one in recent times was Andrew Raven, who lived in Dean Street from 1994. Ardtornish Estate on the Morvern peninsula looking across the Sound of Mull was purchased by Owen Hugh Smith in 1930 and inherited by Andrew's mother, Faith. She, her husband John Raven, a noted amateur botanist, and their five children spent school holidays there. Andrew grew to love the area, absorbing his family's commitment to sustaining rural development in the Highlands, supporting productive links between land use, environmental protection, community and culture.

Raven studied architecture and furniture design, but his growing interest in conservation and land use, and his increasing responsibilities at Ardtornish, led him to study for a postgraduate diploma in Land Economy. For a time he worked as a commercial land agent but his wider interests led him to join the council of the Rural Forum whose aim was 'working for a better future for rural people in Scotland'. He gave up his well-paid career in the private sector to become Director of Land Management at the John Muir Trust, a young charity conserving wild places for people and nature.

In 1996 The Deer (Scotland) Act was passed and in 1999 Raven was appointed to chair the Deer Commission for Scotland. In spite of a diagnosis of cancer, he spent six years building the organisation into a professional, efficient outfit, with clear strategic direction. His pragmatism was crucial in finding a path through the controversies that dog the management of Scotland's wild deer populations. His leadership abilities, commitment to conservation, and understanding of the complexities of rural politics, led to invitations to serve on other significant bodies. In spite of the pressures this brought, Raven's commitment to public service meant he said yes more often than no, which included serving as Chair of the Forestry Commission in Scotland.

Sadly, his cancer brought his early death in 2005. An obituary said of him: 'He had a very modest, warm and generous personality, utterly free of pretension, interested in people. His rare and special skill was perhaps to link these qualities to a very practical mastery of land-use economics, and a sound grasp of politics with both a small and a capital "p".'

Following his death, his widow, Amanda Game, supported by the Raven family and others established The Andrew Raven Trust, a charity to help Scottish communities, particularly those in rural areas, to develop sustainable land management. A major part of the Trust's work has been an annual weekend held at Ardtornish House at which a selected group of rural policy makers, community leaders, specialist scientists and artists meet to explore a specific theme in relation to sustainable rural development. See http://andrewraventrust.org/annual_weekend

DEAN TERRACE - NANCY LOUDON OBE

1 Nancy Loudon, 1986
2 No. 18 Dean Terrace
3 *Handbook of Family Planning*, published 1985

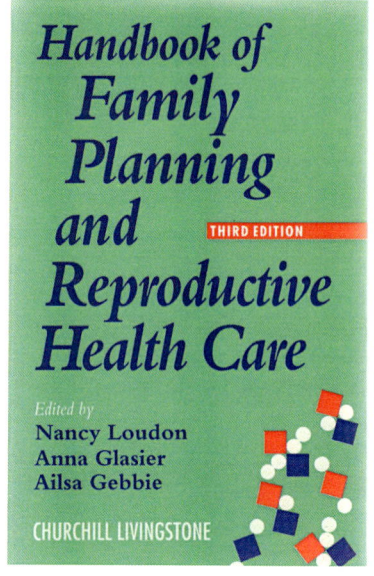

In 1839 the prejudice of the day led to Stockbridge resident, James Young Simpson being told he would not be appointed to the post of Professor of Midwifery unless he married. While one might have presumed that such prejudice in the field of midwifery would have been long passed by the early 1950s, sadly it was not so. Nancy Mann who was working as a registrar specialising in obstetrics at Simpson's Maternity Hospital was forced to resign her post by the professor in charge when he heard she was engaged, as he told her there was no place for a married woman in obstetrics.

Nancy was born in 1926 on the Black Isle, Inverness into a large farming community. She was Dux of Fortrose Academy and then studied medicine at Edinburgh University during the 1940s. In 1954 she married John Loudon, a fellow obstetrician, who, ironically, two years later was appointed to the job she had been forced to give up. She went to work at the Edinburgh Mothers' Welfare clinic, the first family planning clinic in Edinburgh, housed in an old shop, with only a cold tap, and a waiting room furnished with wooden benches. In 1957 a bequest enabled the clinic to move to No. 18 Dean Terrace, where it operated for over 50 years. In the 1960s and 70s Loudon and her dedicated team faced huge battles as many of the older medical professionals were initially hostile to the new developments.

In 1972 Loudon took over as Principal Medical Officer at the time when the clinic was a branch of the Family Planning Association. In spite of widespread opposition to the concept of 'family planning' and new methods of contraception, the clinic provided support and advice to women who often were ignorant or confused about sexual matters. Even by 2009 one woman said: 'I wanted the pill as I was sleeping with my fiancé. I could not go and see the family GP. So I got the train to Edinburgh [from Fife]. Of course it was inconvenient, but I wanted the pill.'

Among Loudon's many achievements at the clinic was establishing the Lothian Abortion Referral Service, which reduced distressing delays for women seeking abortion. Loudon pursued a wide range of academic medical interests and in 1985 published the influential *Handbook of Family Planning*. She was chairperson of the UK National Association of Family Planning Doctors and held many other national medical roles. When she died in 2009 an obituary said of her: 'Nancy was not afraid to challenge the establishment when the needs of women were threatened and could cut through red tape and bureaucracy with her critical thinking and persuasive manner. The "Cinderella" medical speciality of Family Planning has now become firmly established in the UK with the Faculty of Sexual and Reproductive Healthcare; at the roots of its development and hard-won achievements were intelligent and articulate pioneering women like Nancy Loudon.'

DUNROBIN PLACE - JAMES GILLIES

THE HALLELUJAH ARMY SILVER BAND, EDINBURGH.

ASSAULT ON A SALVATIONIST IN EDINBURGH.

At the Edinburgh Burgh Court to-day, James Flynn, residing in Milnes Court, Lawnmarket, was brought before Bailie Anderson on a charge of having on Wednesday, in Howe Street, assaulted James Gillies, residing in Dunrobin Place, by striking him on the face. Gillies deponed that he was a member of the "Hallelujah Army," and that the assault, which was quite unprovoked, was committed while he and a part of the "Army" were marching down to Stockbridge. There was a disorderly crowd following them, of which the prisoner was one. They were frequently very much disturbed and annoyed while in the streets. He had known members of the "Army" go home black and blue through being assaulted. Two young women, named Sarah Jane Bell, who said she was an "officer" in the "Army," and Annie Wallace, gave corroborative evidence.—The accused said he and a number of others were in the habit of following the "Army," but it was for the purpose of protecting them. (Laughter.)—The magistrate said it was a very peculiar mode of protecting them.—The prisoner then said that when he went to the meeting that young man (Gillies), who was called "The Major," refused to let him in. The magistrate said there appeared to have been no provocation in the case.—Flynn, who had been twice previously convicted of assault, was sentenced to 15 days' imprisonment.

1 Hallelujah Army Silver Band, Edinburgh, c.1910
2 Evangelical street meeting, c.1890
3 *Edinburgh Evening News* report, 1881

James Gillies who was living in Dunrobin Place in 1881, joined the recently formed Hallelujah Army, an evangelical Christian movement similar to the Salvation Army, which also began proselytising in Scotland at that time. Hallelujah Army members travelled around Scotland, preaching the Word of God in the streets and were frequently attacked, often by Roman Catholic youths, (The Salvation Army similarly came under attack in its early years in Scotland.) In autumn 1881 the members marched through Stockbridge to its Mission Hall in Allan Street in Stockbridge, where they had arranged to hold their meeting and the 'army' was followed by a disorderly, jeering rabble. At the hall, Gillies was punched in the face trying to stop a young man intent on trouble entering. This was nothing new as in court Gillies explained: 'We are much disturbed and annoyed while in the streets. I have known members go home black and blue through being assaulted.'

Two months later another man was in court charged with assaulting Gillies, this time in Galashiels: 'The assailant struck Gillies several blows, and the female soldiers were in great alarm, and but for the timely arrival of the police serious violence would have been done.' A few months later, 'about 3,000 young men and boys attacked the Hallelujah Army in Dunfermline and a terrible scene ensued. In the Kirkgate the members of the army and their followers were completely mobbed and were jostled about. At Guildhall Street, the place of meeting, members of the army as they passed in were subjected to very rough treatment; several of the women were badly squeezed, while the Rev. Jacob Primer, who has all along identified himself with the movement, came in for very unseemly handling. After the army had passed into the hall the crowd surrounded the entrance and it was with great difficulty that the police force, notwithstanding that their numbers ware augmented by the night man, kept them from breaking into the hall.'

Whether Gillies remained an active member of the Hallelujah Army in spite of the attacks on him is not known, although the group remained in existence in Edinburgh through to the late 1920s. The attacks on the 'army' eventually passed and by 1910 it, together with other evangelical groups, became an accepted part of Edinburgh life: 'On Saturday night the Hallelujah Army paraded for their usual march and open-air service. While the band was passing the Tron Church playing a funeral march the crowd was so dense as to stop for the time all traffic. Many of the people were so impressed by the playing of the favourite hymn, Abide with Me that they gathered round, and the bandsmen had some difficulty in playing their instruments. On arriving at Parliament Square, where the open-air services are usually held, there were not less than a thousand persons present.'

GLENOGLE HOUSE - MARGARET MAXTON

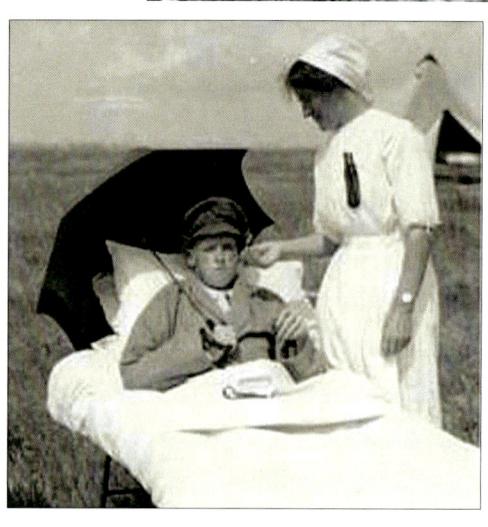

1 Nurses in mosquito nets, Salonika, 1918
2 Outdoor hospital ward, Salonika, 1918
3 Greek Medal of Military Merit

Margaret Maxton was born in 1880 and grew up with her five siblings at No. 2 Glenogle House, the last street built in the Stockbridge Colonies. Her father was a wholesale shirt and collar manufacturer. She attended Moray House College to train as a teacher, but in 1904 became a nurse and spent three years as a probationer at St Pancras Infirmary in London. In 1908 she returned to Edinburgh and worked at the Royal Infirmary before being appointed school nurse at Stockbridge School in Hamilton Place in 1913.

In December 1914 Maxton successfully applied to join the Queen Alexandra's Imperial Military Nursing Service and in May 1915 was posted to the Colchester Military Hospital, which took in wounded servicemen. Her work would have included applying dressings, feeding meals to the sick and wounded, talking to the patients, comforting the dying, and writing letters of condolence. 'Shell shock' would have been another challenge.

In early 1918 she was posted to Salonika in Northern Greece. While she would have experienced hardship and heartbreak while working at Colchester, it is unlikely anything could have prepared her for conditions in Salonika. She arrived at the start of the unbearably hot summer that brought hordes of mosquitoes and as the nurses worked mainly in tent hospitals, all had to wear elbow length gloves, puttees, and hats with net veils to try to avoid malaria. While the winter brought relief from insects, freezing temperatures meant the nurses had to work wearing balaclavas, scarves, coats and gum boots. One nurse wrote: 'Food was scarce. Breakfast consisted of two tablespoons of oatmeal, no milk, two small slices of bacon with one red stripe through it and two slices of bread and jam, tea with sugar to taste. Lunch - bully beef, rice and syrup. Dinner - soup, meat - rabbit often - leeks and pudding, and every sister had to dress for dinner, that is, in her best mess frock, cape and cap. We had no butter or potatoes for about five months.'

Maxton was awarded the Greek Medal of Military Merit 'in recognition of distinguished service' and sailed home from Salonika in March 1919. The Principal Matron reported her to have been, 'a conscientious and reliable sister – a good nurse - highly interested and hardworking – very kind and attentive to her patients.' There is no record of what Maxton thought of her war experiences but an Australian nurse who served there at the same time wrote: 'This damnable country, enervating and malaria-sodden, soul-blasting and mind demoralising, is like the harlot who with false graces and charms, lures to destruction. And we have paid her toll in deaths, ruined constitutions and broken spirits'.

Margaret Maxton returned to her work as a school nurse but nothing further has been traced of her life after 1920. Perhaps while in Salonika she met an attractive Australian or Greek and left for sunnier climes.

HAMILTON PLACE - JAMES MACLAREN

1 Front of brochure for Hamilton Place Academy, c.1830s
2 One of the pair of 12 inch terrestrial globes given to James Maclaren by his pupils
3 Advert for Hamilton Place Academy, 1846

In 1835 James Maclaren opened Hamilton Place Academy, a private school, at No. 8 Hamilton Place. Ten years later the school moved to No. 10 and he and his family lived at No. 11. Both were three-storey houses (replaced by tenements, Nos. 46-52 around 1900) and the school had a playground behind. Maclaren was born in Perthshire in 1805 and described by his granddaughter as 'a red-headed Highlander and in spite of having a big nose, good-looking.' He studied at Edinburgh University and then took a teacher's degree. In 1833 he married Elizabeth Hume; they had two girls and four boys.

The school took day pupils aged 8 to 14, and also boarded ten boys paying around 40 Guineas each annually. There were six teachers who taught, 'a complete English, Classical, and Mercantile Education, combining the Practical and Scientific Branches with the Languages and General Literature, in which pupils are thoroughly prepared either for Domestic Usefulness, Military Schools, the Counting-House, or University. Religious training is of primary importance.' One of those educated at Maclaren's school was Alexander Graham Bell, inventor of the telephone.

The six Maclaren's children's lives were intertwined with the school. They and their parents ate with the boarders and all were educated there when young. The pupils were woken at 6.30am and from 7am had an hour and half of lessons before breakfast. Then three more hours of class from 9am. At midday they had lunch followed by another two hours in class. Dinner was at four and afterwards 'they enjoy themselves in recreation, walking or playing, till six o'clock.' They then had tea before two hours of homework. After supper at 9pm they went to bed. 'Saturday afternoon is generally devoted to short excursions into the country, when the weather permits, thus affording an excellent opportunity for constant observation on Natural Phenomena.'

Maclaren was well liked by his pupils. In 1835 they presented him with a pair of 12 inch terrestrial globes, 'in testimony of gratitude and affection, and of the very high estimation in which they hold Mr Maclaren as their teacher.' A different form of terrestrial globe was recalled by his granddaughter, Elizabeth Ross: 'He often came to see our mother in our flat in East Claremont Street, always bringing with him the biggest orange he could get. It had first to do duty as a geography lesson - the earth was round like this orange, flattened at the poles, and it had the equator put round it, latitude and longitude marked on it; it was peeled and divided up, and the first geography lesson was happily over.'

Two sons became doctors and two teachers. At this period in Scotland marriages were not celebrated in church but usually in the bride's father's house, so No. 11 Hamilton Place was the venue for both daughters' marriages. James Maclaren died in 1885.

HENDERSON ROW - WILLIAM MACAO

1 Signature of William Macao
2 Entry from Post Office Directory, 1806
3 Grave memorial for William & Helen Macao, St Cuthbert's Graveyard

William Macao, who died at No. 11 Henderson Row on 31 October 1831, had a remarkable career. His first job in the early 1770s, when aged 19, was as a servant to Dr David Urquhart on his estate on the Black Isle, near Inverness. Then, in 1778, Urquhart's neighbour, Thomas Lockhart, a Commissioner of Excise, employed Macao as his footman at his house in George Square in Edinburgh. When Lockhart died just two years later, his widow arranged for Macao to be employed as a servant by the Board of Excise. From that lowly post Macao rose to become the Board's Accountant of the Superannuation Fund. This progression would be notable in itself. What makes it extraordinary is that William Macao was the first Chinese person to settle in Britain.

He is only the fifth Chinese recorded as coming to Britain, and the first to settle. The four who visited before were considered so exotic that they were taken to meet the king and had their portraits made. Yet the place of Macao in the history of the Chinese in Britain remained unknown until this author's research brought to light his remarkable story. (*The Chinese in Britain – A History of Visitors & Settlers*, published by Amberley)

Macao was the first Chinese to wed a British woman, marrying Helen Ross of Invercassley in 1793. They had three children: Ann, Henrietta and William Ross, who later became a Writer to the Signet. Macao also was the first Chinese to be admitted into the Church of Scotland, becoming an elder at the Rose Street church.

Macao's story has one further extraordinary twist. In 1818 a foreign merchant in London came across a clause in the Scottish Parliament Act of 1695 establishing the Bank of Scotland that stated that all foreigners (aliens) who purchased bank shares would, 'thereby become a naturalised Scotsman … and as such, a naturalised British subject'. The merchant, and over 140 others, including Macao, bought the requisite shares on the presumption that this endowed British citizenship. The government were outraged at this potential undermining of their power to bestow citizenship and eventually it was agreed that a court case should be brought by one of those who had bought shares to determine whether the clause still had force. The Bank of Scotland selected Macao and in January 1819 Lord Alloway ruled that the clause stood, and Macao was thereby a naturalised Scotsman. However, Alloway left undecided whether this also meant Macao was a naturalised British subject and on appeal, the earlier ruling was overturned. However, this still means that for almost two years William Macao has the unique status of being the only individual since the Act of Union to have been legally decreed a Scottish citizen, as since 1707 all other citizens of Scotland have been legally designated British. Britain's first Chinese Scottish gentleman is buried alongside his wife in St Cuthbert's graveyard.

HERMITAGE PLACE - CUMBERLAND HILL

STOCKBRIDGE WORKING MEN'S INSTITUTE.—LECTURE by Mr CUMBERLAND HILL, THIS EVENING, MARCH 12, at Eight o'clock. Subject—"Reminiscences of Stockbridge." Tickets, 3d and 6d; Members Half-price—to be had from Mr Somerville, Bookseller, and Mr Porter, Bookseller, Howe Street.

GREAT PUBLIC MEETING OF THE WORKING CLASSES.

A PUBLIC MEETING of the WORKING CLASSES will be held in BRISTO STREET CHURCH (Rev. Dr Peddie's), on MONDAY EVENING, April 4, to consider the propriety of PETITIONING PARLIAMENT against the OPENING of the NEW CRYSTAL PALACE on SABBATH ; and also to consider what Steps should be taken to Secure to the Working Classes the Half-Holiday on Saturday, now generally adopted in Manchester.

The Right Hon. the LORD PROVOST in the Chair.

The following Working Men will take part in the proceedings:—Charles Hill, baker; Alexander Fraser, blacksmith; John Cameron, saddler; Cumberland Hill, late painter; John Scarlett, coachman; John M'Gregor, cabman; Robert Westwater, joiner; Job Auld, mason.

A large attendance is earnestly requested, as a crisis in the Sabbath Question has arrived which affects the Working Classes more than any other portion of the community.

DEATH OF ST CUTHBERT'S POORHOUSE CHAPLAIN.

Mr Cumberland Hill, chaplain of St Cuthbert's Poorhouse, Edinburgh, died yesterday at his house in Hermitage Place, Edinburgh, of inflammation of the lungs. Mr Hill, who was in his 82d year, and had been chaplain for 30 years, was only last month provided with a colleague and successor, and received a retiring allowance from the Board. The deceased chaplain was a native of Stockbridge. Originally a working painter, he followed out the higher branches of his calling, devoting much time to sketching the architectural antiquities of the town. He subsequently became a city missionary, and afterwards poorhouse chaplain. His taste for antiquities was displayed in the volume which he published in 1887, under the title of "Memorials and Reminiscences of Stockbridge, the Dean, and Water of Leith." Mr Hill was for many years connected with Dean Street U.P. Church, where he was elder, session-clerk, and precer.

1 Advert for lecture, 1867
2 Advert for meeting, 1857
3 Sketch of the rear of the house on corner of Church Street and India Place in which the artist David Roberts was born (now No. 8 Gloucester Street) by Cumberland Hill
4 Hill's Obituary in the *Edinburgh Evening News*, 19 Feb 1891

In 1867 Cumberland Hill gave a lecture entitled 'Reminiscences of Stockbridge' in the newly built Stockbridge Working Men's Institute in Brunswick (St Stephen) Street and later delivered further lectures on the subject in the Dean Street United Presbyterian Church, where he was an elder. In 1874 he published this historical material as *Historic Memorials & Reminiscences of Stockbridge*. In 1887, when he was 77, Cumberland published an expanded edition of his book, commenting that, 'in writing this small volume I have been luxuriating in the sweetest joy of the aged – living in the past.' Throughout his life, Cumberland had a fascination with Stockbridge's past and was also known for his sketching of Edinburgh's architectural antiquities, although only those that he included in his book survive.

Cumberland was born in Edinburgh in 1810. His father was a labourer and he became a house painter. In 1837 he married Martha Carmichael and they lived at No. 1 Bedford Street. There they had a son and two daughters. By the 1840s his business had expanded and he employed a couple of men. He also was appointed Chairman of the Edinburgh Operatives and General Benefit Society, which introduced life assurance and sickness benefit schemes for working men, and was a committee member of the Edinburgh Total Abstinence Society.

In 1861 Cumberland was appointed as a City Missionary at £70 pa. Such posts were introduced by churches to provide for the spiritual and material welfare of those in need. In 1861 Cumberland and Martha moved to one half of No. 2 Hermitage Place (later renamed Raeburn Street). Living with them were their son John, a jeweller, his wife, Elizabeth, and their new baby, also named Cumberland, and their two unmarried daughters: Martha, a seamstress, and Marion who was still at school. In 1863 Cumberland was appointed chaplain of St Cuthbert's Poorhouse in Lothian Road. Sadly, a few months later John died and Elizabeth left, leaving grandson Cumbernauld in the Hills' care. In 1872 Marion married James Brown, a tobacconist, and they had a son, Robert. Tragedy struck again when James died, so by the 1881 census both fatherless boys were living with the family in Hermitage Place.

Hill lectured on a range of historical subjects to a variety of groups, including 'Antiquities of the Village of the Water of Leith' in aid of the Water of Leith Library and 'Old Edinburgh Doctors and their patients' to members of the Edinburgh Total Abstinence Society.

As chaplain at the poorhouse he attended the annual New Year celebration: 'At about one o'clock over 400 inmates of St Cuthbert's Poorhouse sat down to the New Year's dinner, which consisted of mutton-pie, plum-pudding, bread and beer. In the evening they assembled in the hall, where they were treated to bread, cheese and ale, and passed a pleasant hour or two in singing and dancing.'

HUGH MILLER PLACE - KENNETH VYNER

1 Stanley Vyner and Kenneth Vyner, 1939 (Edinburgh Collected)
2 National Fire Service Overseas Contingent practising transporting a fire engine by landing craft, 1944

In March 1944 a call went out throughout the National Fire Service (NFS) for volunteers to join a new unit designated the Overseas Contingent that was being formed in readiness for D-Day. Its planned role was to cross the Channel and follow the troops as they advanced through Normandy, providing a fire fighting and fire prevention service. Only men were eligible to apply and although there were many applicants, only 120 were selected. One was Kenneth Vyner, who was working as a fireman in Edinburgh.

Vyner was born in 1908 and attended Leith Technical College before joining the Edinburgh Fire Service. On average in the 1930s Edinburgh Fire Brigade received around 1,400 call-outs, some minor but others in which the fire-fighters risked their lives. At the outbreak of the Second World War Vyner, his wife, Charlotte and their one child were living at No. 23 Hugh Miller Place. In August 1941 all fire-fighters became part of the National Fire Service (NFS) when Edinburgh and other local authority fire brigades were amalgamated with the national Auxiliary Fire Service.

Five Overseas Contingent groups were created and the men trained together in the South of England. While training, they helped with fire-fighting during the German flying bomb and rocket attacks. The special training given to the members of the Overseas Contingent was aimed at bringing them to a high level of physical fitness. In many ways it mirrored the training given to soldiers attached to 'commando' units except the firemen did not receive weapons training. The instruction even included sessions in foreign languages. An advanced element of the training involved embarking and disembarking their pumps and other vehicles on and off landing craft.

Eventually it was decided just to send one group, which included Vyner. Thus, in January 1945 he was part of the single Overseas Contingent sent to France where it was attached to the Twelfth (US) Army Group. The firemen fought petrol and oil fires, steered their way over mined roads to emergency jobs, and dodged snipers' bullets. At one point 500,000 gallons of petrol from underground tanks that had been stored in a town well had to be pumped out; a fortnight's job. On another occasion the contingent had to deal with a fire from a collision between two petrol trains. "We had many an odd job to do.' remarked Section Leader Vyner. 'On one occasion we had a rush job to pump out two motor torpedo boats which had been in collision in the Channel . It was all in the day's work.'

After seven months of hectic activity the men returned from France and the Scottish members were given a welcome parade at the NFS Headquarters at Craiglockhart. Vyner then returned to fire duty in Edinburgh and became an Assistant Inspector. As well as his fire-fighting activities he was treasurer of the South-Eastern Fire Brigade Orphans Fund. Vyner died in 1969.

INDIA PLACE - ROBERT CHAMBERS

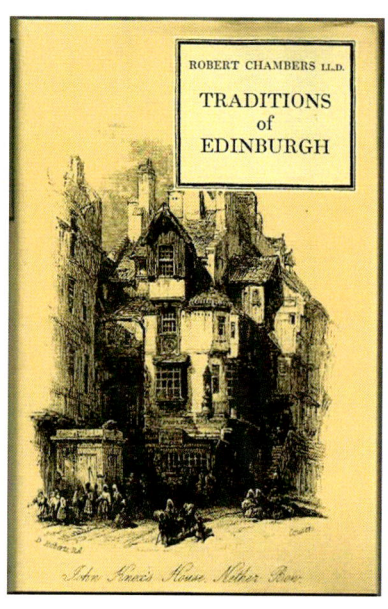

1 *Traditions of Edinburgh* by Robert Chambers, originally published 1823, revised edition published 1869
2 Robert Chambers, 1863
3 Advert for *Walks in Edinburgh*, 1829
4 Advert for Robert Chambers Subscription Library, No. 4 India Place, 1823

Robert Chambers was born in Peebles in 1802. He and his elder brother were both born with six fingers on each hand and six toes on each foot, and their parents attempted to correct this abnormality through operations. Unfortunately, while William's was successful, Robert was left partially lame. On leaving school Robert took a job as a clerk but this did not work out and William, who had opened a subscription library and bookshop in Broughton Street, suggested Robert try selling second-hand books, which he then did from a stall in Leith Walk.

In 1822 Robert rented No. 4 India Place and opened his own subscription library and bookshop. New books were expensive and subscription libraries enabled patrons to access more books than they could ever realistically afford. While Robert was living above the library he launched his writing career. He made the acquaintance of Walter Scott and in 1822 published *Illustrations of the Author of Waverley, Being notices and anecdotes of real characters, scenes, and incidents supposed to be described in his works*. This was followed by *Traditions of Edinburgh* (1823) and *Walks in Edinburgh* (1825). In this latter book he wrote: 'Farther to the west lies Stockbridge which gives name to a sort of village, now surrounded, and partly destroyed, by the encroaching limits of the rapidly-extending city. The glen here formed by the Water of Leith was, till lately, a beautiful and sequestered natural scene; but its echoes, which formerly answered only to the melody of birds and the fall of waters, are now disturbed by the rude sound of the mechanic's hammer, and almost destroyed outright by the alterations in the character of the ground.'

In 1828 he passed the running of the India Place library on to his other brother, James, and opened another library in Hanover Street. At this time he was living at No. 3 Upper Dean Terrace. In 1832 William and Robert decided to publish a weekly 16-page journal, reasonably priced at one penny. The contents included history, religion, language, and science, and the journal's success led William to close his Broughton Street library to focus on the new journal. Within two years the journal was selling over 80,000 copies a week and the brothers set up a publishing firm. William managed the firm while Robert continued his literary projects and James ran the Hanover Street library. For a few years from 1834 Robert lived at No. 28 Ann Street.

Robert's literary output was prodigious and successful. His other books included *Book of Days*, 'a miscellany of popular antiquities in connection with the calendar, including anecdotes, biographies, curiosities of literature, and oddities of human life and character' (1862-1864).

W. & R. Chambers Publishers became one of the country's leading firms and in 1865 William was elected Lord Provost of Edinburgh. Robert died at St. Andrews in 1871 and William in 1883.

KEMP PLACE - JAMES COLVILLE

1 Plaque in Glenogle Park, Stockbridge Colonies
2 James Colville, illustration accompanying his obituary, *Edinburgh Evening News*, 11 Jan 1892
3 Advert, 1872
4 Hugh Miller Cottage, 2023

In 1861 Edinburgh's masons and joiners went on strike in support of a reduction in their working hours from ten to nine hours. The employers held out against the 1,500 workmen and although the joiners returned to work, the masons continued their strike. Masons in Dundee also joined the strike and the Chairman of the Edinburgh masons, James Colville wrote a letter to them that ended: 'There must be no surrender. Two or three good men are perfectly able to carry anything if they just stand true to one another.' Continuing the strike was courageous as many had families to support, including James Colville who had four young daughters.

Eventually the employers gave way but Colville and a small number of other workers decided they wanted to work for themselves so established The Edinburgh Cooperative Building Company (ECBC). This aimed to build affordable houses for workers and give fair employment to men in the building trades. Colville was appointed manager and the company raised funds by selling 10,000 £1 shares. Land that had been part of James Haig's whisky distillery in Canonmills was purchased and building began. In the 1871 census Colville records that he was managing 17 masons, 25 joiners, 41 labourers, 3 blacksmiths and a clerk.

In 1863 Colville, his wife, Elizabeth, and their four young daughters moved into Hugh Miller Cottage, on Glenogle Road. It was a cottage and shop - probably first used as an office by Colville - at the end of the first two colonies on Glenogle Road and named in honour of the geologist and journalist who had championed the Cooperative's cause. By 1881 three of Colville's daughters were working: Isabella as a dressmaker, Catherine as a shopkeeper and Elizabeth as a teacher. Susan was still at school. The Colvilles later moved to No. 32 Bell Place. James continued to oversee all the the Cooperative's building that expanded to build on other sites, including properties in Dalry Road built to house Caledonian Railway workers, where there is a plaque: 'Erected by the Edinburgh Co-Operative Building Company Limited - James Colville Manager 1870.' In 1886 Colville was made a Justice of the Peace and thus became Edinburgh's first 'workman magistrate'.

The Colvilles finally moved to No. 16 Kemp Place and James retired in 1890, aged 76. He died in early January 1892 and his wife a fortnight later. During Colville's management the company built over 1,500 houses in Edinburgh and Leith. It was said that the company's success was due to, 'the able and energetic manager, James Colville, whose genuine interest in cooperation makes him a ready helper to all who desire to advance the common cause.' His obituary described him as 'a well-known and familiar figure in and around Stockbridge for the last 30 years, whose work in connection with the co-operative movement entitles him to a foremost place in the history industrialism.' The third terrace is named in honour of Colville.

KERR STREET - JAMES CRIGHTON

TO THE ELECTORS OF ST BERNARD'S WARD.

GENTLEMEN,

I beg to offer you my best thanks for your having Elected me one of your Representatives at the Council Board of this City.

I have the honour to be,
GENTLEMEN,
Your most obedient Servant,
JAMES CRIGHTON.

6 Spring Gardens,
4th Nov. 1856.

POLICE COMMISSION.

The annual election of General Commissioners of Police took place yesterday, when the following gentlemen were returned:—

WARDS.   GENERAL COMMISSIONERS.
1. John Howison, Rose Hall.
2. Robert Stephenson, Grange Villa.
3. William Brunton, 40 George Square.
4. William Wilson, 165 Pleasance.
5. Peter Jamieson, 6 Nicolson Square.
6. John Cochrane, M.D., 17 Argyle Square.
7. Simon F. Wood, 2 Salisbury Street.
8. Robert Hogg, 37 Abbey Hill.
9. Andrew Dodds, 129 High Street.
10. James Ford, 184 High Street.
11. John Greig, senr., 433 Lawnmarket.
12. Thomas Monteith, 302 Lawnmarket.
13. George Lorimer, 18 Graham Street.
14. William Tullis, Viewforth.
15. James Leggat, Port Hopetoun.
16. Peter Robertson, 7 Torphichen Street.
17. David Smith, W.S., 2 Ainslie Place.
18. James Crighton, 1 Kerr Street.
19. Andrew Thomson, M.D., 24 Dundas Street.
20. James M'Knight, W.S., 12 London Street.
21. George Hill, 6 Saxe Coburg Place.
22. Robt. Oliphant, 17 Young Street.
23. John W. Mackie, 108 Prince's Street.
24. James Stewart, 34 Hanover Street.
25. Charles M'Pherson, 12 South St David Street.
26. William Dick, 8 Clyde Street.
27. Robert Brown, 5 Picardy Place.
28. William Milne, 24 Greenside Street.
29. Alex. Thomson, 16 Union Place.
30. Edward Mitchell, 2 Leopold Place.
31. John Gibson, W.S., 53 Inverleith Row.
32. Capt. P. Hay, 25 St Bernard's Crescent.

WANTED, a Stout Active Man as PORTER. Apply to James Crighton, grocer, 1 Kerr Street, Stockbridge.

1 Advert inserted by James Crighton, 1856
2 Kerr Street - No.1 was the projecting shop on corner, c.1900
3 List of Police Commissioners, 1852
4 Advert, 1855

James Crighton was born in Berwickshire in 1808. He came to Edinburgh aged 16 and worked as an assistant in a grocer's shop. In 1832 he opened his own small grocers at No. 4 Glanville Place. Across the road at No. 1 Kerr Street was a larger shop on a prime corner site and in 1841 Crighton leased it and moved there, advertising as a grocer, tea and wine merchant. He subsequently traded there for 45 years. He remained single so never bought a house, but instead moved between rented flats, including in Glanville Place, Kerr Street, N.W. Circus Place, Spring Gardens and, finally, Dean Terrace.

In 1852 Crighton was elected as the St Bernard's Ward's Commissioner of Police. This unique system was introduced in Edinburgh in 1805 and consisted of elected individuals from the various wards who oversaw policing matters and regulated the police force. As well as ensuring, 'a more regular police for apprehending vagrants, suppressing begging, removing nuisances', the commissioners were responsible for overseeing the lighting and cleaning the streets, regulating hackney coaches, and control of weights and measures. A few years later he successfully stood for election to the Edinburgh Council as representative of St Bernard's Ward and served in that capacity until his death. In all the 33 years Crighton served on the City Council he was only opposed once, an unsuccessful challenge by a member of the temperance movement. This was a unique achievement, showing the high regard local people had for him because of his commitment to the locality. In 1885, 'James Crighton made motion expressing great disappointment at the abandonment by the Town Council of their proposal to take adequate powers in for the purpose of abolishing the mill-lades on the Water of Leith, and regretted that sanitary improvement, so urgently required, would thus be indefinitely delayed.' One of his proudest achievements was creating Stockbridge Park as a recreation space.

This was a time when most of what now falls within state-supported social work was sustained by charitable patronage, both financial and expertise, and Crighton gave of both. He served on the management committees of a range of number of charitable institutions including the Trinity Hospital and the Western Reformatory Institution (formerly the Dean Bank Institution for the Reformation of Female Juvenile Delinquents), which helped reform girls and young women who had been discharged from prison. His work for the latter involved helping raise funds for new premises to house 40 young women at Dalry.

Crighton retired in 1887, sold his business and died two years later. Like many, his funeral service took place in his home: 'The funeral of the late Mr Councillor Crighton took place this afternoon from his house in Dean Terrace. Service was conducted in the house by the Rev. Andrew Keay, Free Church, Stockbridge. Among those present was Provost Boyd.'

LESLIE PLACE –
SERGEANT MAJOR DAVID NELSON

1 Sergeant Major David Nelson, Seaforth Highlanders of Canada, Vancouver, c.1914 (Photo - Richard Broadbridge, City of Vancouver Archives)

2 Wounded or invalided soldiers from the 16th Battalion Canadian Empire Forces convalescing in England, 1917. Nelson is second from the left in front row

David Nelson fought in the Boer War and the First World War, and survived both. He was born in Leith in 1871, one of seven children. His father was a messenger at the Parliament House and after living in Brunswick (St Stephen) Street for a time the family moved to No. 4 Leslie Place. When aged 14, David joined the Seaforth Highlanders as a band boy. He was an outstanding athlete and for a number of years served on the army's gymnastic staff.

In 1898 he was part of the force led by General Kitchener that fought in Crete and in 1899, when war was declared on the Boers, sailed with the 2nd Battalion to Africa. At the Battle of Magersfontein in December 1899 when his battalion was under heavy enemy fire, he rescued his injured colonel and then returned to carry a second colleague to safety. In October 1902 when Edward VII travelled by train from Balmoral to Aberdeen, on his arrival, 'a small company were admitted to the station near the Royal saloon…..three non-commissioned officers of the Gordon Highlanders were presented by His Majesty with the D.C.M. for gallantry in South Africa. The first to receive the decoration was Sergeant-Major David Nelson.'

Early in the 1900s Nelson emigrated to Canada, where he married Elsie Gertrude Nelson and they had four children. He worked as an Immigration Inspector. In 1914, when the British Empire declared war on Germany, although now aged 43, Nelson re-enlisted. He was promoted to Regimental Sergeant Major and sailed to England in October. 'Although he was not the usual strident type of Sergeant Major, but gave orders in a quiet deliberate way; his authority was never questioned or trifled with. Whenever possible, he smoked a pipe, moving it from side to side as he gazed into the distance.' He was a stickler for the rules and avoided any unauthorised articles in his kit. What the troops had, he had, and nothing more. His lighter side was seldom seen although on New Year's Day, 1915, he amazed the men in the sergeants' mess, by producing a penny whistle and playing reels.

In February 1915 he saw action in France with the 10th Canadian Infantry Battalion, including an attack on an entire German Division at Kitchener's Wood in April during the Second Battle of Ypres. In July 1915 he was wounded by fragments from an exploding shell and spent time in hospital. When he returned to active duty he trained troops in both England and Canada during 1916 and 1917. However, from the end of 1917 into 1918 he was back fighting and took part in the campaign in Africa, where he came down with malaria. In March 1918 he was released from service as, 'Being no longer physically fit for War Service.' He was suffering from depression that today probably would be diagnosed as post-traumatic stress disorder. Nelson did not return to Canada but lived in London, working for The Reading Corporation Tramway Company.

MACKENZIE PLACE - EMMA STIRLING

1 Advert, 1887
2 Emma Stirling, c.1880
3 Hillfoot Farm, Aylesford, Nova Scotia, Canada, 1889

In 1878 a children's nursery opened at No. 10 Mackenzie Place where working mothers could leave their children under the age of seven for a fee of two pence a day. The nursery was established by Emma Stirling and the following year she also opened a number of children's homes around the city, including an Infants' Home at No. 11 Mackenzie Place. (Both properties later were demolished.) The homes catered for girls and boys, and each housed small numbers of children with the older children taking care of the younger children. In 1884 her informal arrangement was structured as the Edinburgh and Leith Children's Aid and Refuge Society. Stirling also opened a 'Shelter from Cruelty' in the Old Town and her concern at the plight of children in danger helped bring about the 1888 Prevention of Cruelty to Children Act. Her homes were invaluable to many. In 1882 Arthur Delaney, whose wife had died leaving him with three young children, lost his job so arranged for his children to live in Stirling's homes.

In 1886 Stirling leased a farm in Nova Scotia and took around 100 children from Scotland there, believing that Canada would offer the disadvantaged children a better start in life. Unfortunately, not all parents were consulted about their children's move to Canada. In 1886 Arthur Delaney, who had remarried, went to Mackenzie Place to collect his children but was told they were no longer there. His demands to know their whereabouts went unanswered. Even the society's trustees were unable to get Stirling to divulge the whereabouts of Delaney's children. It later transpired that when Delaney had first begun seeking the return of his children, Stirling had moved them in secret before shipping them off to Canada. Delaney took the case to court and it ruled that neither Stirling nor the society had the right to have taken the children without parental agreement, and the children should be returned. However, Stirling still refused to say where the children were. The perturbed Society trustees paid for a private detective to travel to Canada to trace the children, but without success. All the distraught Delaney eventually received was a paltry sum of damages from the Society.

To avoid the court actions by aggrieved parents in Scotland and the infuriated Society's trustees, Emma Stirling remained in Canada, although even there she was unpopular with Nova Scotians who felt her child immigration to be inappropriate. The final straw for her work in children's welfare came in April 1895 when, under mysterious circumstances, her Canadian house and its barn were burnt down. She closed the project, retired to the USA and died there in 1907. In the early 2000s Patricia Delaney Dishon, a descendent of Delaney, began researching the story (*The Delaneys of Edinburgh*, 2012); she discovered that the three children had been put into an orphanage in Canada and subsequently placed with families, two as servants.

MALTA GREEN - WILLIAM CUSHNIE

Surgeons,	Sir George Ballingall, Deacon.
Goldsmiths,	Messrs James Naysmith, do.
Hammermen,	William Dick, do.
Skinners,	John Cox, do.
Furriers,	John Welsh, do.
Wrights,	William Nelson, do.
Masons,	Robert Paterson, do.
Tailors,	David Robertson, do.
Bakers,	Alexander Porteous, do.
Fleshers,	Adam Wilson, do.
Cordiners,	William Whitehead, do
Websters,	James Kerr, do.
Hatters,	Alexander Campbell, do
Dyers,	William Cushnie, do.

TOWN COUNCIL.—The Deacons of the several Incorporations having been yesterday introduced, and having taken the requisite oaths, the following were unanimously elected as Ordinary Council Deacons for the ensuing year:—

Messrs Alex. Henderson,	Deacon of the Goldsmiths
Alex. Ritchie	Skinners
Gordon Brown	Wrights
Peter Lorimer	Masons
George Thomson	Baxters
William Cushnie	Bonnetmakers

1 List of elected Edinburgh Guild Deacons, 1827
2 Report of new Deacons on the Town Council, 1828
3 Malta Green Cottage, 2023

Each of Edinburgh's 14 trade guilds annually elect a Deacon and until the Scottish Reform Bill of 1832 introduced elections for all councillors, six formed part of the Town Council by right. The eight guild Deacons not appointed to the council were known as Extraordinary Deacons and joined the council meetings for certain topics of business, and for the annual elections of councillors and office-bearers. In 1827 William Cushnie, who had a dyeing workshop, was elected Deacon of the Dyers and Bonnetmakers Guild and served on the Town Council.

Cushnie was born in 1784 and on completion of his seven-year apprenticeship with a dyer, successfully applied for his Burgess ticket. Only burgesses were allowed to trade in the city and this enabled him to open his own dye works in Lothian Street in 1817. In 1832 he moved his dye works from Lothian Street to newly erected premises in Malta Green. 'Mr Cushnie begs to inform his customers and the public generally, that by the ample accommodation he has now obtained, and from the peculiar construction of the Premises, which have been erected by himself, solely for the purpose of Dye Work, and the introduction of several pieces of new machinery which his long experience and practice have alone suggested, he is now enabled to obviate the numerous difficulties which he, as well as others in the same profession, have hitherto had to contend with. He continues to dye, clean, scour and dress Satins, Velvet, Gauzes and Lace. Crumb cloths, carpets, Hearth Rugs, English Blankets and Gentlemen's Clothes, cleaned and dressed as usual.' He also had a shop in Frederick Street.

Around 1840 Cushnie had Malta Green Cottage built next to his dye works. It included a greenhouse as he was a keen gardener; in 1842 he received a commendation at Edinburgh Horticultural Society's show for his 'two fine specimens of Statice puberula, covered with flowers.'

When he retired he passed the business to his son George. However, George died in 1847 so Cushnie sold the business to William Donald, who had been an apprentice at the works.

Cushnie was elected Deacon 21 times between 1827 and 1872 and also was elected a Commissioner of Police. He served on the board of a property investment company and was treasurer of St Cuthbert's Workhouse. In 1849 he was one of the committee that accompanied 100 children from the workhouse on its annual excursion. 'The train reached Dunbar about half-past nine and after surveying the ruins of the ancient castle, the children were conducted to a field east of the town, where they partook of a substantial repast. Several hours were subsequently spent in the happiest manner in pastimes of various descriptions, in which the managers took part. On their return to town in the evening, on parting, the children gave three cheers for the managers.'

Cushnie lived to the grand old age of 96.

MALTA TERRACE - KENNETH MACLEAY

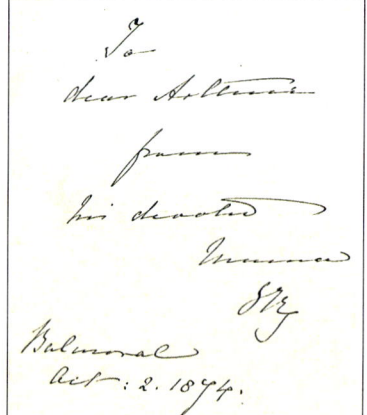

1 *William Ross* by Kenneth Macleay, 1866 (Royal Collections)
2 Kenneth Macleay, c.1845 (photo - David Octavius Hill & Robert Adamson, National Portrait Gallery)
3 Inscription by Queen Victoria in a first edition of *Highlanders of Scotland* she presented to her son Prince Arthur - 'To Dear Arthur from his devoted Mother VR Balmoral Oct. 2, 1874'
4 *Prince Alfred* by Kenneth Macleay, 1864 (Royal Collections)

On 30 June 1876 during a brief visit to Edinburgh, Prince Albert visited No. 3 Malta Terrace, 'for the purpose of inspecting the finished portrait of his Royal Highness which Mr Kenneth Macleay has had the honour to paint for her Majesty.' Prior to moving to live at Malta Terrace in 1868 following the death of his wife, Macleay had resided with her at No. 26 Hamilton Place and it was while living there that he received his first commission from Queen Victoria.

Kenneth Macleay was born in Oban in 1802, the son of a surgeon, and from a young age painted miniatures on ivory. In 1822 he moved to Edinburgh to study for a year at the Trustees' Academy and then set up in business and by 1830 was considered the leading miniaturist in Scotland. He worked primarily in watercolour, and, partly in reaction to the impact of photography on the miniature business, also produced larger portraits.

In June 1864 Victoria asked Macleay to produce a 'cabinet' portrait (about 6 x 4 inches) of her son, Prince Alfred and was so taken by it, had him paint portraits of her two other sons. She was particularly fond of the portrait of Alfred and commissioned a miniature version, but asked that Prince Alfred's tie be changed from white to black. Macleay did not feel such a change worked and sent the ivory miniature to the queen, with a letter explaining why he had decided not to make the change. The Queen was not amused. She immediately returned it to Macleay with a handwritten note: 'The Queen does not like this miniature as well as the original and she wishes Mr Macleay to alter it by and large.' The artist repainted the tie.

Fortunately for Macleay his initial disobedience did not sour his relationship with the queen. In 1865 she commissioned him to portray her favourite servants at Balmoral, a project that took Macleay four years. From this developed a more significant commission that was the highlight of his career: a series of portraits of representatives of the more important Highland clans. The portraits of retainers and clansmen were exhibited in London in 1869 and then reproduced in chromolithograph by Vincent Brooks (London's premier lithographer) as illustrations to the two-volume *The Highlanders of Scotland* (1870).

Macleay died in 1878: 'The funeral of Mr Kenneth Macleay took place yesterday afternoon from his residence in Malta Terrace, Edinburgh, to the West Church burying ground. The burial service was conducted according to the rites of the Episcopal Church. The funeral was attended by the members of the Royal Scottish Academy and a number of students of the life school. The Queen has written to one of the members of the Academy expressing her regret at Macleay's death and her condolence with his family on the sad event.'

What became of Queen Victoria's portrait that Prince Albert visited to view is a mystery for it does not appear in records of Macleay's art works.

MARY'S PLACE - ALEXANDER EDGAR

Alexander Edgar of Wedderly and of Stockbridge near Edinburgh

Profile & Legacies Summary

Will of Alexander Edgar [late of Wedderly plantation in Trelawny and now residing at] Stockbridge near Edinburgh proved 21/03/1821. He said that under his marriage settlement of 10/07/1797 with Ann Gordon he had settled 30 'negroes' in trust to secure her an annuity of £300 p.a. currency but that she had joined him in the sale of Wedderly with 221 acres and 117 enslaved people ('slaves') in trust to John Mitchell late of Jamaica 'for behoof of the late William Green' of Jamaica for £19,588 14s currency or £13991 18s 7d sterling payable in instalments on which there was balance of £15,238 11s 1d currency and a further £2,447 1s 4d owing from William Green (both of which appeared to be the subject of chancery proceedings in Jamaica). He appointed trustees including his wife, Henry Raeburn 'portrait painter in Edinburgh' and Raeburn's son Henry Raeburn jun. for his estate including the balance due to him from the sale of the Wedderly estate, and the Grangepen estate or plantation part of the Farm Pen in St James formerly the property of his late brother Dr Handyside Edgar, the latter to be sold subject to his wife's annuity for the benefit of his eldest son, also named Alexander.

1 *Sale of Slaves by Auction*, print 1787
2 *Portrait of Alexander Edgar* by Henry Raeburn, (National Trust for Scotland, Fyvie Castle)
3 Information from the website of The Centre for the Study of the Legacies of British Slavery, University College London

Alexander Edgar's family had long been plantation owners in Jamaica and his father owned the Wedderly plantation in Trelawney. At this time Scots owned 30% of the estates in Jamaica, all of which were worked by enslaved labourers. Edgar's father, who died when Alexander was an infant, had two illegitimate daughters from a relationship with an enslaved woman. Alexander inherited the plantation and when he married Anne Gordon in Jamaica in 1797, a marriage contract was drawn up in which he settled 30 'negroes' in trust to secure Anne an annuity of £300 p.a.

The couple left Jamaica soon after the wedding and Edgar sold his plantation estate and 117 enslaved people, having arranged that the money would be paid in instalments over the next decades. In 1814 they moved into the newly built No. 6 Mary's Place that was advertised as: 'That elegant house consisting of dining and drawing room, parlour, five bedrooms, two light bed closets (with windows), kitchen, scullery, catacombs, officer-houses with water pipes, a large garden and other accommodation necessary for a genteel family.' They had a number of children already and others were born in the house, and eventually their 11 children lived there, looked after by three servants. The Edgars became friends with Henry Raeburn, and Alexander Edgar was one of a number of wealthy Scottish slave owners that Raeburn painted. Such was their relationship that Raeburn and his son agreed to be the trustees of Edgar's estate. Following his death in 1820, the Raeburns oversaw the payment of the significant sum still outstanding from the sale of the Wedderly plantation, including launching legal proceedings in Jamaica. The Raeburns also arranged the sale of another plantation that Edgar had inherited from his brother and this transaction included the sale of 87 slaves - 42 women and 45 men.

Thus the comfortable life enjoyed by the Edgars came from the substantial profits made from slavery. Three daughters married sons of slave owners in Jamaica: Eliza and Mary married the brothers, George and James Archer, both of Great Pond, St Ann's, and Louise married Samuel Jackson of Sod Hall, whose father was a member of His Majesty's Council of Jamaica. It is likely that all received or inherited money from the reparation paid as part of 1833 Slavery Abolition Act in which all slave owners received money to compensate them for the loss of their 'property.' The pay-outs varied from colony to colony based on the value of slaves to their owners, but in total the British Government authorised payment of £20 million to slave owners – equivalent to well over £60 billion today. Of course no freed slaves received compensation for their years of unpaid labour and suffering, and with nowhere else to go and no money, their 'freedom' was mainly tokenistic as their abused lives changed little.

Anne Edgar lived in Mary's Place until her death in 1841.

NORTH WEST CIRCUS PLACE – BARCLAY TODD

EDINBURGH NORTHERN CO-OPERATIVE SOCIETY.

The quarterly meeting of Edinburgh Northern District Co-operative Society was held in Free St Bernard's Hall, Henderson Row, last night. Mr Barclay Todd presided over a large attendance. The chairman mentioned that the half-yearly report, which had been issued to the members, was of a very encouraging nature. It stated that business had continued good. The cash drawn during the past half-year amounted to £41,626, which was an increase on the same period last year of £3765, or 10 per cent. A dividend of 3s 8d per £ was declared on general purchases, and 2s 4d per £ on fleshing purchases. The present membership was 2354, and the share capital £28,620. The report was adopted.

1 Edinburgh & Northern District Co-operative committee - Barclay Todd, middle row, third from right 1899
2 Newspaper report, 1898
3 *The Independent Order of Good Templars*, Staffordshire Pottery Figurine, 1870

The first documented consumer co-operative, the Fenwick Weavers' Society, was founded in 1769 in East Ayrshire and the concept was later developed by many, including Robert Owen at his cotton mills at New Lanark. In 1889 at the East Scotland Co-operative Conference Association in Free St Mary's Hall, Broughton Street, Barclay Todd, the Chairman of the Edinburgh & Northern Co-operative, 'spoke of the moral effect of co-operation' and 'his belief that the increasing powers of the working class would accomplish wonders never dreamed of by the leaders of co-operation.'

Todd spoke from personal experience for he had risen to a position of influence through his membership of co-operative movements. Born in 1844 in Kinross where his father was a shoemaker, by the time he was 14 Todd was working as a house painter on the remodelling of Kinnaird Castle in Victorian baronial style. Perhaps this led to similar work at Duns Castle, for in 1867 he married Mary Guicharde, the daughter of a butler at the castle.

They moved to Edinburgh, where Todd got a job as a painter's clerk and measurer with the Edinburgh Co-operative Building Company (ECBC) in the construction of the Stockbridge Colonies. They rented a flat at No. 3 Johnston Place (Raeburn Place) and their first child was born there in 1868. Between then and 1885 they had three daughters (one of whom died when an infant) and five sons. They lived in Stockbridge for over 30 years but like many with limited resources moved between rented properties, including No. 7 Saunders Street, No. 8 Rintoul Place, No. 1 Dunrobin Place and from 1895 at No. 19 N.W. Circus Place.

David Rintoul, a mason and chair of the ECBC, also became chair of the Edinburgh & Northern District Co-operative Society (ENDCS), which had a shop in Brunswick (St Stephen) Street and in the late 1860s he was instrumental in rescuing it from possible failure. By the mid-1870s the store was flourishing and at some point time Todd joined the Co-op's committee and was president in the 1890s when it opened a large bakery and a laundry, and initiated insurance schemes for horses and for glass.

Todd also was a leading member of the Edinburgh branch of The Independent Order of Good Templars, a popular temperance movement, and as such a leading advocate of a campaign to limit the number of pubs in the city. Unusually for the time, the Good Templars admitted women on an equal footing with men and as President of the ENDCS Todd helped establish a local branch of the Scottish Co-operative Women's Guild and provided premises for the fifty women members to meet.

In 1899 Todd coordinated an amalgamation of the ENDCS and St. Cuthbert's Co-operative Society but sadly died the following year, and thus never saw the combined co-op grow to become one of the largest societies in the British co-operative movement.

PERTH STREET - SADIE AITKEN MBE

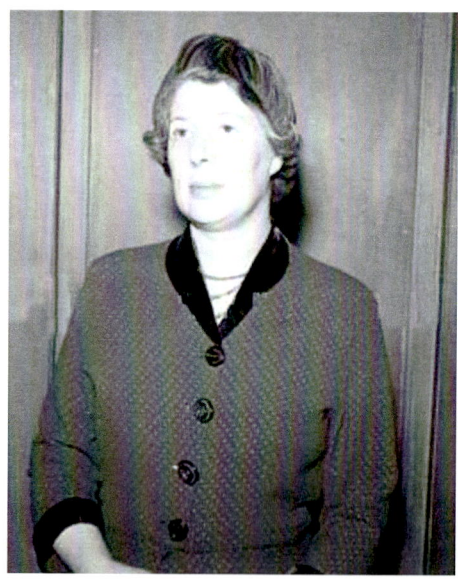

1 Gateway Theatre programme for *An Inspector Calls* by J. B. Priestley, 1953
2 Sadie Aitken, c.1940s
3 Sadie Aitken & Moultrie Kelsall, the theatre's Chairman, outside the Gateway Theatre, 1961 (*The Scotsman*)

In 1946 the Broadway cinema and theatre in Elm Row (now student flats) was gifted to the Church of Scotland. Originally built in 1882 as the New Veterinary College it had been a cinema and a theatre from around 1910. Remarkably the Church decided that it should continue as such and it was renamed the Gateway Theatre. Knowing that Sadie (Sarah) Aitken who was working for Church's Social Services had an interest in theatre, they asked if she would be interested in managing it. After checking that she would continue to be a Church of Scotland employee, Aitken agreed and became the first woman in Scotland to have a theatre licence.

Aitken was born in 1905. While growing up at No. 19 Perth Street she fell in love with the theatre while performing in a fundraising pageant. In 1927 she began working for the Church of Scotland and around the same time joined the Edinburgh branch of the Scottish Community Drama Association (SCDA), becoming its secretary until the 1970s. Through the 1930s and into the 1940s she took on amateur and professional acting roles, and was an early proponent of community arts activity, running drama activity for young disadvantaged boys at the Little Theatre.

At the Gateway Theatre Aitken presented both amateur and professional theatre, inviting companies such as Glasgow Citizens and Perth Theatre to perform, and to finance her ambitious plans continued to show films, though she tried to feature art-house films that might not otherwise have been seen in the city. She had a key role in the development of the Edinburgh Festivals. In 1948 she persuaded Robert Kemp, a Scottish playwright, and Tyrone Guthrie, an English theatrical director, to mount a production of Sir David Lyndsay's *Ane Satyre of the Thrie Estaitis* in the Church of Scotland's Assembly Hall as part of the Edinburgh International Festival, and mounted shows as part of the Fringe. She was renowned for being resourceful: 'If we needed to dress an actor as a tramp she would depute someone from wardrobe to go down to the Cowgate and find a good second-hand outfit which was fumigated when brought back.'

In 1953 the Church decided to hand the building over to a fully professional independent company. Aitken remained as manager and Robert Kemp was appointed artistic director. Over the next 12 years the theatre hosted performances that included plays by contemporary Scottish dramatists and starred many of Scotland's finest actors. The theatre closed in 1965. 'No history of any company at the Gateway could be complete without a tribute to Sadie. Her marvellous sense of humour, her unfailing willingness to help and her passionate devotion to the theatre make her one of the very few real characters in the business.' Sadie Aitken continued to act for television and film, worked with the SCDA and was a BBC arts critic. She died in 1985: 'Warriston Crematorium was packed with mourners. In true theatrical style it was a full house with standing room only as Sadie took her final curtain'.

PORTGOWER PLACE – THOMAS & FRANCIS COLLINSON

1 Advert for concert, June 1914
2 Thomas Henry Collinson
3 Francis Montgomery Collinson (right) taking notes from a traditional singer, c.1940s
4 Chorus, orchestra, singers and Thomas Collinson, conductor, who performed Handel's *Messiah* in the Music Hall on New Year's Day, 1908

As part of the celebrations of the silver jubilee season of the Edinburgh Royal Choral Union in December 1907, Thomas Collinson conducted the first performance in Scotland of Bach's *Mass in B Minor* at the McEwan Hall, and a few days later, on New Year's Day, conducted Handel's *Messiah* in the Music Hall. Later that month as a finale to the silver jubilee season, the Hallé Orchestra was engaged and Collinson conducted it and a choir of 333 voices in a concert featuring Schubert's *Song of Miriam* and Mendelssohn's *Lobgesang*.

For forty years Collinson was a significant figure in Edinburgh's musical life. Born in Alnwick, Northumbria in 1859 he studied the organ, and in 1883 was appointed conductor of the Edinburgh Royal Choral Union. He was also appointed organist and choirmaster of St Mary's Episcopal Cathedral and organist to the University of Edinburgh; playing at the first graduation ceremony held in the newly opened McEwan Hall in 1897. At the concert to mark the opening of the Usher Hall in March 1914, Collinson began with an introductory organ recital, including music by Handel, Ole Bull and Bach's *Grand Passacaglia in C minor*.

Collinson was an inspired choirmaster but on a few occasions his judgement of a voice was wrong. A young Joseph Hislop asked Collinson to assess his voice and Collinson's considered verdict was, 'You have a genius for music but your voice will never take you into the professional ranks'. Hislop ignored the advice and became an internationally renowned operatic tenor.

Collinson married Annie Wyness in 1891 and they had three sons and two daughters. The eldest son, Francis studied music with his father and at Edinburgh University, and became a theatre musical director in London, conducting for both Cole Porter and Richard Tauber. He was an avid folk music collector and when working for the BBC 'discovered' the great traditional English singers, Bob and James Copper from Sussex and Harry Cox from Norfolk, and recorded them and others. In 1951 he was appointed the first musical research fellow of Edinburgh University's School of Scottish Studies, focusing on traditional song in both Scottish and Gaelic. He published important books on Scottish music, including *The Traditional and National Music of Scotland* and *The Bagpipe: The History of a Musical Instrument*.

Francis wrote how his father challenged the snobbery that there once was against the bagpipe: 'On occasions of national importance, such as memorial services to deceased royalty or to great figures of state, my father used to engage the pipe-major stationed at Edinburgh Castle to play a complete piobaireachd towards the end of the service. The majesty of a piobaireachd played in a cathedral has to be heard to be believed.' Thomas Collinson died at No. 5 Portgower Place in 1928 and Francis in Galashiels in 1984.

RAEBURN PLACE - JAMES SIMPSON OBE

1 No. 40 Raeburn Place - note the car turntable in the front garden
2 James Simpson
3 Glanville Place tenement
4 The Botanic Cottage. Designed by the renowned architects John Adam and James Craig and built in 1764-5, it was the chief gardener's house and stood at the main entrance to the original Botanic Garden. After the Garden moved to Inverleith in the early 1820s, the cottage became a private home, then later offices and a van rental shop. By the mid-2000s it had been abandoned and set on fire. The building was saved, taken down and rebuilt in today's Botanic Garden.

James Simpson nearly became a soldier, but decided at the last minute to follow his father as an architect, and trained in the offices of Ian Lindsay in Edinburgh and Bernard Feilden in Norwich, both leading conservation architects of their day. He married Ann Bunney, daughter of Herrick Bunney, organist of St Giles for 50 years, and in 1975 they moved into No 40 Raeburn Place, where they brought up their daughters Hannah and Kate and lived for 45 years. Ann was an art historian, who spent her career in the Scottish National Gallery of Modern Art".

In the early years of architectural practice, Simpson taught architectural conservation in the College of Art and began to lecture widely, as far afield as Iran, Russia and Burma. He later developed a particular interest in the preservation of Scotland's heritage in India, particularly in the city of Calcutta. In 1977 he formed an architectural partnership with Stewart Brown. Over forty five years, Simpson & Brown's reputation grew steadily and James' projects included urban work at Stirling Tolbooth, Law's Close in Kirkcaldy and Alderman's Fenwick's House in Newcastle; castles and houses like Rosslyn, Kinlochmoidart and Yester; churches like St Mary's Dundee, Yester and Kilberry; and a number of William Adam houses, including Arniston, Tinwald and The Drum.

Simpson has been involved with architectural and urban conservation through bodies like the Cockburn Association, the Architectural Heritage Society, the Edinburgh New Town Conservation Committee and the Scottish Redundant Churches Trust (now Historic Churches Scotland). He has served on a number of public bodies, including the Ancient Monuments Board and the Edinburgh World Heritage Trust, and was a co-founder with Oliver Barratt of the Cockburn Conservation Trust (now part of the Scottish Historic Buildings Trust), one of whose early projects was the rescue in 1979 of the then derelict tenement in Glanville Place, where the trust managed to acquire six empty flats for 25p!

His last and most unusual project was close to home: the transferring stone by stone and timber by timber of the 1760s Botanic Cottage from the original Botanic Garden site in Leith Walk, and its fastidious rebuilding in the Botanic Garden in Inverleith.

Like so many who live in Stockbridge, Simpson has cared about its protection and not least about the appropriateness and quality of new projects in the area. He was one of those who opposed the building of a stand for the Edinburgh Academicals ground on Comely Bank Road with shops below, although admits to not too much disappointment that it went ahead as he appreciates the design by Michael Laird Architects. That Simpson is open to new ideas that can be harmoniously integrated with the old can be seen at No. 40 Raeburn Place. Look closely at its front garden and you will spot the car turntable the Simpsons installed to resolve the difficulty of backing their car out on to busy Raeburn Place.

REID TERRACE - JOHN THOMSON

RAILWAY ACCIDENT.—While the 6.5 A.M. train to Granton from the Waverley was standing in Trinity Station till tickets were collected a goods train, which fortunately had slowed down, ran into the rear of the stationary train, throwing down the passengers, most of whom received a severe shaking, and many rather serious cuts and bruises.

1 Former Trinity Railway Station, 1969 (photo - Kenneth Williamson)
2 John Thomson, 1913
3 Newspaper report, Nov 1898
4 Staff at another Scottish North British Railway station, c.1900 - perhaps an impressive beard or moustache was thought essential for the job of station master! (photo - John Alsop collection)

On 20 November 1913 John Thomson, who lived with his son at No. 9 Reid Terrace, retired after 41 years working for the North British Railway. Two presentations were made at the railway station to mark his retirement. The railway company presented him with an umbrella and a purse of gold sovereigns, and 'Mr Graham Yooll presented him with a purse of gold sovereigns on behalf of the private residents in recognition of his unfailing courtesy during his time at the station.'

Thomson began working for the railway company in 1872 at Alloa; probably joining the company when he was about thirteen. He initially would have been designated a 'railway lad'; boys who assisted in a general way. There was a fairly common path of promotion for those who proved satisfactory and Thomson moved to the next level, which was as a shunter, overseeing goods wagons being moved around the depot. Having learnt about signals operation, his next promotion was to signalman, and he then moved up the staffing ladder to passenger guard. The top rung for men such as Thomson was as a station master and he gained that promotion in 1881, taking charge of Trinity station on the Granton line in 1895.

Station masters had responsibility for managing the safety and care of the station, and overseeing the staff, and had significant social standing in the local community. Trinity was a stylish area that had mainly been developed in the early 19th century as a mansion house district. Many buildings were 'second homes' to rich families in the city and treated as a country retreat, so he would have worked hard to ensure his station was kept spotless, and all passengers treated with respect.

However, in 1898 Thomson's career almost came to an end. On 1 November a passenger train from Edinburgh to Granton was stopped in the station while tickets were being checked when a goods train ran into its back. Fortunately the goods train had slowed, but the collision shocked the passengers, of whom 21 complained of injury. A Board of Trade enquiry reported that the accident was due to irregularities in temporary single line working between Granton and Trinity Junction, which had been instituted in October due to damage to the sea wall from a strong gale. Although the station's signal porter was judged to have been primarily responsible, Thomson came in for censure as he had decided that during the single line working the signals provided for the protection of trains at the platforms need not used. 'John Thompson, who had sanctioned the disuse of the signals, must be held to be guilty of grave error of judgement, and to have been great measure responsible for the accident, which should be a warning to all men implicated to obey to the letter all the rules drawn for their guidance.'

No doubt Thomson was censured but he kept his job, possibly through the intercession of local station users who clearly held him in high regard.

RINTOUL PLACE - SIR JAMES CAW

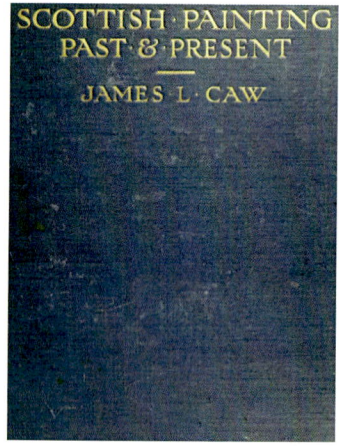

1 *Bust of James Lewis Caw* by Benno Schotz, 1928 (National Galleries Scotland)
2 *Raeburn, Masterpieces in colour* by James Caw, published 1909
3 *Scottish Painting, Past & Present, 1620-1908* by James Caw, published 1908

Although James Lewis Caw only rented a house in Rintoul Place in the Stockbridge Colonies for a short time around 1885, it was while living there that he received the news that changed his life: 'At a meeting of the Board Manufactures last night, Mr James L. Caw, 29 Rintoul Place, Edinburgh, was appointed curator of the National Portrait Gallery in place of the late Mr J. M. Gray.'

Born in Ayr in 1864, Caw apprenticed in engineering at the West of Scotland Technical College and on leaving college became employed as a draughtsman, first in Glasgow and later in Edinburgh. In his spare time he developed a keen appreciation for Scottish art and began to contribute articles and criticism on art subjects to various journals. Through this work he became friends with key artists of the day, including James Guthrie and William McTaggart. He also began to exhibit his own watercolours.

His recognised authoritative art perspective landed him the curator post. The National Portrait Gallery had opened just six years earlier and Caw set about organising the gallery's collection to provide a cohesive exhibition of Scottish portrait history. Appropriately, given his brief time in Stockbridge, his first major monograph that appeared in 1901 was on the work of Henry Raeburn. In it Caw sums up Stockbridge's famous artist: 'Born a painter of character, Raeburn was at his best where character, intellect, and shrewdness were most marked. Yet axiomatic though it may sound, this implies great gifts. To seize the obvious points of likeness, and make a portrait more living than life itself is comparatively easy; but to grasp the essential elements of likeness and character, and, while vitalising these pictorially and decoratively, to preserve the normal tone of life is difficult indeed. Of this, the highest triumph of the portrait-painter's art as such, Raeburn was a master.' Caw's other publications included *Scottish Painting, 1620-1908,* the first serious study of his country's art.

Caw was appointed the first director of the National Galleries of Scotland in 1907, and he made a number of astute purchases of recent art, including Paul Gauguin's spectacular *Vision after the Sermon* (*Jacob and the Angel*) and Claude Monet's *Poplars on the Epte.*

In 1909 he married Anne McTaggart, the daughter of the artist, William McTaggart. From 1916 until 1933 he also was the art critic of *The Scotsman.* In 1930, when inaugurating a scheme through the Education Authority for the teaching of appreciation of art, he said: 'Not only does art introduce a new and rich interest into life, but it indirectly quickens and refines observation of the world about us. The idea behind the scheme is to awaken appreciation of the beautiful things in life.' James Caw retired from the National Galleries in 1930 but continued to have an active career, organising exhibitions and publishing until his death in 1950.

ST BERNARD'S CRESCENT - WILLIAM MOWAT-THOMSON

1 William Mowat-Thomson in his house in St Bernard's Crescent, c.1980
2 William Mowat-Thomson at the piano, c.1960
3 Advert for Theatre School of Dance & Drama, No. 106 St Stephen Street, 1980
4. Interior of Mowat-Thomson's house, 2021 (photo - McTear's Auctioneers)

William Mowat-Thomson was born on a farm in Orkney in 1933 and fell in love with Balfour Castle, a great Victorian pile on the island. It inspired in him a passion for fine furniture and antiques, one that he pursued throughout his life. He also became interested in yoga and took dancing lessons. His dance talent led his teacher to suggest that he train professionally as a ballet dancer and he moved to Edinburgh to study at the Scottish Ballet School. He was a talented pianist and to fund his training accompanied dance classes. He began dancing professionally but his interest in the diversity of dance styles led him to decide instead to become a dance teacher.

In the early 1970s Mowat-Thomson opened the pioneering Theatre School of Dance and Drama in Shandwick Place and in 1976 bought No. 106 St Stephens Street - erected in 1867 as a home for the Stockbridge Working Men's Club - and moved his school there. He and others taught dance in a variety of styles to adults and children, and he initiated Scotland's first full-time dance course. Mowat-Thomson would correct dancers' postures with a gentle tap of his silver-topped cane. He also was employed as a pianist by many dance companies to accompany classes and rehearsals. His school studios were used by artists for rehearsals and making work, particularly during the Edinburgh Fringe, including such luminaries as David Bowie and Lindsay Kemp.

Mowat-Thomson also ran the first Yoga Teacher Training course in Scotland in 1974 and established a yoga centre in the St Stephens Street building. In 2000 he sold the Theatre School to one of his former pupils, Tracy Hawkes, who continues to run a flourishing dance academy there.

His love of antiques, particularly from the Georgian period, meant that he was at his happiest scouring antique shops for treasured items, where his charm often secured a good deal - quite a feat with notoriously hard-nosed dealers. He bought statues and columns, oil paintings, swords and chandeliers to decorate his house in a traditional country house style, and adorned spaces with antiquarian books, dinner services, jugs, Bonnie Prince Charlie memorabilia, and all manner of smaller items. For a time, alongside his dance and yoga centre, Mowat-Thomson ran two antique shops at different periods, in Thistle Street and the Grassmarket. He lived at various houses, including Stobs Castle near Hawick, and finally in St Bernard's Crescent where he housed his outstanding collection of paintings, furniture and collectables. The house was renowned for the stylish dinner parties that he gave. Usually, afterwards he would play on his grand piano while guests admired his objects.

Following his death in 2019, aged 86, his vast antiques collection was auctioned and sold for over £360,000. One of his former dance pupils said of him; 'He was a maverick and a patient, generous visionary.'

ST BERNARD'S ROW - MARY JAMESON

EDINBURGH INSTITUTION FOR UNWANTED CATS, 18 ST BERNARD'S ROW.

The object of the Institution is to reduce the number of Stray, Diseased, and Unwanted Cats, and in view of the May Term, when so many Cats are carelessly and cruelly turned adrift, the Public are reminded of the Institution. Animals belonging to people unable to pay are taken in Free, but those who can are asked to contribute, as expenses are heavy. An increase of Annual Subscribers, Monetary Gifts by will and otherwise, now needed to carry on the work.
Open Daily.
MARY HOPE JAMESON.

EDINBURGH COMEDY COMPANY'S DRAMATIC ENTERTAINMENT.

In the Royal Halls, 88 Pitt Street, last night, a concert and dramatic performance was given by members of the Edinburgh Comedy Company in aid of the Stockbridge Cat Institution. "Old Jan," a playlet with a Dutch setting, was cleverly performed by Mr William Duns, Miss Hope Jameson, and Miss Grace Purves. The second piece, "The Rehearsal," would more properly have been called a sequence of gags than a farce, but although the material was disjointed, those taking the leading parts made a good appearance. Mr Jack Chisholm made a dignified Sir Ronald Warren; Messrs William Duns and Francis Mathieson kept the fun going, the former as a sort of nondescript traveller, and the latter as an old actor. Miss Margaret Haynes as "Ethel Bertram," an American tourist, was quite successful.

1 Advert inserted by Mary Jameson seeking financial support, 1906
2 First edition of *The Cat*, the magazine of the Cats Protection League, 1934
3 Banner for 'The Animals' Friend' being paraded through London, 1909
4 Review of fundraising show for the Stockbridge Cat Institution, 1919

'Many a neighbourhood at this season suffers in ear as well as in sentiment, by the miserable squallings of half-starved and perishing wretches.' In response to this problem, Mary Jameson established her Edinburgh Institution for Unwanted Cats at No. 18 St Bernard's Row. In 1912, a reporter from the *Edinburgh Evening News* visited Miss Jameson: 'I expected to find a lady who took a languid, patronising interest in the concern and who, over a cup of tea in a luxurious drawing room, would talk tiresome platitudes and quote dull figures from a printed report. On the contrary, I found an enthusiast in the midst of her life work. My ring at the bell disturbed her in the process of sending a stray cat to its last long sleep. She said: "Cats have been much neglected in Edinburgh. The indifference to their sufferings, as a rule, and the gross cruelties perpetrated upon them, are a disgrace to culture, civilisation, and Christianity."'

All that has been traced about Mary Hope Jameson before she established the Edinburgh Institution for Unwanted Cats in 1905, was that she was born in France in 1857 and that her great-grandfather was William Jameson, who established the brick-making trade in Portobello. At the time she began her work there were large numbers of stray cats, many suffering from disease, injury or malnutrition. While stray dogs were rounded up and humanely killed, the public authorities ignored the cat problem, so they were left to die in the street. There also were many poor families who ended up with unwanted kittens. Jameson said of her work: 'When I founded this useful institution, over 20 years ago, the work was overwhelming, poor people getting rid of their cats and kittens free of charge, and others bringing in large numbers, the institution being open morning, noon, and night, and all day on Sundays.'

Jameson ran the institution almost single-handed. Part of the house was used to hold the abandoned cats and when it came time to put a cat down, it was she who administered the chloroform. Another room was a cat mortuary where the deceased animals - on average 100 a week - were kept until being collected by the dustmen. If a cat was brought to her that clearly was a lost pet she would pay for an advertisement in the hope of reuniting the cat with its loving owner: 'Cat (tabby), small, found near Queen Street. Apply Cat Institution.' If unclaimed within a week she reluctantly would put the unfortunate pet down.

While she funded much of her work with her own money, the scale of the work meant she constantly needed to raise additional funds, often through fund-raising events such as one in 1912: 'Musical and Dramatic Entertainment in aid of funds, Wesley Hall, Hamilton Place. Admission 1s and 6d.' In 1930 Jameson began work to establish a Scottish branch of the Cats' Protection League that had been established in London in 1927, but died in 1931 before the final arrangements were completed.

SAUNDERS STREET – GEORGE KEMP

1 Masons working on the Scott Monument. George Kemp & David Lind possibly the two seated men in top hats, 1843 (photo - David Octavius Hill, Capital Collections)
2 George Meikle Kemp, 1843 (photo - David Octavius Hill)
3 Scott Monument under construction, 1844 (photo - David Octavius Hill, Capital Collections)

For five days in 1836 George Kemp worked feverishly in his Saunders Street flat on an entry for the design competition for a monument to Sir Walter Scott, who had died in 1832. Kemp was not an architect, although it was his ambition to be one, but he had significant knowledge of the Gothic architectural style that was the form required for the monument. Some years earlier a proposal he had submitted for the restoration of Glasgow Cathedral was rejected due to his not being an architect so he submitted his design for the Scott Monument under the pseudonym John Morvo.

Kemp was born near Biggar in 1795, the son of a shepherd, and left school when just 11 to work as a herd boy. Around that time he visited Rosslyn Chapel and fell in love with Gothic architecture. He later trained as a carpenter and then travelled around, repairing wooden agricultural and industrial machines. On his travels he expanded his knowledge of the Gothic form by visiting key buildings, including cathedrals in France. In 1826 he moved to Edinburgh and lodged at No. 18 Bedford Street. Six years later he married and moved to Saunders Street, and got a job with the architect William Burn, producing drawings and architectural models.

Kemp's design for the Scott Monument was chosen as the winner with the organisers praising the 'imposing structure of beautiful proportions, and in strict conformity with the purity of taste and style of Melrose Abbey, from which the author states it is in all its details derived.' Given Kemp had never built anything before, a safe pair of hands to oversee the construction was required and the builder David Lind was selected. By coincidence, Lind had begun his career by building a tenement in Bedford Street and was living there at the time Kemp lodged in the street. In 1831 Lind received his first major commission: to build the extension to the Royal Institution building on the Mound (now The Royal Scottish Academy) designed by William Henry Playfair.

On 15 August 1840 the Scott Monument's foundation stone was laid and construction began. In 1842 Lind moved from Bedford Street to 1 Port Hopetoun at the Union Canal Basin, where he opened a large builder's yard for his expanded business. As the monument rose up, so did Kemp's reputation, and he was approached about several potentially lucrative architectural commissions.

On 5 March 1844 Kemp went to meet Lind at Port Hopetoun to discuss the project. It was a foggy evening when Kemp set off to walk home and he never arrived. The following Monday his drowned body was found in the Union Canal. In spite of many theories - suicide, a drunken fall, an attack, a misstep in the fog - the circumstances of Kemp's death remain a mystery. In the autumn of that year, one of Kemp's sons placed the finial on the top of the Scott Monument, marking the completion of his father's sole building.

SAXE-COBURG PLACE - WILLIAM HOLE

1 William Brassey Hole painting the Frieze for the Scottish National Portrait Gallery, c.1900
2 Detail from Hole's Frieze for the Scottish National Portrait Gallery
3 *Jesus healing a leper,* from the series of paintings by Hole published in the book, *The Life Of Jesus of Nazareth*, 1906

In 1859 a perceived threat of invasion by France led to the creation of a number of volunteer militia units. Like elsewhere, many in Edinburgh were formed by groups such as advocates and bankers and the first unit of the Edinburgh City Artillery Volunteers mainly consisted of artists, including the portrait painter, John Watson Gordon, and it was this unit that the painter, William Brassey Hole joined in 1876. By this time the volunteer regiments had become primarily social affairs and many only joined for the dressing up and military pomp, and social contacts. 'The annual ball given by the officers of the 1st Edinburgh City Artillery Volunteers was held last night in the Waterloo Hotel. There were about 250 ladies and gentlemen present.'

Hole had just married Elizabeth (Lizzie) Lindsay and they had moved into No. 30 Saxe-Coburg Place. They had six children while living there. Hole attended Edinburgh Academy and on leaving school apprenticed with an engineering firm. However at 19, having had a painting accepted by the Royal Scottish Academy, he used a small legacy to travel to Europe to research and sketch. In Italy he met the Scottish artist Erskine Nicol, who encouraged him to take up art professionally. By the time of his marriage he had established a studio at Picardy Place from where he ran a private art school, the Edinburgh Atelier, giving life drawing classes for both male and female students. He gained a high reputation as an etcher, one critic describing his etchings as 'perhaps the most wonderful translations of colour and handling, of design and conception and spirit, into another artistic medium ever made, and entitle their author to rank with creative artists of the highest class.'

In 1897 he was appointed to carry out the mural decoration of the central hall of the Scottish National Portrait Gallery on a theme illustrating Scottish history. It took Hole three years to complete the work that included large panels illustrating Scottish history from St Columba to James IV and war and peace through the arts of music and poetry. A critic described this work as 'one of the most notable essays in mural decoration ever accomplished in this country'. He also designed the zodiacal ceiling, reflecting his interests as a keen amateur astronomer.

In the spring of 1901 Hole spent time in Palestine that resulted in eighty watercolours that were published as *The Life of Jesus of Nazareth*. These watercolours became an archetype for 'Sunday School' illustrations for decades after.

Perhaps Hole attended the 'smoking concert' held in 1909 to celebrate the 50th anniversary of the foundation of the Edinburgh City Artillery Volunteers. However, sadly, the playing at soldiers gave way to a grim reality with the outbreak of the First World War, in which one of Hole's sons died fighting on the Somme. The loss hit him hard and may have affected his health as he died in 1917

SILVERMILLS - LAUDER FAMILY

1 *Self Portrait in the Venetian Style* by Robert Scott Lauder (Hospitalfield, Arbroath)
2 *Portrait of John Lauder* by Robert Scott Lauder (Museums & Galleries Edinburgh)
3 *Portrait of James Eckford Lauder* by Charles Lees (Royal Scottish Academy of Art & Architecture)
4 Silvermills House, 2023

The area around Stockbridge has had tanneries since the 16th century. These took in raw animal hides and skins and by steeping the skins in an astringent liquid prepared from bark, removed the matter that could cause putrefaction and decomposition, to produce leather for use. The process created a strong stench and thus it was an advantage to have them sited away from residential areas. In 1809 when John Lauder announced the building of a new, large steam-powered tannery and leather works just behind the present St. Stephen's Church, the developers who had planned to build housing nearby were incensed, arguing that the works, 'would be offensive, noxious and disagreeable to the neighbourhood' Legal attempts to stop it failed so the original plan to complete the west end of Fettes Row with curved sections meeting the bottom of St Vincent Street was abandoned as the tannery blighted all adjoining residential development.

In 1820 part of the land next to the tannery was purchased from Lauder for the building of St Stephen's Church; one hopes that with the tannery closed on Sundays, its congregation were spared the worst of the smell.

Lauder was born at Scrogbank, Traquair in 1768 and married Helen Tait in 1796, and they lived at Silvermills House, This had been built in 1760 for Nicol Sommerville, a painter. It was to the west of the tannery but still quite close, although perhaps Lauder had become impervious to the tanning odours after so many years. At that time, 'Silvermills House was graced with pillared gateways and shaded by an avenue of venerable elms.' Alongside his large tannery, Lauder also had a leatherworks and was, 'well known as a maker of good buff gloves.' Gloves were an indicator of a person's social and economic status, so for the well-off nothing but the best quality would do.

John Lauder died in 1838. He and Helen had five sons and a daughter, all of whom grew up in Silvermills House. Three of the sons trained in the leather business. William, the eldest, became a leather merchant in London, while John took over the tannery and Walter the leather-making business. The two other sons, Robert Scott and James Eckford, became artists.

By 1830 Robert Scott Lauder's art had earned him election to the Royal Scottish Academy. In 1833 he married Isabella Ramsay Thomson and they then went abroad, accompanied by his younger artist-brother, James. Robert then lived in London for a few years, exhibiting work widely. He returned to live in Edinburgh in 1849. Rather appropriately given his middle name some of his most successful historical paintings were based on the works of Sir Walter Scott. James Eckford Lauder also exhibited annually and was elected to the Royal Scottish Academy in 1846. He produced historical and literary subjects until the late 1850s, but when he then turned to landscape struggled to find a market for his work. Both Robert and James died in 1869.

SPRING GARDENS - WILLIAM BRODIE

1 Buchanan Memorial, Dean Cemetery
2 *Portrait of William Brodie* by John Phillip, c.1850 (Aberdeen Art Gallery)
3 Birth announcement, 27 November 1854
4 Greyfriars Bobby, sculpted by William Brodie in 1872

In 1841 William Brodie, aged 26, was working as a plumber in Aberdeen when he married Helen Chisholm. Over the next four years they had three daughters but their next child was not born until nine years later; a gap explained by the fact that from 1847 until late 1853, William lived in Edinburgh and Helen in Aberdeen. The reason for their living apart was that William had begun modelling figures that were much admired and in 1847 moved to Edinburgh to train as a sculptor.

After a four year course of study at the Trustees' School of Design he stayed on in Edinburgh, and began exhibiting work. In 1853 James Buchanan, a prominent Glasgow merchant and patron of the arts, paid for Brodie to travel to Rome to extend his knowledge. While in Rome Brodie had created the work, *Corinna, the Lyric Muse* and when it was exhibited in March 1854 a critic said: 'The most beautiful of the busts is No. 709, *Corinna* by William Brodie. This will gain new admirers to Mr Brodie by all who look upon it. The gentle beauty, and intellectual expression, harmonises well with the story that her gentleness and beauty, no less than her talents, secured for her the laurel wreath, even when Pinder was a competitor.'

On his return from Italy Helen and the children joined him in Edinburgh and the family moved into No. 6 Spring Gardens (now 27 N. W. Circus Place) and there on 27 November 1854 Helen gave birth to a son. He was christened James Buchanan Brodie in honour of Brodie's benefactor. Later the family lived in Cambridge Street.

Brodie swiftly established a successful practice specialising in portrait busts, public monuments and architectural sculpture, and at one point employed '8 Men & 8 Boys'. He was elected Associate of the Royal Scottish Academy (RSA) in 1857 and from 1876 until his death acted as its secretary.

Among his most significant works is a classical mausoleum in Dean Cemetery for his early benefactor James Buchanan; it includes a colossal bronze bust of Buchanan and a bronze door with a relief of a female mourner. In 1871 while making statues of characters from Walter Scott's *Waverley* novels for the Scott Monument, Brodie was commissioned by Lady Burdett-Coutts to make a statue of the city's famous faithful terrier, Greyfriars Bobby, who was still keeping watch over his owner's grave in Greyfriars Kirkyard after many years. She donated a number of dog fountains and wished to place one outside Greyfriars Kirk with a statue of Greyfriars Bobby on top. Bobby died soon after being immortalised by Brodie, and today it is his most viewed work, even if few who pat Bobby's nose know who sculpted it.

Brodie died in 1881. His son James, who had been born in Spring Gardens, moved to America and died in Oregon in 1915.

TEVIOTDALE PLACE - RACHEL HAZELL

1 Rachel Hazell (photo - Sarah Mason)
2 *Bound* by Rachel Hazell (photo - Susan Bell) 'An accessible collection of creative bookbinding projects. Whether you have already tried your hand at bookbinding or are a complete beginner, let Rachel's knowledge and passion motivate you to explore the many possibilities of book art.'
3 Rachel's Little Free Library in Teviotdale Place (photo - Rachel Hazell)

Edinburgh has always valued books and respected all of those who are involved: writers, publishers, printers, binders, booksellers and libraries. Robert Chambers in his 1823 book, *Traditions of Edinburgh* wrote: 'The precincts of St Giles's being now secularised, the church itself was, in 1628, degraded by numerous wooden booths being stuck up around it. Yet, to show that some reverence was still paid to the sanctity of the place, the Town-council decreed that no tradesmen should be admitted to these shops except bookbinders, watchmakers, jewellers, and goldsmiths.'

While almost all bookbinding is now done by machine there are still individual bookbinders who ensure the craft thrives. One is Rachel Hazell who has lived at Teviotdale Place since 2012. She trained in Bookbinding at the London College of Printing and completed Masters degrees in Book Art at Camberwell College of Art and Printmaking at Edinburgh College of Art. She says, 'books, words and the power of imagination have always been central to my life. The day I was taught how to make my first book, I knew I'd be a bookbinder for the rest of my life.'

Her passion is enabling others to discover the creative pleasure of making books through a variety of workshops and on-line courses. Hazell describes herself as 'The Travelling Bookbinder' and her love of travelling began when her mother encouraged her to visit a pen pal in West Africa when she was 15. Her travelling has taken her to Antarctica three times and, in 2008, she worked there as Assistant Post Mistress at Port Lockroy Post Office and as penguin monitor. She has delivered workshops from Napa Valley to Shetland, and her passion for travel has led her to develop bookbinding workshops linked to maps. One in Venice included taking her workshop participants to a library to handle 15th-century navigational books, maps and atlases. A workshop entitled, 'How To Write A Love Letter' offers participants the opportunity to create 'a locked letter, a contemporary version of something that might have been delivered by a messenger on horseback, secured with a royal seal!'

In 2009, Todd Bol of Hudson, Wisconsin, built a small model of a one room schoolhouse where people could leave books for others to read. Named, the Little Free Library, the idea has been taken up around the world and Hazell has created one in the front of her house. 'The local community has totally embraced it,' she says. 'Visitors walking by get curious and stop to have a look and take a picture. As a book artist, sharing books with people is at the heart of my work so to have a library on the garden fence, where people can take a book or leave a book, day or night, delights me.' Teviotdale Place's Little Free Library is one of over 36,000; appropriately there is even one in Antarctica.

When not travelling, Hazell divides her time between Teviotdale Place and a house on Iona.

UPPER DEAN TERRACE - HELEN MARSHALL

Helena Marshall
January 1st 1871.

Wednesday 6th
Went out on an expedition to the Bernini, had a snowball match and slide down an ice hill. walked home a distance of 12 miles. fearfully tired.
Thursday 7th
Remained at home because of rain.

THE BLYTH SCHOOL AND CLASSES FOR GIRLS (formerly Rutland Square Classes), RE-OPEN October 1st in the New Premises, 15 Rosebery Crescent, close to Haymarket Station. Prospectus on application. Pupils enrolled Tuesday and Thursday, 2 till 4 o'clock. Miss E. GOWAN and Miss HELEN MARSHALL, Principals.

1 Front of diary, 1871. Although christened Helen, at this time she called herself Helena
2 Extract from diary recounting visit to Roseg Glacier, Switzerland, 6 August 1873. The week before Helen had been informed her services were no longer required.
3 Advert for the Blyth School, 1901
4 Watt Institution and School of Arts, Adam Square, c.1885

In 1869 Mary Burton, a campaigner for women's rights, persuaded the Watt Institution and School of Arts in Adam Square to admit women students. One of the first students was eighteen-year-old Helen Marshall who lived at No. 5 Upper Dean Terrace. Her father was a coal merchant but earlier had owned ironworks in Russia. Helen's mother had been born in Russia where there was a colony of British residents, and Helen also was born there in 1851.

Helen kept a diary (now in the Centre for Research Collections, University of Edinburgh) that offers an insight into the breadth of subjects studied by the first women at the Watt Institution. These included geology, botany, zoology, English grammar, Renaissance Italian art and scientific experiments. 'Wednesday - Saw electrical experiments in the dark which caused great excitement. Gave in exercises on magnetism. Friday - Heard a lecture on Charles Lamb.'

While the diary contains details on events Marshall attended – 'Visited Hamilton's Excursion (a series of dioramas including depictions of European cities and battles) and enjoyed it amazingly' – there is almost nothing on her emotional state except for occasional allusions. 'At Dr Page's soirée danced a polka with Mr King. Engaged myself to Mr Miles for a country dance. Couldn't make out Mr Nicol's meaning in not having once asked me to dance. At length he asked me for the next dance but I told him I was already engaged at which he expressed great sorrow. My partner came edging his way up and told me he would be obliged to relinquish the next dance as he couldn't waltz. Without taking time to reply, with a jump, minus the orthodox hop and skip I reached Mr Nicol's side and told him as I was now disengaged I could be his partner so we had the next dance together and a tremendous long affair it was too.' The next day she wrote: 'Was in a quandary all day at Nicol's strange behaviour'.

Oddly, the diary makes no reference to her parents' separation which meant Helen and her mother had to move to Buccleuch Place. However, she does recount an unfortunate occasion while working as a governess. She travelled to visit an aunt in St Petersburg and later was employed to accompany children travelling in Europe. While in Switzerland she was dismissed without warning: 'Was startled by Mrs T. making her appearance in the midst of lessons, beckoned me ominously into the boy's room, and there announced that my services wouldn't be required after September. I coolly replied, "Very well" and so the matter ended.' Her diary entry for the next day relates: 'Awake all night. Formed good resolutions for the future.'

Her resolve led Marshall to return to Edinburgh where she became a teacher, and by 1901 headmistress of a small girls' school in Rutland Square. She died in 1909.

VEITCH'S SQUARE - HELEN WHITELAW

ASSEMBLIES, dance practices, &c.; J. Whitelaw's quadrille band; now booking engagements for the season; piano or harp accompaniment; terms.—Veitch's Square, Stockbridge.

SALE OF DAIRY STOCK.

OLIVER & SON, LTD., are instructed by Mr A. WHITELAW to Sell his DAIRY STOCK at VEITCH'S SQUARE, STOCKBRIDGE, on
TUESDAY, 1st June.
24 COWS (some in Full Milk, others Fat.)
CHESTNUT HORSE, 17.2 (suitable for Lorry.)
USEFUL VAN COB.
2 DRAFF CARTS, BOX VAN (Good), 2 MILK VANS, MEAT COOLER, Nearly New (140 Gals.), MEAL CHEST, 2-WHEELED DOGCART (nearly new), BLOCK and TACKLE, GRASS RAKE, SET CART HARNESS, 3 SETS VAN HARNESS, TURNIP CUTTER, BARROW, STABLE UTENSILS, &c.

1 *Cowshed* by Frederick William Elwell, 1922 (Beverley Art Gallery)
2 Advert for James Whitelaw's quadrille band, 1895
3 Advert for the sale of Whitelaw's dairy, 1915

The father of Helen Burton was a thatcher near East Calder and like many daughters of larger rural families she was sent to work when only 12 years old as a servant at an inn in Mid-Calder. In 1859, aged 19, she married Walter Whitelaw, the son of a ploughman, and they leased a dairy in Cramond. In 1874 they moved to Stockbridge and rented a dairy in Veitch's Square on the bank of the Water of Leith that consisted of a house, stables for two horses, sheds for equipment and a byre that held about 30 cows.

This was one of many byres sited throughout the city to provide fresh milk to residents - those that ran them often were termed 'cowfeeders'. As most were close to houses the cows were kept confined all the time and were a significant health risk. There were a number of other byres in Stockbridge, including two in Allan Street and one in Bedford Street where 20 cows were kept. Not all were well maintained. William Wilson, a cowfeeder in Silvermills, was taken to court and fined for 'failing to keep his cow-house or byre in a thoroughly clean and wholesome condition.' The city worked to close down the cowsheds in the city but even by 1900 there were still 115 in the city, containing around 3,000 cows.

The Whitelaws had eight children and the 1881 census records that the two eldest boys were working; Alexander (18) for the North British Railway and Peter (15) as a clerk. Four other boys, aged 4 to 13, were at school although no doubt they also helped in the dairy. The only daughter was still an infant and a seventh son had just been born. At that time Walter employed two young women, one as a dairy maid and another as a general dairy servant. It is likely that Helen helped with the milking given the number of cows they had. The milk would have been put into large churns and delivered to local shops. Customers brought their own containers into which the milk was ladled. Milk deliveries to the houses of the better-off was more often provided by shop owners.

Soon after the arrival of the eighth child tragedy struck. In 1882 Walter died, though only in his mid-forties, leaving Helen with a dairy to run and five children still under the age of 10. To help, both older sons gave up their jobs. In 1891 the oldest son, Alexander married Janet Orr and they and Helen then ran the dairy, employing a van driver, a byre man and two dairymaids. The third son, James, became a musician and had a band that played at local dances and social events around the city.

In 1900 Helen, then in her early sixties, retired from the business and moved to live in a flat in Great Junction Street. Alexander ran the dairy until his death in 1915. The dairy then was leased by Walter Ramage until its closure around 1925, at which point the cows gave way to motor vehicles as many of the premises in the square became 'motor car houses'.

APPENDIX - STREET NAMES

1 Looking down former Church Street (now Gloucester Street) to Kerr Street. The building on the right, on the corner with India Place, was the birthplace in 1796 of the painter, David Roberts. The house was built around 1790 from the stones of demolished buildings in the Old Town.
2 'Fear God Onlye, 1605' An old stone lintel incorporated into the house

In 1882 the council declared that a number of street names would be changed. The Dunlop family who lived in Brunswick Street were passionate antiquarians and the father, John, wrote to *The Scotsman* in protest.

'What has Stockbridge done? Of what crime or misdemeanour have its inhabitants been guilty that the scourge of civic change should fall so much more heavily on "our village" that on the rest of Edinburgh, and that twelve of our streets should have their well-worn names blotted from memory? We are a quiet people in Stockbridge, but we have an attachment to our native places and to our native streets. Concerning the largest alteration, which is to blot out six names, and substitute one new street - viz. "Stockbridge Street" for them all, there is no use including North West Circus Place in the number as it is not, properly speaking, in old Stockbridge.

Again, concerning our Brunswick Street, which is proposed to become an appendix of St Stephen Street, I only wish to remark that no one has known it more intimately that I have done for the last forty years, and during all that time I have never known of any mistake occurring through its having a name-sister in town. If change is inevitable would it not be more just and more graceful to retain the old name by the larger population and proprietorship? The electors are in the proportion of about 25 to 1 in Stockbridge compared with Hillside. This would minimise greatly the annoyance and expense of change.

Concerning Church Street, the intention to change its name to India Lane is not easily understood, seeing there is a pair of Indias amongst our street nomenclature already. The contiguity of Stockbridge to India is not in any way remarkable and there is surely no startling resemblance among us to the dusky inhabitants of that very warm country to account for this inscrutable preference. Church Street and Lane are the remains of the kirk road from Granton and Stockbridge to the West Kirk when that church was the only place of worship in all its wide parish. Church Street retains traces of its name - Anglicised it is true - the more's the pity. In Church Street, too, David Roberts was born. Near his birthplace is that of Sir Henry Raeburn. If a new appellation was wanting could the street not have been named after either of its gifted sons? Though had they been alive, both would have protested against such a change. In their day, Church Lane was pleasantly famous for the smell of its sweet briar and wild roses on the June Sabbath days. So far as I have been able to investigate Church Street is perhaps the oldest road in the suburbs of Edinburgh.'

Dunlop's protest saved N W Circus Place and other streets from being renamed Stockbridge Street, but Brunswick Street was amalgamated into St Stephen Street, and Church Street and Church Lane were eventually renamed Gloucester Street and Gloucester Lane.

Information drawn from *The Place Names of Edinburgh* by Stuart Harris (1996)

Allan Street - named for Thomas Allan of Allanfield who feued the street
Ann Street - named for Henry Raeburn's wife
Arboretum Avenue (original entrance to Inverleith House) - named when Botanic Gardens was extended as trees were planted there
Avondale Place - Scottish place name
Baker's Place - possibly named in link to Stockbridge Flour Mills that were there
Balmoral Place - Scottish place name
Bedford Street - derivation unknown
Bell Place - named for David Bell, joiner and third chair of the Edinburgh Co-operative Building Company (ECBC)
Bridge Place - where the original footbridge to the Colonies was sited
Brunswick Street (renamed St Stephen Street) - named for Frederick, Duke of Brunswick
Carlton Street - as built in 1824 possibly commemorating George IV's visit with reference to Carlton House in London, his home before his accession
Cheyne Street - probably named by Captain Cheyne who lived at No. 19 and may have feued the land
Church Street/Lane (renamed Gloucester Street/Lane) - road up to the West Kirk (St Cuthbert's Church)
Claremont Street (renamed Saxe-Coburg Street) - Claremont was the Surrey home of Prince Leopold of Saxe-Coburg
Clarence Street - named for William, Duke of Clarence
Collins Place - named for James Collins, first chairman of the ECBC
Colville Place - named for James Colville, mason & first manager of the ECBC
Danube Street - derivation unknown
Dean Street - related to the Dean Estate - was old road to Dean Village.
Dean Bank Lane - Dean Bank the traditional name for steep bank on west of Water of Leith
Dean Park Crescent, Mews, Street & Terrace - related to the Dean Estate
Deanhaugh Street - was main street in the original Deanhaugh village
Dunrobin Place - Scottish place name
Glanville Place - derivation unknown
Glenogle Colonies, House & Street - possibly named in compliment to John Haig on whose land the Stockbridge Colonies were built as he lived at Glenogle, Perthshire
Hamilton Place - named for Mrs Hamilton, original owner of Nos. 10/11.
Haugh Street - 'haugh' a Scottish word for flat area next to a river

Henderson Row - named for Alexander Henderson, Lord Provost in 1823
Hermitage Place (renamed Raeburn Street in 1968 to avoid confusion with Leith Street) - derivation unknown
Hugh Miller Place - named for Hugh Miller, stonemason, geologist, journalist and champion of the cause for housing reform
India Place - named in relation to British colonies
Johnston Place (no longer exists – was name for tenement block in Raeburn Place on corner with St Bernard's Row) - derivation unknown
Kemp Place - named for William Kemp, Governor of the Poors House & active in the ECBC
Kerr Street - possibly named for the developer of the street
Leslie Place - named for Count Leslie of Deanhaugh House
Mackenzie Place - possibly named for Samuel Mackenzie, a painter and pupil of Henry Raeburn
Malta Green & Terrace - named in connection with Malta House
Market Place (renamed St Stephen Place) - entrance to Stockbridge Market
Mary's Place - derivation unknown
North West Circus Place - generic name linked to Royal Circus
Perth Street - Scottish place name
Portgower Place - derivation unknown
Raeburn Place & Street - named for Henry Raeburn
Reid Terrace - named for Hugh Gilzean Reid, a newspaper editor who supported the group of stonemasons who formed the ECBC
Rintoul Place - named for David Rintoul, mason & second Chair of the ECBC
Saunders Street - possibly named for John Saunders who had links to Henry Raeburn
St Bernard's Crescent & St Bernard's Row - named in connection with St Bernard's House where Henry Raeburn lived
St Stephen Street - named in connection with St Stephen's Church
Saxe-Coburg Place - named for Prince Leopold of Saxe-Coburg
Silvermills Lane - possibly relating to silver being milled there once.
Spring Bank Gardens (now N. W Circus Place west side) - perhaps in reference to the springs at the two wells
Teviotdale Place - Scottish place name
Upper Dean Terrace - related to the Dean Estate
Veitch's Square (in earlier times known as Virgin Square and Veitch's Court) - derivation unknown

OTHER EDINBURGH BOOKS
by Barclay Price

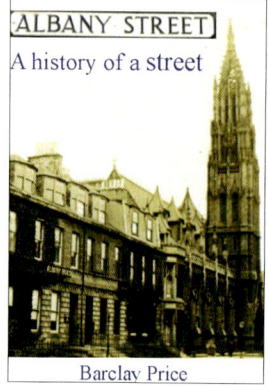
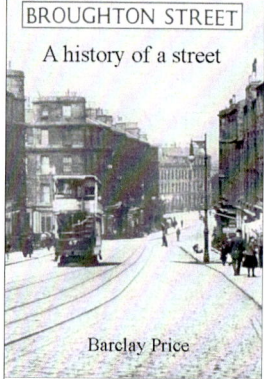
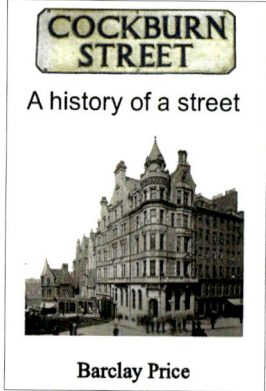
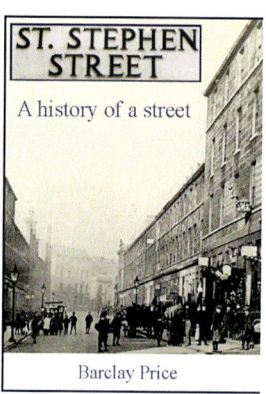
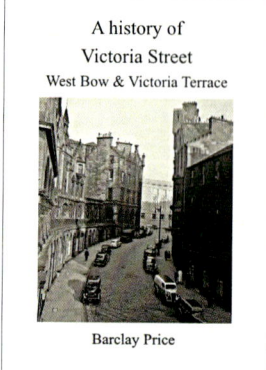
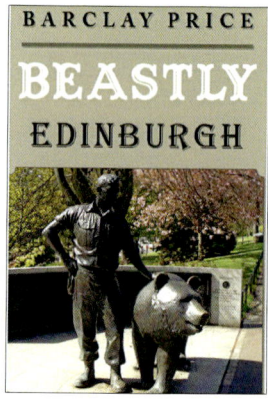

About the author
After retiring from working in the arts Price developed an interest in local history research. He has self-published five previous books on the history of local streets: Albany Street, Broughton Street, Cockburn Street, St Stephen Street & Victoria Street. These can be purchased/ordered from Golden Hare Books in St Stephen Street or by emailing *albanystreetedinburgh@gmail.com*

Amberley Publishing have published three other books by Price: *Beastly Edinburgh* and *Beastly Glasgow*, a history of animals in those cities, and *The Chinese In Britain – A History of Visitors and Settlers.*

INDEX

Abolition of Slavery Act (1833), 177
Adam, John, 184
Adam, William, 185
Adamson, Alexander, 19
Adamson, Robert, 126, 140, 175
addiction, treatment, 91–93
Ainslie, John, 10
air raid shelters, 89
Aitken, Sadie, 180, 181
Akram family, 99–101
Albion Halls, 37
alcohol, licensing, 93
Alfred, Prince Consort, 174, 175
Allan St, 27, 47, 52, 55, 78, 81, 108–109, 151, 207
allotments, 87
Alloway, Lord, 157
anaesthetics, 141
Anderson, Andrew, 81
Anderson, David, 98
Anderson, Mary, 123
Anderson, Sir R R, 43
Ann St, 11, 22, 23–25, 111
Anti-Prohibition Lobby, 93
Arakhamia-Grant, Ketevan, 80, 81
Archer family, 177
archery, 69
Ardtornish House, 146, 147
Athol St, 16
Atkinson, Robert, 63
Avondale Place, 112–113

baby-farming,' 125
Baker's Place, 115
ballet, 191
Balmoral Castle, 175
Balmoral Place, 29, 116–117
Bank of Scotland shares, 157
Barratt, Oliver, 185
baths, public, 77, 133
Beattie, William Hamilton, 35
Bedford St, 19, 22, 25, 27, 159, 195
Begbie, Thomas, 24, 34
Bell, Alexander Graham, 155
Bell Place, 119, 165

Bells Mills, 7, 17
bicycles, 66, 67, 72, 73
billiard halls, 79
bingo halls, 82, 83–85
Blyth School, 204
Boast, Anna, 71
Boer War, 169
Bol, Todd, 203
Bonnar, Thomas, 31
bookbinding, 203
The Book of Old Edinburgh (Dunlop), 128, 129
bookshops, 103, 163
Botanic Cottage, 184, 185
bowling, 77
Bowton, John, 41
Bradman, Don, 73
Braidwood, John, 39
Braidwood, Thomas, 39
Brandon St, 33
Bridge Place, 28, 29
Broadbridge, Richard, 168
Brodie, William, 200, 201
Brodie family, 201
Brooks, Vincent, 175
brothels, 135
Brown, Revd Alexander W, 126, 127
Brown, James, 159
Brown, Janet, 139
Brown, Robert, 19
Brown, Stewart, 185
Brunswick St (St Stephen St), 19, 23, 95, 97, 120
Buchanan, Francis, 59
Buchanan, James, 201
Bunney, Ann, 185
Burdett-Coutts, Angela, 201
Burgess, Jane, 131
burgesses, 173
Burn, William, 41, 195
Burr, Alexander, 108
Burton, Mary, 205
buses, 64, 65
byres, 207
Byrne, W, 8

cabmen, working conditions, 63
cafés, 101–103
Calcutta Cup, 68, 69, 71
Caledonian distillery, 25
Cameron's English Academy, 40, 41
Campbell, Janet, 61
Campbell, Robert, 39
Canada, 168, 169, 171
Canonmills, 7, 34
Carlton St, 21, 123
Carmichael, Martha, 159
Carnegie, Andrew, 45
Carnegie, Capt David, 95
cars, 66, 67, 139
Carstairs, Jane, 141
Carstairs, Wilhelmina, 140
Cassie, Veronica, 117
Cassie family, 117
Catholic Apostolic Church, 142, 143
Cats' Protection League, 193
Caw, Sir James L, 189
Chambers, Robert, 45, 103, 162, 163
Chambers, W & R, Publishers, 163
charitable institutions, 38–39
charity shops, 105
Charlotte St, 21
chemists, 98, 99
chess, 79–81
Chesser, John, 35, 43
Cheyne St, 37, 79, 125
childbirth, 109, 141
child care, 170, 171
Chinese residents, 157
Chisholm, Isabella, 201
chloroform, 141
churches, 36–37
Church Street/Lane, 7, 37, 209
Church of Scotland, 127, 181
church schools, 43
cigarettes, 91
cinema, 82, 83
Claremont Street (Saxe-Coburg St), 36, 37, 126, 127
Clarence St, 129
Clark, Ros, 51
Clark, R & R, printers, 33–35
Coates Curling Club, 76, 77

Cockburn, Henry, Lord, 41
Cockburn Conservation Trust, 185
Collinson, Francis, 182, 183
Collinson, Thomas, 182, 183
Collins Place, 131
Colville, James, 164, 165
Colville, Susan, 97–99
Comely Bank, 75
contraception, 149
Cook, William, hairdresser, 54, 55
Cooper, Barbara, 145
co-operatives, 97, 178, 179
Corson family, 99, 100
cowfeeders, 206, 207
Craig, James, 17, 184
Craw, Matthew, 17
Crawford, William, 133
Crichton, surgeons, 25
cricket, 68, 69, 71, 75, 103
Crighton, James, 75, 166, 167
crime, 58–61, 67, 97–99, 119, 125, 139
Crimean War, 33
Crolla family, 101
Cullen family, 41
curling, 76, 77
Cushnie, William, 173
Cuthbert, Jane, 93

dairies, 206, 207
Dallas, Elmslie W, 136, 137
dance, 191
Dangerous Drugs Act (1920), 91
Danube St, 21, 135
Davidson, Thomas, 129
Dawson, John, 97
Deaf & Dumb Institution, 38–39
Deanbank House, 9, 137
Dean Bank Institution, 38–39, 167
Dean Bank Lane, 137
Dean Bank Lane Mews, 139
Dean Bridge, 17, 22, 23
Dean Cemetery, 201
Dean estate, 23
Deanhaugh House, 9–11, 13, 14, 15, 21–23
Deanhaugh St, 5, 7, 36, 37, 98, 99,

214

101, 141
Dean Park, 75
Dean Park Crescent, 143
Dean Park Meuse, 63
Dean Park St, 144, 145
Dean St, 17, 19, 22, 57, 82, 83, 141, 147
    churches, 37, 159
Dean Street School, 42, 43
Dean Terrace, 19, 59, 148, 149, 205
Dean village, 7
Deer Commission, 147
Delaney, Arthur, 171
dentistry, 115
de Quincey, Thomas, 90, 91
Deuchar, David, 12
Dishon, Patricia Delaney, 171
Disruption (1843), 37, 127
Docherty, Elizabeth, 131
Donald, William, 173
Donaldson's Hospital, 39
Donaldson's School, 39
drapers, 103
draughts, 80, 81
drugs, 91
Drumsheugh, 8
Drysdale, Alexander, 39
Duck Race, 85
Dundas House, 33–35
Dunlop, Alison, 128, 129
Dunlop family, 129
Dunrobin Place, 29, 150, 151
Durham, Thomas, 139
Dyers & Bonnetmakers Guild, 173
Dykes, Robert Davidson, 79, 80

East India Company, 123
East of Scotland Model Marine Engineers Club, 77
East Scotland Co-operative Conference Association, 179
Edgar, Alexander, 176, 177
Edgar, Anne (née Gordon), 177
Edgar, Ann (later Leslie and Raeburn), 11, 13, 15
Edinburgh Academicals rugby ground, 27, 69, 70, 71, 185

Edinburgh Academy, 23, 40, 41–43, 197
    Sports Ground, 68–71, 80–81
    Stockbridge Club, 50, 51–53
Edinburgh Atelier, 197
Edinburgh City Artillery Volunteers, 197
Edinburgh Community Service in Unemployment, 53
Edinburgh Co-operative Building Company, 29, 165, 179
Edinburgh Festival Fringe, 85, 181
Edinburgh Harriers, 79
Edinburgh High School, 41
Edinburgh Institution for Unwanted Cats, 193
Edinburgh & Leith Children's Refuge, 170, 171
Edinburgh Lying-In Institution, 109
Edinburgh (Masson), 110, 111
Edinburgh North Church, 37
Edinburgh & Northern District Co-operative Society, 29, 96, 97, 178, 179
Edinburgh Old Cross, 11
Edinburgh Operatives & General Benefits Society, 159
Edinburgh Police Bill (1832), 59
Edinburgh Royal Choral Union, 183
Edinburgh Savings Bank, 99
Edinburgh Total Abstinence Society, 159
Education (Scotland) Act 1872, 43
Elder, Ann (later Raeburn), 13
Elim Pentecostal Church, 37
Elizabeth, Queen Mother, 52, 53
Elizabeth St, 21
Elliott, Helen, 81
Ellison, Mr, 37
Elwell, F W, 206
Engler, Millie, 82
entertainments, 82–85
Excise Board, 157

Fairley, Henry, 87
Falshaw Place, 28, 29
Family Planning Association, 149

Fenwick Weavers' Society, 179
fires, 54, 55, 161
fire stations, 54, 55
First World War, 71, 87–89, 91, 145, 153, 169, 197
fishmongers, 94
football, 75
foot races, 69
Forestry Commission, 147
Forth Road Bridge, heating, 35
Fowler, Ben Gunn, 47
Free Protesting Church of Scotland, 127

Gallie, George H, 71
Game, Amanda, 147
Gardenstone, Lord, 31
Gardiner, William, baker, 94
Gateway Theatre, 180, 181
Gatheral, James, 86, 87
Gibb, John, 23
Gilbert, Mrs, 78
Gilchrist, Robert, 17
Gillies, James, 151
Gilliland, James, 12, 13
Glanville Place, 100, 101, 167, 184, 185
Glegg, Capt Henry, 122, 123
Glegg family, 123
Glenogle Baths, 77–79, 132, 133
Glenogle House, 153
Glenogle Park, 29
Glenogle Rd, 33, 34
Gloucester St, 7, 37
Golden Hare Books, 85, 102, 103
golf, 74, 75
Goll, Otto, barber, 99, 144, 145
Goll family, 145
Gordon, Anne, 177
Gordon, John Watson, 197
Gordon, Mary, 23, 91
Gormley, Antony, 27
Graham, James Gillespie, 39
Grand Theatre (later cinema), 82, 83, 93
Grange Cricket Club, 23, 72–73, 75
Grange Dyvours Club, 73

Gregor, Susie, 85
Greyfriars Bobby, 200, 201
Grieg, David, 61
Grieg, Mr, 95
Grindlay, Janet (Jessie), 141
Guild Deacons, 172, 173
Guthrie, Sir Tyrone, 181

hackney cabs, 63
Hadden, Thomas, 34, 35
Haig distillery, 29, 33, 165
Hallelujah Army, 150, 151
Hallidie, Andrew, 64, 65
halls, community, 45, 48–53
Hamilton Place, 37, 41, 45, 49–51, 54, 55, 57, 59, 97
Hamilton Place Academy, 41, 155
Hannah, William, 115
Hannah family, 115
Hardy, Thomas, 35
harriers, 79
Harris, Eoghan, 26, 27
Haugh St, 79
Hawkes, Tracy, 191
Hay Brothers, 37
Hazell, Rachel, 202, 203
Henderson, David, 23
Henderson Row, 35, 36, 37, 47, 64, 65, 67, 157
Heriot, George, 43
Hermitage Place, 159
Hermitage St (Raeburn St), 20
Hill, Cumberland, 3, 7, 9, 10, 11, 158, 159
Hill, David Octavius, 126, 140, 175, 194, 195
Hislop, Joseph, 183
Historic Memorials & Reminiscences of Stockbridge (Hill), 3, 158, 159
hockey, 70, 71
Hofmann, Wolfgang, 85
Hole, W B, 196, 197
Hope, Sir John, 75
Horner, Leonard, 41
Horse, Rider, Eagle (Bridge), 26, 27
horse transport, 63–65, 67

hotels, 93
Howell, John, 41
Hugh Miller Cottage, 165
Hugh Miller Place, 29, 160
Hume, Elizabeth, 155
Hurd, Robert & Partners, 53

ice-skating, 77, 83
Independent Order of Good Templars, 178, 179
India Place, 16, 27, 45, 102, 163
Inglis, Mrs, 23
Inverleith Hall, 51
Inverleith House, 9, 23
Inverleith Park, 23, 77, 87
Inverleith Pond, 77
Ipswich, Queensland, 121

Jackson, Samuel, 177
Jamaica, 177
James, Paula, 134
Jameson, Mary Hope, 192, 193
Jameson, William, 193
John Muir Trust, 147

Keay, Revd Andrew, 167
Kemp, George Meikle, 194, 195
Kemp, Robert, 181
Kemp Place, 165
Kerr St, 63, 64, 97, 166, 167
King, Jessie, 124, 125
Kirkwood, James, 10, 16, 24
Koltanowski, Georges, 79, 80

Laird, Michael, Architects, 70, 71
laudanum, 91
Lauder, John, 199
Lauder, Robert Scott, 198, 199
Lauder family, 198, 199
laundries, public, 35, 46–47, 53, 77
Lazarowicz, Mark, 100
Learmonth, Lord Provost, 23
Learmonth estate, 75
Lees, Charles, 198
Leitch, Hepburn, 113
Leitch family, 113
Leith police, 119

Leslie, John, Earl of Rothes, 11, 13
Leslie Place, 21–23, 66, 168
libraries, 44, 45, 103, 163, 202, 203
Lind, David, 194, 195
Lindsay, Elizabeth, 197
Lindsay, William (internee), 145
Lindsay, William & Sons, 33, 34
Little Free Library, 202, 203
Little Zola, 82
Lockhart, Eliza, 127
Lockhart, Thomas, 157
lodging houses, 113
Lorimer, Robert, 34, 35
Lothian Abortion Referral Service, 149
Lothians & Edinburgh Abstinence Programme, 90, 91, 93
Loudon, Nancy, 148, 149
Lowlands Licence Act (1788), 33
Lugton, Thomas Polson, 51, 95, 102
Lyndsay, Sir David, 181

Macao, William, 156, 157
Macao family, 157
MacConnell, Alexander, 57
MacGibbon & Ross, architects, 99
Macintosh, I T, 78
McIver, Sir Lewis, 81
Mackenzie, Sir Compton, 35
Mackenzie, Forbes, 93
Mackenzie, Robert, 71
Mackenzie Place, 26, 27, 171
Maclaren, James, 155
Maclaren family, 155
McLeay, Kenneth, 174, 175
MacNamara, Patrick, 131
MacNamara family, 131
MacPherson, Fanny, 35
McPherson, Robert, confectioner, 94
Macrae, Ebenezer, 61
McTaggart, Annie, 189
Mak family, 101
Malta Green, 172, 173
Malta Green Cottage, 67, 173
Malta House, 9, 91, 93
Malta Terrace, 175
Mancini, Remo, 100

Mansfield Traquair Centre, 142, 143
Marr, Charles, 67
marriages, 4, 51, 155
Marshall, Helen, 205
Marshall, William, 204, 205
Marton, May, 82
Mary's Place, 177
Mason, Sarah, 202
Mason family, 89
Masson family, 111
Maxton, Margaret, 153
Maxwell, James Clerk, 41
Melrose, Alexander, 17
Mentiply, Rachel, 119
Michael Laird Architects, 27, 185
midwifery, 109, 149
Military Service Act (1918), 87
milk, 66, 67, 206, 207
mill lades, 9, 19, 24, 27, 33, 167
Milne, James, 21, 37
Milne, John, 37, 127
Mineral St, 21
model boating, 76, 77
Morham, Robert, 79
motor buses, 64, 65
motor cars, 67, 139
The Mound, heating, 35
Mowat-Thomson, William, 190, 191
Muir, David, 121
Munro, James, 103
Murray, Ebenezer, 93
musicians, 183

Nasmyth, Alexander, 31
Nasmyth, Robert, 115
National Fire Service Overseas Contingent, 160, 161
National Galleries of Scotland, 188
National Portrait Gallery, 188, 196, 197
National War Memorial, 34, 35
naturalisation, obtaining, 157
Nelson, Elsie Gertrude, 169
Nelson, Sir Hugh, 120, 121
Nelson, Mr, cyclist, 67
Nelson, Thomas Jnr, 45
Nelson, William, 31

Nelson Halls, 45
New Town, 17, 41
Nicol, Erskine, 197
Nightingale, Florence, 111
Nor' Loch, 7
North, Christopher, 23
Northern District School, 43
North West Circus Place, 45, 90, 103, 179, 201
Noyce, Dora, 134, 135

opium, 91
Orkney, 191
Orme, Emily, 111
Osmond Tearle Shakespearean Company, 83

Palace Sports Club, 83
Patriot Hall, 9, 28, 29, 97
Patten, James, 73
pawnbroking, 97
Pearson, Thomas, 125
Peattie, H, 14
Peddie, James, 19–21
Peddie & Kinnear, 37
Pentland Club, 85
Perth St, 77, 181
pharmacies, 98, 99
Philip, William, 19
Phillip, John, 200
photography, 137
Playfair, W H, 37, 195
police, 59–61, 119, 166, 167
police boxes, 60, 61
Poole, W, 30
Portgower Place, 183
Post Office, 99–101
pregnancy, 109
Presgrave, Charles, 101
Primer, Revd Jacob, 151
Pringle, A S, 71
prostitutes, 135
publishers, 163
pubs, 92, 93
putting, 77

Raeburn, Ann (nee Edgar) (wife), 11, 12, 13, 15
Raeburn, Ann (nee Elder) (mother), 13
Raeburn, Sir Henry, 2, 12, 13–15, 63, 77, 176, 177, 188
   as developer, 13–27
Raeburn, Henry jnr, 15, 207
Raeburn, Robert, 11, 12, 13, 15, 33, 59
Raeburn family, 13, 15, 21
Raeburn Mews, 67
Raeburn Place, 17, 185
   Halls, 48, 51–53, 77
   shops, 47, 95, 99, 101, 103, 105, 144, 145
Raeburn Short Hole Club, 77
Raeburn St, 20
railway accident (1989), 187
rationing, wartime, 88, 89
Reid, Hugh Gilzean, 29
Reid Terrace, 29, 187
restaurants, 101–103
Rintoul, David, 179
Rintoul Place, 189
Ritchie, Eliza, 115
Ritchie, Hugh, 107
'Road Vigilants,' 67
Robbins, Catherine, 49
Robertson, Alexander, 18
Robertson-Durham, James, 139
Rocheid family, 23, 77
roller-skating, 77
Rose, James, 137
Rose family, 137
Ross, Elizabeth, 155
Ross, Helen, 157
Ross, James, 29
Ross, Walter, 9, 10, 11, 13, 31
Ross, William, 174
Ross's Folly, 10, 11
Royal Botanic Gardens, 23, 184, 185
Royal Highland Society, 75
Royal Institution, 195
Royal Scottish Academy, 195
   rugby, 68, 69, 70, 71

Ruhleben Prison Camp, 144, 145

Sabbatarianism, 63, 93
St Bernard's Bridge, 20, 21, 129
St Bernard's Chapel, 37
St Bernard's Church, 37, 127
St Bernard's Crescent, 19, 21, 23, 191
St Bernard's FC, 74, 75
St Bernard's Free Church, 36, 37
St Bernard's House, 9, 10, 11, 13, 15, 21
St Bernard's Row, 79, 83, 192, 193
St Bernard's School, 42, 43
St Bernard's United Free Church, 127
St Bernard's Well, 8, 9, 30, 31
St Cuthbert's Co-operative Society, 62, 96, 97, 179
St Cuthbert's Poorhouse, 159, 173
St George's Free Church, 37
St George's Well, 9
St Giles, 203
St Mary's Episcopal Cathedral, 143, 183
St Stephen's Church, 37, 85, 199
St Stephen's School, 37, 43, 121, 129
St Stephen St, 21, 22, 23, 27, 36, 67, 83, 85, 101, 105
St Vincent's Chapel, 36, 37, 49, 85
Salonika, 152, 153
Salvation Army, 151
Ane Satyre of the Thrie Estaitis (Lyndsay), 181
Saunders St, 16, 26, 27, 56, 59, 195
Saxe-Coburg Place, 77, 137, 197
Saxe-Coburg St, 36
schools, 155, 204, 205
   art, 197
   dance, 191
   female students, 129
Schotz, Benno, 188
Scott, R, 8
Scott, Sir Walter, 11, 13, 35, 41, 137, 163, 199
Scott, William, 65

Scottish Co-operative Women's Guild, 179
Scottish & Newcastle Brewery, 33
Scottish Painting, 1620-1908 (Caw), 188, 189
Scottish Parliament Act (1695), 157
Scott Monument, 194, 195, 201
Seaforth Highlanders, 169
Second World War, 31, 89, 161
Shaw, G B, 35
Shelter Halls, 45
Shepherd, T H, 40, 124
shinty, 75
shops, 94–105
Silvermills, 7, 27, 32, 34, 35, 66, 67, 198, 199
Simpson, James, 185
Simpson, Sir James Young, 140, 141, 149
Simpson, John, 55
Simpson & Brown, 185
Simpson's Maternity Hospital, 149
Sitwell, Edith, 35
The Sixpenny Waverley, 35
6 TIMES (sculptures), 27
slave owners, 177
Sleep, Wayne, 52
Smith, George, 43
Smith, John, 57
Smith, William Allan & Co, 35
smoking, 91
Somerset Cottage, 92, 93
Somerville, Robert, 45, 103
spirit merchants, 93
sports grounds, 23, 68–81
Spring Gardens (NW Circus Place), 45, 90, 103, 201
Standard Life offices, 35
Starforth, John, 29
'Steamies,' 46, 47
Stein, John, 33
Stevenson, Flora, 43
Stewart, Archibald, 113
Stockbridge
    early shops, 23
    expansion, 17–21
    first bridge, 17, 18, 21
    industries, 32–35
    origins, 7–9, 11
    social conditions, 25–27, 109
Stockbridge Brae, 7
Stockbridge Church, 36, 37, 85
Stockbridge Colonies, 28, 29, 33, 116–117, 119, 131, 132, 133, 165, 179
Stockbridge Free Church, 36, 37
Stockbridge House, 52, 53
Stockbridge Library, 44, 45, 81
Stockbridge Market, 23, 95
Stockbridge Mills, 15, 33, 55–57
Stockbridge Mutual Service Club, 53
Stockbridge Park, 74–75, 167
Stockbridge school, 39, 42, 43
Stockbridge Working Men's Institute, 48, 49
Stocks, Lumb, 108
Sutherland Hussey Harris Architects, 26, 27
Swanson, John, 138, 139
swimming baths, 77, 79, 132, 133

table tennis, 81
Tait, Helen, 199
Talon, Thomas Knox, 36
Tanfield Hall, Howard Place, 127
tanneries, 199
taxis, 67
Taylor, Henry Ramsay, 45
Telford, Thomas, 23
temperance movement, 93
tenements, 17
tennis, 73
Teviotdale Place, 29, 202, 203
theatre, 83, 85
The Theatre School of Dance & Drama, 191
Theatre Workshop, 49–51
theft, 59, 61
Thomson, Flora, 109
Thomson, Isabella Ramsay, 199
Thomson, James, 55
Thomson, John, 29, 186, 187
Thorburn, Thomas, 64, 65

Tillie, Frank, 86, 87
Todd, Barclay, 178, 179
tolls, 63
Tombleson, W, 124
toy shops, 105
Traditions of Edinburgh (Chambers), 162, 163, 203
trams, 35, 64, 65
transport, 62–67
Traquair, Phoebe Ann, 142, 143
Traquair family, 107, 143
Trinity, 187
Trotter, George, 19
Tudor Cinema, 82, 83
Turbineus (cat), 110, 111

United Presbyterian Church, 37
Upper Dean Terrace, 205
urban conservation, 185
Urquhart, David, 157
Usher Hall, 183

Valentine, David, 118, 119
Valentine family, 118, 119
Veitch's Court/Square, 9, 206, 207
Victoria, Queen, 141, 174, 175
Vyner, Kenneth, 160, 161

Walker, G, 8
washhouses, public, 46, 47, 133
Water of Leith, 9
   first bridge, 7
   flooding, 19
   ford, 7–9, 17
   industries, 33–35
   laundry use, 47
   mill-lades, 9, 19, 24, 27, 33, 167
   pollution, 25
   village, 7
Watson, J H D, 71
Watson-Gordon, John, 90, 91
Watt, D, 79
Watt Institution & School of Arts, 204, 205
Wells, H G, 35
Wemyss, James, 145

Wesley Hall, 37
White, Alexander, 87
White, Letham, 145
Whitelaw, Helen, 207
Whitelaw family, 207
Wilkie, David, 21
Wilson, Christian, 109
Wilson, John of Elleray, 23
Wilson, Robert, 65
Wilson, William, 17, 207
wine and spirit merchants, 93
women
   childbirth, 109
   compositors, 35
   crime, 125, 167
   cycling, 67
   education, 129
   laundry, 47, 53
   police officers, 61
   public posts, 43
   smoking, 91
   sport, 70, 71
   students, 205
   suffrage, 89, 111
   swimming, 79
   temperance, 179
   wartime work, 87–89
Wood, Charles, 50, 51
Woolworths store, 53, 102, 103
Workmen's Compensation Act, 57
workmen's strike (1861), 165
Wright, Robert, 43
Wylie, James, 81
Wyness, Annie, 183

Yeats, W B, 35
York Place, 13, 15
Younger, William, 33